Tidings from Zion

Tidings from Zion

Helen Bentwich's Letters from
Jerusalem, 1919–1931

Edited by
Jenifer Glynn

I.B.Tauris Publishers
LONDON ● NEW YORK
in association with
The European Jewish Publication Society

Published in 2000 by I.B.Tauris & Co Ltd
Victoria House, Bloomsbury Square, London WC1B 4DZ
175 Fifth Avenue, New York NY 10010
Website: http://www.ibtauris.com
in association with the European Jewish Publication Society

In the United States and Canada distributed by St. Martin's Press
175 Fifth Avenue, New York NY 10010

The European Jewish Publication Society is a registered charity which
gives grants to assist in the publication and distribution of books relating
to Jewish literature, history, religion, philosophy, politics and culture.

ISBN 1-86064-349-3

A full CIP record for this book is available from the British Library
A full CIP record for this book is available from the Library of Congress

Library of Congress catalog card: available

Typeset in Garamond by A. & D. Worthington, Newmarket
Printed and bound in Great Britain by Creative Print and Design (Wales)

Contents

Illustrations

Introduction

When my aunt Helen Bentwich died, I was anxious that her store of letters and photographs should not be thrown away. No-one else wanted to give them a home, so I was showered with a pile of boxes, some with neatly sorted bundles, some in total chaos. It seemed intrusive to read these intimate relics then, so I just looked at the wonderful photographs before pushing them all into a cupboard. That was in 1972, but 20 years on I felt it was time to look further.

I realized that the series of letters which she had bundled, all written to her mother from Palestine between 1919 and 1931, were sorted with a view to writing a book which she did not live to complete. There was rare and candid material there which I felt could make a small but worthwhile (and entertaining) contribution to the story of Palestine under the British Mandate. I was happy to find that Dr Sidney Brichto agreed, and I am very grateful both to him and to Colin Shindler of the European Jewish Publication Society for the support and encouragement which have made this book possible.

All letters, methinks, should be as free and easy as one's discourse.

Dorothy Osborne, 1653

Prelude

Helen Franklin's bookplate shows a handsome desk chair, with a dog sprawled over it and a hockey stick across the arms; another dog is standing on the desk with his front paws on the windowsill, looking out at English countryside and a hockey pitch. A later bookplate, designed in 1920 for her and for her husband Norman Bentwich, is divided into two arches, one showing a scene in Jerusalem and the other an English farm. The symbolism is perhaps stronger than was intended, for marriage brought a division into her life. It was marriage that took her to Palestine in 1919 at the age of 27, and through all her 12 years there the yearning for England was poured into her weekly letters. Because she never expected to stay in Palestine so long – always hoping Norman would change his job – Helen remained something of an outsider there, a critical spectator, not fitting into any of the many groups that formed the strange society of Palestine under the British Mandate. Yet when she eventually settled in England, love of Palestine drew her back almost every year.

Helen's parents, Arthur and Caroline Franklin, both came from Jewish families who had been in England for some generations and felt themselves rooted in England, but they were formidable travellers with a particular interest in seeing, and thoroughly investigating, Jewish communities wherever they went. This interest naturally took them to Palestine (then under Turkish rule), and Helen had joined them on their visit in the spring of 1914. It was unusual tourism. Caroline, who was an active member of the Buckinghamshire Education Committee and was involved,

1

through the Anglo-Jewish Association, with the Evelina de Rothschild School in Jerusalem, kept a note-book of 'Visits to schools,
interviews opinions &c' – eight schools, three hospitals, and an
orphanage, together with notes on Zionism and a report of a
meeting on social work. An introduction to the American Ambassador to Turkey took them to official parties where they met the
Turkish Governor of Jerusalem, the Arab Mayor, and the Mufti,
as well as prominent Jews. They even joined the Ambassador's
party on a visit to the Mosque at Hebron, escorted by 'police and
soldiers who were all nervousness and excitement'.[1] More con-
ventionally, they toured the land in a carriage drawn by two horses
(there was only one motor car in the country, and the roads were
terrible), and they loved the scenery, the flowers, the bazaars, and
the variety of people.

They saw the thousands of Russian pilgrims who flocked to
Jerusalem for Easter – many who came that year were to be
stranded there for the rest of their lives by the war – and the Nebi
Musa procession, when crowds of Moslems[2] come into Jerusalem
from Nablus, Hebron and the surrounding villages, and after a
service in the Dome of the Rock, march with much shouting and
singing and music along the Jericho Road to the reputed tomb of
Moses, on the plain near the Dead Sea. On that occasion Caroline
noted phlegmatically in her diary, 'We came home and on the way
passed a man who had been stabbed. We stopped and sent him to
the hospital in our carriage. We started to walk but our carriage
was soon back again.'

This visit, with its mixture of social work, official activities and
thorough – even sometimes hazardous – travel, foreshadowed
many of Helen's later interests in Palestine. For Helen and her
mother were very alike, and their close understanding made the
weekly letters lively and unrestrained. Helen had a diploma in
social work from Bedford College London and, although in 1914
she was not keen to spend her holiday getting involved in social
problems, she showed her mother's enthusiasm and urge to
organize when she went back to Palestine to live.

On the way to Jerusalem, the Franklins had spent some days in
Cairo, where their friend Norman Bentwich was a lecturer in the
Law School. Norman, 'the idealist lawyer' as C.R. Ashbee called
him, had been there for two years, hoping that the Egyptian

service might give him a background of Middle East expertise and contacts which would help him find work where he really wanted to be – in Palestine. His hopes were to be realized in an unexpected way when the war took him to Jerusalem with Allenby, and he stayed on to work as legal adviser in the British post-war administration. In 1914 he looked after the Franklins attentively for much of their time in Cairo, and when he was in England on leave later that year he and Helen became engaged. On his visit home the following summer they were married, on 7 September, and Helen went back with him to Cairo.

The Bentwiches, though they were also a Jewish family well established in England, had a very different outlook from the Franklins. The most important and permanent influences in the upbringing of Norman and his brother and nine sisters were Zionism and music. Norman's father Herbert was a lawyer, an admirer of Herzl, a friend of Solomon Schechter, and a delegate to Zionist conferences. His mother (who died in May 1915) was a pianist, the winner of gold and silver medals at the London Academy before she married at 18 and gave up her career for her large family; each child was taught an instrument, and she took them to concerts and practised each day with them in turn. Their house became a meeting place for enthusiastic Zionists and for musicians from Central and Eastern Europe.

In some ways it was a strange marriage, because Helen had no great feeling for either music or Zionism. She took some months making up her mind to marry Norman because she knew that after the war it would mean living in Jerusalem, and the idea came as a shock. At the time of their marriage Norman was 32, and convinced, after abandoning earlier thoughts of academic life or the English Bar, that his future lay in Palestine. Helen was 23, equally full of energy and idealism, though hers was undirected, a youthful urge to put the world to rights. But they shared a passion for social and racial justice, and something of a pioneering spirit. In her position as a government official's wife in the strange and stressful society of the British Mandate, Helen never found a fully satisfactory outlet for her energy and ability. Later they were to have a base in Hampstead while she had a distinguished career in Labour politics and the London County Council, and Norman's

work was split between the Hebrew University and various
international organizations. They had no children.

Arriving in Cairo with some experience as a VAD (Voluntary
Aid Detachment) helper in a hospital in Aylesbury, Helen worked
first with some of the sick and wounded from Gallipoli. When
that crisis was over and the hospitals emptied she became a typist
in the Ministry of Finance. In the last days of 1915 Norman joined
the newly formed Camel Transport Corps, starting in a camp not
far from Cairo, but soon trekking further and further into the
Sinai Desert. As they were increasingly unable to meet, Helen left
Cairo in August 1916, deciding she could do more useful war-
work in England. It was to be two and a half years before she
could join Norman again, when he became Senior Judicial Officer
in the Occupied Enemy Territory Administration (OETA) which
governed the part of Palestine then under British rule.

Helen had a colourful wartime meanwhile, first as a foreman at
Woolwich Arsenal, where she was so shocked at the women's
working conditions that she started organizing them into a union;
caught signing up new members during a slack period on the
night-shift, she was dismissed for 'Bolshevik tendencies'. She then
joined the Land Army, and for the rest of the war worked happily
in Hertfordshire, ending as a welfare officer riding a tempera-
mental motor bicycle all over the county. She led a contingent of
land girls in the Lord Mayor's Show, and rode on a cart-horse into
the courtyard of Buckingham Palace when they were inspected by
King George V. The Land Army work turned out to be useful
training for her future life; in recruiting rallies she learnt to make
public speeches – a skill she was to need later in politics – and the
land experience was helpful for her work in Palestine.

In January 1919 Helen managed to get permission to join
Norman in Palestine on the grounds that she was a trained social
worker, needed because the social problems had intensified in the
war. But there were also fundamental changes in Palestine since
1914, for the Turks had entered the war on the side of the Germans and had been defeated by the British under Allenby, ending
a rule which had lasted 400 years. The British government, from
mixed political and idealistic motives, had stated in the Balfour
Declaration (1917) that they 'view with favour the establishment
in Palestine of a national home for the Jewish people', and there

were plans for the current military administration to be succeeded by a British Mandate, which the Jews hoped might nurture such a home.[3] A Zionist commission, representing the Jews of the Western allies, had arrived in Palestine in 1918 to prepare the ground and to help the existing Jewish population recover from the traumas of war; the commission also acted as an intermediary between the military administration and the Jews of Palestine. But the Versailles principle of self-determination inspired Arabs as well as Jews. A letter to Lloyd George in March 1919 pointed out that the Peace Conference had 'laid two eggs – Jewish nationalism and Arab nationalism; these are going to grow up into two troublesome chickens'.[4]

Helen was more concerned with immediate social needs than with long-term strategy. Proud of her wartime experiences and her pre-war practice as a manager of a girls' club and the founder of the first company of Girl Guides in east London, she was keen to sort out Jerusalem. With youthful confidence she analysed problems and suggested solutions in her first week, but her views naturally developed over time. Since there was no censorship, she wrote very freely and often critically – until she learnt that in a 'secret and confidential' document which was circulated in the Administration by a hostile official who was attacking the Balfour Declaration and the Zionist Commission, 'the wife of a highly-placed British officer who was a Jew' was quoted as being similarly critical in letters to her mother.[5] She was more careful after that.

The chapters that follow are based on her spontaneous and free-ranging letters. They reflect the mood of the moment – noticeably tense in times of hot weather, sometimes overflowing with irritations that disappear the following week; often slightly self-mocking; impulsive and quick to criticize in the early days, more mature and understanding later. She wrote long letters every week to her mother, and often to her father too, but it is only the letters to her mother that have survived. If the letters seem light-hearted in a world full of problems, remember that they were written as cheerful letters home, to a family already aware of the situation in Palestine. 'One wants the most exuberant & unsquashable of spirits to live here for any length of time,' Helen wrote, and she tried to show that she qualified. But under the surface of trivialities and gossip there runs the story of two idealists increasingly baffled by human perversity and frustrated by the realities of Middle Eastern politics.

Helen herself used the letters as a source for the volume of autobiography which she was drafting in her last years, and I have used this manuscript when it gives extra insights. It was designed to follow her earlier book, *If I Forget Thee* [6] — an odd title because that book ended just after her arrival in Jerusalem, which is where this one begins.

---

[1] Caroline Franklin's diary.

[2] I have kept the old spelling 'Moslem' to be consistent with Helen's letters.

[3] About half of the 60,000 population of Jerusalem, but only about 10 per cent of the 700,000 population of Palestine, was then Jewish.

[4] Letter from Richard Meinertzhagen, intelligence officer; see Meinertzhagen's *Middle East Diary* (London: Cresset Press, 1959), p 17.

[5] Norman and Helen Bentwich, *Mandate Memories* (London: Hogarth Press, 1965), p 47.

[6] Helen Bentwich, *If I Forget Thee* (London: Elek, 1973); the title is from Psalm 137, verse 5: 'If I forget thee, O Jerusalem, let my right hand forget her cunning.'

1919

Launching into Troubled Waters

27.1.19

My dear Mother

Here I am in Jerusalem – such a Jerusalem as one couldn't have conceived 5 years ago. Motor cars & lorries tearing through the streets day & night; clean & decent bazaars inside the walls; law & order everywhere (due, of course, to Norman) & free access to the Holy Church & the Mosque of Omar, both of which I visited to-day as easily as one goes into Westminster Abbey. It's a greatly improved place – and above all, the old Fast Hotel,[1] where we are now staying, has been taken over by the Navy & Army Canteen Board, & is run for officers & their wives at the rate of 7/- a day, with excellent food (masses of it after an inside trained to our meatless England) & very clean & comfortable.

I went to the Law Courts with Norman, which are half of the Russian Hospice – do you remember, a huge building? The lower half is the American Red Cross, who have a very cheery personnel of about 70 in all ... This morning I went to see Miss Landau [at the Evelina de Rothschild School]. Do you remember Miss Landau's Hodge, with the green turban? He was shot by the Turks for being too faithful to the English. Miss Landau is the one feature of Jerusalem that has undergone no change – I sat there for 2 hours nearly, & she poured forth conversation at me, & it was as impossible to quell it as to dam a waterfall. However, I gleaned a good many facts – chiefly that a Rescue Home is badly needed for

the bad girls in Jerusalem to be sent to, that there is a large opening for agricultural & horticultural work among the girls, & that
some sort of co-ordinating organization among the charities is
badly needed. Then I went to the Zionist people, & got a list of
all the women's & children's institutions that take Jews, which I
shall visit as soon as I can. And then I'll have more idea about
what's wanted. I had a long talk with a hairy old man called Kahn
through an interpreter – he saying I must learn Hebrew first, &
me saying that the lives of babies & the souls of girls were more
important, & that I meant to get going on that right away. I firmly
refused to go on any committees yet awhile – they spend all their
time meeting & writing reports, I think, & do nothing ... There's
no lack of work – but there may be lack of power to do what is
needed, & an utter impossibility of getting any two people to take
an interest in each other's affairs. Perhaps it's only in the exterior
that Jerusalem has changed after all – there are still missionaries
disguised as the Syrian & Palestine Relief;[2] & still bigots, both in
the Orthodox party & the Zionists. If *only* one could be a thorough despot! ... I'm about the only woman here not in uniform,
& I mean to get land work going straight away, to wear it again.
How I hate a skirt! But I fear my fine clothes will arrive home as
they left for the most part – jerseys & tweeds are the order of the
day here, & there doesn't seem much chance of a social life.
Norman works from 8–8 at present.

It was a backward and divided country, suffering from years of
neglect and struggling to recover from wartime horrors, and from
the destruction and starvation and deportations that the Turks had
inflicted in the course of their defeat. 'The Turk,' Storrs wrote,
'when he struck his flag and the Camp in which he had bivou-
acked rather than settled for four hundred years, carried with him
in his retreat money, records, registers, drugs and surgical instru-
ments, much furniture, all food – and generally everything that
could be of the smallest use to the City or to its liberators.' An
article in *The Times* written by C.R. Ashbee in 1919 described
Jerusalem as 'a picturesque but filthy mediaeval town with
sprawling suburbs; ill-timbered, unwatered, with roads inconven-
ient and leading nowhere; and, for the rest, a government that no
longer functions and a city whose inhabitants are cut up into
innumerable jarring sects'. Helen felt herself in a no-man's land in

the middle of these jarring sects, English among the Jews and Jewish among the English.

The Jewish Community, although only some 65,000 in the whole country, was divided among many factions. With the self-contained orthodox communities, Helen had very little contact or sympathy. These included ultra-orthodox anti-Zionists (both Yiddish-speaking Ashkenazim from Russia and central Europe, and Ladino-speaking Sephardim descended from the Spanish dispersion) who refused to use Hebrew for any purpose except prayer; and also religiously orthodox Zionists who as a matter of principle talked only Hebrew. Helen's socialism, her feeling for women's role in society, and her love of work on the land should naturally have drawn her more to the secular Zionists – but she shrank from their earnestness and dedication and admired them only from a distance, never with any urge to be involved. And as she wrote later, her horror of nationalism, fed by the First World War and its aftermath, made her respond to Zionism not as a political movement, but only as a 'spiritual and cultural force that would help to keep Judaism alive in the modern world'.[3]

Adding to the racial and linguistic mix among the Jews, some old people's homes were supported by the Jews in Hungary and other European countries; groups of houses exclusively for the use of families where the men did nothing but pray all day were supported by money collected in Europe and America. And although David Yellin, as early as 1904, had started a teachers' association to encourage teachers to use Hebrew, there were schools in Palestine maintained by Jews in other countries, where the language of that country was the language of instruction – German was becoming less important, but Miss Landau's school (the Evelina de Rothschild School) was supported by the Anglo-Jewish Association, and taught in English, while the schools of the Alliance Israélite taught in French.

The Christian community was as divided as the Jewish. The majority belonged to the Greek Orthodox Church, but there were Roman Catholics, Protestants, Greek Catholics, Armenians, Abyssinians, Copts and Nestorians. Constant conflicts broke out amongst these communities over the Holy Places, particularly over the Church of the Nativity at Bethlehem and the Church of the Holy Sepulchre in the Old City; British soldiers were posted in these places to keep the peace. Many of the male clerks in the Administration were Christians, having been educated at one or other of the English mission schools – the pupils from these schools knew English well, and understood English ways, even to playing cricket. An English mission high school for girls was started soon after the Occupation, but in these early days most of the female clerks in the Administration were Jewish, having been to Miss Landau's school.

It was two years since the Balfour Declaration had committed the British government to 'view with favour the establishment in Palestine of a national home for the Jewish people' and to 'use their best endeavours to facilitate the achievement of this object, it being clearly understood that nothing shall be done which may prejudice the civil and religious rights of existing non-Jewish communities in Palestine'. But the form the national home would take had not been defined. Some thought Balfour was thinking of 'a gentle sanctuary, in which the despised Jews of Eastern Europe would find peace and religion';[4] others, that he was foreseeing 'an independent sovereign Jewish State'.[5] The Bentwiches' vision lay somewhere between the two; they wanted a home for the Jews but, fearing the extremes of nationalism – a fear which Norman shared with Helen – they hoped with endless optimism for some sort of co-operation. In 1941 Norman was still writing of the need for 'a federal system of the Semitic countries', involving Jews, Arabs and English.[6] This is near to the interpretation that Lloyd George, in his memoirs, said Balfour meant: 'some form of British, American or other protectorate, under which full facilities would be given to the Jews to work out their own salvation and to build up, by means of education, agriculture and industry, a real centre of national culture and focus of national life'.[7] But in 1919 the Balfour Declaration had made both the Christians and the Moslems of Palestine feel worried and threatened, and old tensions between them gave way to a defensive grouping against the Jews. There were plenty of divisions among the Arabs of Palestine, but opposition to Zionism and fear of Jewish immigration brought a veneer of unity.

Helen started tackling the more accessible problems:

2.2.19: I'll try & tell you what I've been doing since Tuesday. In the morning I went to see a very good girls' workroom, with 170 girls doing army-contract needlework – chiefly shirts. It's awfully well managed & very model. It's the only really good girls' workshop here. There is a courtyard where I'm going to start some of the girls of the town on vegetable growing, I hope … On Wednesday we went to tea at the OETA Headquarters in what was the German Hospice on Mount Scopus. It's a most beautifully luxurious place, with about 25 officers living & working there, & lots of clerks, including 3 or 4 English lady ones, & about 15 typist girls from Miss Landau's school who are brought up & down every day in a lorry. They were the only girls to learn English, so they are very useful. Now the girls in the school are learning shorthand, & will get very high pay after … Thursday evening I saw an American Zionist who is very sensible and practical, and told him of the 2 things I wanted – a Rescue Home & a land army. He said they'd not enough money, so we are going to ask the American Red Cross to take on the Rescue Home; & either appeal especially for the land army or ask the American Red Cross for it too. Friday the officer in charge of Agriculture in OETA came to lunch, & was very sympathetic to my scheme for planting the waste places of the town with vegetables, working it with Jewish girls, & keeping poultry wherever possible. He'll get me seeds from Egypt, & probably chickens too. Tools are rather a job.

The vegetable and flower patches were thoroughly successful, though they never became self-supporting, and they were consoling at times when other efforts were frustrating; the chickens materialized later.

6.2.19: I find I have no drawing-room conversation, so I entertain my guests chiefly with what it feels like to be a factory-hand, & the easiest way of hoeing turnips … 10 of the unemployed Jewish girls here started to work on the land in an unused garden, hoeing and digging under the guidance of a woman trained at Kinnereth. They were most awfully keen, and we hope soon to have at least 50. They are to get one and a half piastres an hour & to work 6–8 hours a day. We hope to sell the vegetables later on at a profit, & we have got young plants, & borrowed tools, from the American

Red Cross. But we want money for it badly – that's why we sent the cable asking for it. We thought some people in England might like to help such a worthy cause. We can't get much out of the Zionist Commission. It is the *worst run organization* with the *most unsuitable personnel* it has ever been my lot to strike. They have no records of relief, no proper investigators, no proper division of the city, no correlation between the departments of giving relief to orphans, men, girls, widows, or medical, & so there is absolute chaos, & much wasting of money. When one sees the fine men & women – Jewish & Christian – which the Americans have, & their efficient organizations, it nearly makes one weep. Tell Uncle Herbert [Herbert Samuel] how pitifully bad it all is.

Plenty of ammunition there for the 'hostile official's' document.

The land girls were enthusiastic, and two weeks later Helen was able to get the use of a large tract of empty land and to employ 40 more. 'Heaven only knows how we are going to pay the girls,' she wrote, 'we are relying on having money from England, & I *do* hope you'll have been able to get us some.' She visited the gardens every morning to see the progress, first on foot, and later, wearing her land-army uniform, on horseback. 'I'm getting very used to my gee now,' she wrote in May, '& am out on him all & every morning, through the town & round the gardens with the *sais* [groom] carrying a basket of vegetables behind. Our peas are getting quite famous, & I could sell many more than I've got to the English people, who all stop me in the street & ask for them. We pick them young, or else they are stolen, & that's what makes them nice.'

The Bentwiches found a house in the German Colony, a well laid-out suburb to the south of the city, with pleasant gardens and trees. In about 1870 a number of Germans from South Germany had emigrated to Palestine, to live a more Christian and pacifist life than they had felt to be possible under the increasing militarism of Germany, but many remained patriotically German. They had formed small colonies in Jerusalem, Jaffa and Haifa, and two agricultural colonies. After the British occupation in the war all the men and some of the families were interned in Egypt, and thus many of their houses were empty, to be taken over first by the army, and later by British families. 'If the Huns come back to live

– they are only interned in Egypt – we'll have to vacate at once,'
Helen wrote. (The following year, when the Germans were
coming back and the Bentwiches were in another German house,
she wrote without much remorse that 'The Germans, poor things,
are being squashed up in a few houses, & ours is allotted to us for
5 years.')

The house was at the end of the colony, and was then the last
in the town. 'I'm glad I don't live right in the élite Jewish quarter,
everything one did would be discussed & I don't feel that my life
can stand such scrutiny. For instance, if one transgressed on
Saturdays it would be the talk of the town; or if I had men there
without Norman, they'd want to know all about it. Here, nobody
cares *what* I do, & it's ever so much nicer to be right away from
these cliques & communities.' The house had nine rooms and two
loggias (where they slept out in hot weather), but no bathroom.
Helen was allowed to borrow German furniture from store, but
finding it disagreeably heavy and ugly, took very little and used
Norman's camp furniture for the rest.

11.2.19: With the aid of 3 prisoners I got a few more pieces of
furniture moved from another house to mine. Prisoners are a useful form of labour – they work backsheesh, & do all kinds of
manual work, without guards, & quite happily. I take a sort of
family interest in them, because Norman sent them there … It's a
nice house but pretty bare. I'll tell you what there is: in the par-
lour, one red plush sofa carefully camouflaged with Bokhara
embroideries; three shelves of books – 2 of the shelves readable
ones & the other stodge. One fairly large table with a cashmere
shawl on it, a silver casket, & a vase; one little table with writing
things & more embroidery & silver candlesticks; one black rock-
ing chair, one black ordinary chair, & three deck chairs; also two
corners are shut off with Bokhara hangings to make the room
look less bare. There are chintz curtains at present, killed by the
embroideries, so to-day we have been buying black ones. I think it
ought to look rather nice & novel to have black curtains, with
white walls & a black & white stone floor, don't you? Try it! The
dining-room has one table, uncompromisingly ugly & leggy, & 4
black cane-bottomed chairs, & chintz curtains – c'est tout. In the
hall there is one table (borrowed from the law-courts) on which

sits my black rabbit & a clock. In the other room is all the mess & rubbish, so as to keep the two we use very tidy & presentable.

I wish I could find a regular whole-time job to do, in the Government or elsewhere. It makes the days seem so long when you have to think all the time 'what shall I do next.' If you've got real regular work to do you can do so much more in between whiles. I could do a lot if only there were some money, with the Jewish people. Rescue homes, & homes for working girls who are orphans, & further developments of the land work are all badly needed – but it's no use attempting any more on our own, & the [Zionist] Commission has no money to give us. So there's nothing to do but talk & talk & talk – & we breakfast at 7.30, which makes the day longer. I like being in my land-kit & at work in my own garden – it's unambitious, but I'll have to stick at that, I suppose, until we get some money, or until the garden is done. *Do* collect us some money.

Breakfast was at 7.30 because Norman worked a long day. His post as Senior Judicial Officer involved setting up a new judicial system of courts: Magistrates' Courts (with Palestinian magistrates), and District Courts and a Court of Appeal (each with a British president and two Palestinian members). He was also in charge of prosecutions, and was busy trying to get rid of corrupt practices – so successfully that he quoted a headman of a Haifa village who happily said that robbing was now more worthwhile, for with no bribes to pay to police or prosecutors, they could keep everything themselves.[8]

Norman had engaged a cook, with her young adopted daughter to help. 'The old lady is very good at cooking, which we both appreciate; but she hasn't much idea of the things we usually have at home, & when I try to explain, in my new patois of French, German & Arabic, somehow things turn out queer. Both Norman & I like scrambled eggs & don't like omelettes – yet we've had omelettes both mornings because we couldn't either of us say scrambled eggs in any language she knew.' They had a daily housemaid, and Norman's Sudanese batman slept in the cellar under the house. At that time they had no car, so Norman rode daily to his office, and his horse, stabled in the barracks in the town, was brought each morning by his Arab *sais*. Later Helen bought a white Arab horse, quiet and easy to ride; she admitted she was a timid horsewoman, and never so happy on a horse as she had been on a motor bicycle. Though 'It's great riding astride,' she wrote home. 'I should have gone on when I was a kid if I'd ridden that way then.'

17.2.19: The cook does us very proud at meals, & we are very much better off for food than you poor things at home. We live fine!

I went round the town a bit with Norman – it's ripping inside the walls now, because it's all fairly clean, & there are no beggars, & no would-be guides ... Most of the American Red Cross are going up north, to Aleppo, where things are terribly bad. I wish they weren't – they're such a jolly, go-ahead, sane sort of a crowd, & it will make a lot of difference when they go ... I went to the Social Research Meeting again. They aren't so bad – perhaps I say that because they've taken up on their first venture my pet plan, & are all very keen on it. It's just an obvious sort of scheme to divide the town into districts & have a social worker over each, & keep proper records, & work on the family as a basis – things which one would think they would have started with but which they seem to have ignored ... I had a talk with the head of the American Zionist Unit and one of the heads of the American Red Cross here. Particularly I was asking for money for the land-girls, & after very much parley – & a good dinner at the Commission house – they arranged for me to have it from some American fund ... An agriculturalist attached to the Zionist Commission came to see me, & he suggested sending the girls bulb-collecting on the hills when it was too wet to dig, & then he would find a market for the bulbs in England. So to-day I have done that.

We lunched up at OETA HQ, in the German building, with General Storrs – a very solemn & serious affair. Storrs was very nice & polite; but it always makes me want to laugh now to be treated so very much as the lady. It used to alarm me in the old days, but now I see the funny side of them all, & it's harder to treat it as it ought to be treated, than it was when I was so shy. I really enjoy it awfully – they're so solemn. And I do behave quite nicely, really. After that we called on the Mufti, a very nice intelligent man with a jolly twinkle. He had intimated that I was to state what time I desired to honour him, & so we went to-day, as I had

my glad rags on for the General. He had his room furnished in
awfully good taste – white covers to the chairs, & black table-
cloths, & lovely rugs & hangings – & atrocious cheap lace curtains, like lodging house ones …

This Mufti, the influential head of the Moslem community, was 'a
good friend', 'a perfect dear, with such a jolly smile'. It was his
successor Amin Husseini (appointed in 1921) who became pro-
Nazi and disastrous.

The headquarters were in the German Hospice on the Mount
of Olives. Helen described it as a pretentious stone building with
superb views in every direction. It had been planned by the Kaiser
during his visit to Jerusalem in 1899, and he was pictured in
mosaic on the roof of the chapel, with his wife by his side, and a
replica of the Hospice in his hand. Ronald Storrs, the Military
Governor of Jerusalem, was the Bentwiches' host because General
Money, the Chief Administrator, was away at the time.

Storrs, 'the urbane and artful Governor' as Lawrence described
him, played a large part in the life of Jerusalem under the military
administration and in the early days of the Mandate. Jerusalem
owes much to his imaginative despotism, for he decreed that no
buildings should be altered without his permission, that stucco
and corrugated iron were not to be used in that city of stone, and
that there should be no advertisements except on one or two
authorized hoardings in commercial quarters. He founded and ran
the Pro-Jerusalem Society, raising large sums of money for resto-
ration and improvements. Fred Kisch (Chairman of the Palestine
Zionist Executive 1923–31) wrote that 'alone among the English
officials Storrs does try to bring Jew and Arab together as his
guests',[9] though many Jews felt his sympathies were too much
with the Arabs. Helen always found him lively company, and
admired his support of the arts, but was irritated by his snobbery
and sometimes more seriously upset by his pro-Arab views.
'Whatever else he is, he's the most entertaining talker here,' she
wrote that November, 'especially if one doesn't mind what he
says.' He was a good pianist, often accompanying Norman's
violin. Helen was at first critical of him for starting a music school,
which she thought 'futile in a place which is crying out for industries & constructive work'; she became less philistine later, under

the influence of Norman and his sisters. Storrs' house was full of enviable hangings and pottery, and he had a good collection of books which, to Helen's pleasure, he was willing to lend to his friends. (All his fine collection was destroyed in a fire in a riot in Cyprus in 1931 when he was governor there.) Ernest Richmond – 'a ripping person – the son of the artist,[10] and in charge of the preservation of the Mosque & other antiquities, & full of all sorts of town planning & new industry ideas' – had been brought to Jerusalem by Storrs and was sharing Storrs' house at that time; 'controversial' is the adjective Helen used both for him and Storrs. Richmond was an admirer of the Arabs, and later, when he became political secretary (1920–24), a bitter anti-Zionist. But in those early days, when he was in Jerusalem as an architect and not as a politician, he was the Bentwiches' friend.

Helen ended this letter of 17 February with a discouraging general summary:

> ... I'm sure the folk at home who talk so glibly of the Arab & the Jew lying down side by side like the lion & the lamb don't know much of the real feeling here. It's very deep – & the Jews are not as tactful as they might be, out here, in trying to make things easier. It's all rather a mess-up – if only we had some real strong Jews in charge out here, apart from the Government or Administration. Those in it can do nothing, of course – & the Jews outside that we have are laughably pathetic. Money & men & women – that's what we want here. But only the right sort – we've too many wasters & dreamers. Still, despite politics, life flows very happily & gaily, & it's all jolly interesting.

The next letter is typically full of a mixture of social life and social conscience. Although Helen happily admitted that being 'a rare female in a male-run administration is the way to have a very good time', the constant entertaining was not wholly frivolous. 'From the first,' Norman wrote, 'we decided to make our home a meeting place for all sections of Jerusalem society. As long as we lived there, Jews, Christians and Moslems would meet at our house British officers and residents, as well as many of the crowd of tourists who very soon began to arrive.'[11] That week they gave three dinner parties, a lunch party and two tea parties and played

tennis – but also visited workrooms for women, negotiated for
more land for Helen's girls, and discussed the problems of the
5000 or so orphans. The term 'orphan', Helen explained, was used
to include all children whose parents were unable to bring them
up, and sometimes the parents would ask the orphan committee
to take over the care of a child. Children's villages were early
established in different parts of Palestine, and the children trained
to work on the land. There were often arguments about whether it
were better for a child to live in the family environment, however
squalid it might be, or to live in a modern and well-run village.
Helen's view was that the family should be retained as a whole,
and helped to care for its own children, so she was more interested in working among the families than the 'orphans'. She also
told of a curious case, a woman whom a Cairo friend asked her to
help:

24.2.19: She is a woman from Jaffa, an Orthodox Christian, who,
during the war, was starving. Her husband went away to fight, &
she was left with her child alone. So she put on men's clothes, &
went out as a porter. But the Turks took her for a man, & con-
scripted her, & for 9 months she fought in the Turkish army, up
Beersheba way, right in all the fighting. After we came, she came
to Jerusalem, & her husband died. The Syrian & Palestine Relief
ladies gave her work as their door-keeper, but she *would* wear her
soldier's trousers & tarboosh, as she is very proud of having been
a soldier. So these dear ladies were horrified & turned her away.
Since then, she has been cleaning boots outside the Jaffa Gate.
Her child is in a convent. She looks full of life & interest & is
willing to do *any* sort of work – from washing or scrubbing to
carpentering or driving a car.

3.3.19: The unemployment is terrible. There is *no* industry for the
girls. The lace & needlework is an entirely artificial one, & costs a
lot to keep up, & can seldom pay. Everything can be brought in
cheaper than it can be manufactured here – there is at present no
power, no money, no initiative & no power of organization. So
land work seems the only possible thing to start right away. Tools
are our great difficulty – & a common language. I know I should
talk to the girls in Hebrew, but I don't seem able to learn any.
What with having learnt an Ashkenazi pronunciation before, &

some Arabic since, I can't get hold of this Hebrew here at all. So
– prepare for a shock – I find I get on quite nicely in Yiddish …
The General [Money] has come back, & everyone rather rejoices
that Storrs has to go down one, & be merely Governor of Jerusalem. He's not exactly popular … New books here are so rare that
we have to make one last as long as possible – *do* send some more
please.

20.3.19: We have a big fancy-dress party to-night – Miss Landau's
– which is the talk of the town. OETA officers aren't to go in
fancy dress, which pleases Norman. I'm going in my smock &
breeches, & the handkerchief on my head.

Friday we were up betimes, & went off in a box-car, first to
Hebron & then to Beersheba. They do a lot of hunting at Beersheba & the governor has a lot of dogs. When we visited he gave
me one, a carrotty little puppy about 4 months, who is awfully
affectionate & quite a good companion. He will take my evening
shoes and stockings into the box where he sleeps & chew them,
& loves unrolling Norman's puttees.

I went to Miss Landau's school & took 12 girls for Guides –
next week I'll have about 25. Her school *is* a good show, & yet
the AJA [the Anglo-Jewish Association] is always making her re-
duce the numbers; so she has to get rid of the big ones, just at this
time when no work can be found for girls; & they are just sent off
because English Jews can't even pay £300 a year for the girls here.
It's the only thing Anglo-Jewry does for Palestine, beyond the
Zionist Commission (which is a dud as regards funds), Can't you
stir them up to *increase* the school instead of monthly reducing it!

Yesterday we went by car to Nablus with Redcliffe,[12] and
Redcliffe & I went all over the town while Norman did his work.
We visited the Samaritans, of whom there are only 160 left. An
official from the court, who is a Samaritan, took us round. He
took us to his house & gave us tea, & gave us a Samaritan book &
a picture, & then shamelessly asked me if I would ask Norman to
raise his salary! I told him to make his children work; he had
grown-up sons who did nothing. They've no school there, &
seem to think one unnecessary.

In a later letter Helen assured her worried mother that she was not taking backsheesh, and never would. The book was for Redcliffe Salaman, not for her.

Helen reported that at the opening of the music school which Storrs had founded, 'there was the usual "incident", without which nothing in Jerusalem is able to take place'. At the end, the performers started to play what all the British thought was going to be 'God Save the King'; but it turned out to be Hatikvah, the Zionist anthem, and General Money told Storrs and the others to sit down. Miss Landau, who was not a Zionist, sat down too, and many Zionists, feeling insulted, decided to boycott her ball. Helen did her best to act as peace-maker, persuading some to go after all – just as well, for poor Miss Landau had plenty of other problems, with a strike in Cairo stranding the music and the ices. It seems to have been a grand party all the same, with rooms in Japanese style, Miss Landau as a Dutch peasant, and 'one of the Hadassah girls rather beyond the limit as Pavlova – scantily attired to say the least of it. They are rather a queer crew – for the most part, very vapid little bits of fluff, who add considerably to the gaiety of life here, but not to its dignity.'

26.3.19: I went riding with some officers from the graves concentration unit, on a very quiet horse of theirs. They have 25 carthorses, & they go to outlying places, exhume bodies, & drag them in with these horses attached to sand-carts – rather a loathsome job, but very necessary. They are making a fine cemetery on the Mount of Olives.

Norman is a Lt. Col. now, *pro tem* – but if Clarke comes back he'll probably degrade again, Anyway, it dates from October, so we're *multi*-millionaires for a few weeks for a change.

April – the 2nd Saturday: I've talked to a good many people about work for girls, but it's very difficult. Gardening is out of the question in this drought – all the things I've planted are growing *down* instead of *up*, & we aren't allowed to use Government water for watering, & the cisterns are inadequate. It'll have to be some sort of home industries, I think, because it's so hard to get a Jew & Moslem & Christian to work side by side in factories.

We called on the Governor's mother & sister, who are staying up here with him, but fortunately they were out. For heaven's

sake send me a manual on social etiquette. Mrs Storrs [Ronald
Storrs' mother] has been here 2 or 3 weeks, & everyone was horrified I hadn't called before. So when Lady Money came, we
called two days after & the ADC said she wasn't ready. I feel I'm
blighting Norman's career.

I went to see Mr Ashbee, the architect & Town-planner here.
He is making a lot of gardens, & I've offered him my girls. We
went to see the place, all round David's Tower, & the walls round
the Jaffa Gate. It's very fascinating planning gardens, with flowers
from the hills transplanted, & all sorts of experimental places. I'm
keen to take part, but since then politics & other difficulties have
thrust themselves in, so I may have to back out. Nothing can be
done here without politics, & my aim & object in life is to keep
out.

C.R. Ashbee is better known in England in the context of Chip-
ping Campden and the Guild of Handicraft. But he served with a
field ambulance in the Middle East in the First World War, and in
1918 was invited by Storrs to come to Jerusalem to report on the
arts and crafts and to help in new plans for reconstruction. He
became Civic Adviser, and secretary to the conservationist Pro-
Jerusalem Society. His maternal grandfather was Jewish.

3.4.19: There are a lot more wives coming now. It's ever so much
nicer to have a lot of nice English people here – one can't help
feeling so much more at home with them than with anyone else.
Last night we dined at Norman's old Mess. Major Sackville-West
was there – an extraordinarily well-meaning dull man, who has
lived in Constantinople & all sorts of other interesting places &
yet bores one describing them. But he's very kind, & interested in
flowers. He travels all over the country in a carriage, collecting the
Ottoman debt.

We are suffering domestic troubles, as the cook has gone off
home with fever, & the small girl is nursing her there. And Ibra-
him had fever, and then disappeared; so we were left with only
the girl. But – don't let this come to the ears of the Women's War
Agricultural Committees – we take the garden-girls to help in the
house, & they love it for a change, & pull off their shoes &
stockings & do all the washing & scrubbing.

Home papers are too depressing almost to read – starving Germany, & cutting down her army, & then keeping our own conscription & bleeding the nation for armaments makes one feel that, if one could have foreseen the end of the war at the beginning, every decent person would have been a pacifist. I think morally we've lost the war a thousand times over, as a nation.

The Coal Commission is a pretty good indictment of the government & the capitalists, & as such is, to me, very cheering. There's right stuff somewhere in England if we can only overthrow this cynical government before it is too late.

Many apologies for the above – just to let you know that I've not changed really, altho' I'm camouflaged as a Colonel's lady. But a factory agitator is still the bent nearer my heart!

21.4.19: Szold came to dinner. He is a new member of the Zionist Commission – a go-ahead, capable, clever, broad-minded young man, a great improvement on the old lot who were here when we came. He & Bianchini (the Italian) & Friedenwald – another American – ought to pull things up a lot.

Saturday morning we went to the Holy Fire, at the Church of the Sepulchre. Norman hated it, because it was barbaric & irreligious. I can't say I *liked* it – I don't believe any of the spectators did – but I'm awfully glad to have seen it. We were all accommodated in alcoves high up, rather like third tier boxes at the opera, & so were very safe & uncrushed. Storrs & Waters-Taylor sat at the entrance to the Sepulchre, & 12 of the young OETA officers acted as policemen, with lots of gendarmes. Once or twice processions of 'rowdies' shoved their way in & banged about & made everyone afraid of what might happen, but the ringleaders were turned out & all was quiet. Then processions of gorgeously robed priests & patriarchs went round, & the Greek patriarch went into the sepulchre, & there was absolute silence & waiting. And then the people nearest shoved their candles into a hole, & withdrew them alight, & then there was great noise & excitement. Everyone shoved to get their candles lit first, & all the bells rang, & there was singing & shouting. It was quite an impressive sight to see the mass of lighted candles below – only a wretched Armenian bishop behind me would drop hot grease down my neck.

We went to tea with Norman's Jewish interpreter boy, a very clever Sephardi youth. They have a queer ceremony tonight, as the last night of Passover, of beating each other with bunches of green corn, to mean that the next year should be as green & promising as the green corn.

28.4.19 Friday we went to lunch up at OETA with General and Lady Money – she has just come out from England, & seems awfully nice & not too conventional. There are heaps of ladies out here now – I feel quite the oldest inhabitant, having got here before them. Storrs' mother & sister are out here – they called on me the other day, but fortunately I was out. I can manage most of the ladylike business by now, but afternoon-tea at home with callers beats me; I always retreat into the kitchen to see if the water is boiling. Norman is rather grieved over my clothes. He says a wife who dresses in breeches & smocks he can understand, & a wife who wears ultra-chic short skirts & futuristic patterns he can understand; but one who is one thing in the morning & the other in the afternoon is beyond him. He didn't mind until all these others came out, & they are mostly of the quiet country order who get their clothes at the Stores, & so he says mine are too short & too bright. And they can't be lengthened or dyed – the only thing to do is to get leave, & get some more. Meanwhile he blushes to own me in my mauve jumper-dress, or the new green flowery one. Still, I blush still more to own him in his stained & patched tunics & breeches; he will soon be reduced to dispensing justice from his bed, if we can't get to Cairo to get some new breeches.

Two of Norman's clerks came to tea – a Palestinian boy, & a sergeant from Croydon, who is always so proper & respectful I really had him to tea to see if he could say anything except 'Yes madam' & 'No madam.' He talked a lot, chiefly on the superiority of Croydon over Jerusalem. Taken all round, it *is* a much nicer place. There aren't so many foreigners there, nor so much sun, & more drainage & fresh water, & a good deal more civilized enjoyment. Oh, for some more *books*.

8.5.19: Norman now works from 8.30–1, & 3–5, which is much more civilized, & is usually home about 6, for tea. So at last I realize I have a husband, instead of just a lodger. Also, he gets Sundays off, which is great fun … We rode on our gees to Ram Allah, a village 10 miles north of here, & had lunch with a very cheery young deputy governor there, & rode back – an all-day trip about two and a half hours each way.

We called on Mrs Ashbee, who with 4 small daughters has just arrived out here. She seems very nice – but rather overwhelmed at the prospect of housekeeping here for all that family, which is no light task, especially as he's civilian & not military. It's a great mistake to be a civilian here – everything is done for the military, & the rest get a very thin time.

We try not to be quite so gay, because we never have any peaceful evenings & it makes Norman's life one whirl. But it's very hard here, what with all the OETA officers, & other odd English & American friends, & the Jewish people, & Norman's legal crowd. It's much gayer in that way than Cairo, but most of the people are awfully nice, & it's great fun.

I've just started chickens – 12 baby ones & a hen to mind them, & 2 hens to lay, which have produced 3 eggs in 2 days between them. They live in the cellar in true East End style, because they ate the seeds in the garden. But we will make a run, as soon as we have enough wire. [The chickens were later massacred by her dog.]

16.5.19 Cairo: I'm spending a few days once more in Cairo. Norman had to go to Haifa to confer & conspire with generals, & I thought I'd probably be awfully *de trop*, as no other wives were going. I got my permit from Col. Crichton because I said I wanted to collect money from the rich Jews in Cairo for the land girls. The RTO [Railway Traffic Officer] people knew I was going, & I had a *very* comfy journey. It's great to be a lone woman on a journey out here, where there is such a superfluity of males. And if you're a colonel's wife, you get things reserved very easily … Oh, people *do* live in luxury here! The prolific flowering trees & creepers, growing everywhere; the riot of colour in the gardens; the whiteness & tidiness of Gezira houses; the neat suffragis [Arab manservants]; the gorgeous motors, the liveried servants, the *shops*, the *bathrooms*, the nice home sort of food. It has made me sick of roughing it.

I have been perfectly ruthless about my flat. None of the furniture had been allowed to come, so I went for a permit & got it. Then I went to the flat, & found how much more civilized I would be if I had all the proper furniture, & so, perfectly ruth-

lessly to the tenants who had only had it on the understanding
that we would take the furniture at a minute's notice, & who
hadn't been awfully careful of our things, I have had taken away
almost everything, & it will be packed tomorrow, & should be up
in a week. I feel quite excited at the thought of having pretty &
English things in my house.

The furniture, including a piano, made a big difference to the
comfort of Jerusalem life. But enthusiasm for the fleshpots of
Egypt soon faded:

26.5.19 Jerusalem: Cairo *isn't* a healthy place, & after a day or
two I soon went off my food & started pains in the middle, as in
the old days. But being back here is great, & I'm as fit as can be.

Don't say that I find your accounts tame & petty – I often
envy you being in England & among all decent, civilized sorts of
things – there are not many times that I don't really want to get
home back to England & a natural sort of life. For all our gaieties
& entertainments, this life is very artificial, & rather brain-fagging.
Still, it's great fun, & like munitions & the land-work is a fine experience. But it's very abnormal. I expect you are revelling in
roses & rhododendrons by now – & strawberries. Oh ye gods,
strawberries! Still, life has its compensations, & at present we are
very full of apricots. And my lilies & hollyhocks & broom & oleander & snapdragons make my rooms look ever so gay. The great
event is that we have got up most of our crockery & *all* our
books. We *have* got some ripping books – it's such a joy to see
them again after 3 years.

Domesticities are still *very* impossible. I'm becoming a nagging
virago every minute I am in the house, so the only thing to do is
to go out & not notice. Chaya is past praying for – what would
you do if your servant told you, when dinner was half an hour late,
that she'd waited half an hour for you the night before, so it was
your turn this time! And one who reads all your letters & invitations, & who, if you don't go out when you are invited, asks why
you can't go, as it makes it so hard for her. And I've hardly a
handkerchief left. Still, they are all so far *very* honest with big
things – jewellery & money – so I suppose we mustn't grumble at
a few handkerchiefs & underclothes.

27.5.19: Monday & Tuesday [in Cairo] I went round after money again & I only got about £70 in all – stingy beasts. But I'm not worried any more, as I've just been cabled the £1000 I've agitated for, from America.

I've adopted a small woolly white 6-weeks-old puppy called Billy. He is very fascinating & a great joy, tho' he grows so fast I'm afraid he may turn into a mastiff.

Monday I went to a meeting of Jewish people to form a committee for inaugurating an association to promote the foundation of companies of scouts & guides. They *talked* – & got little further. I'm vice-president. They *live* on committees here. However, fortunately they talk in Hebrew, & I'm not expected to understand, & only the important bits are translated for me.

3.6.19: We are frightfully patriotic here, & because it's the King's birthday we have a general holiday & rejoicing, with a grand reception by Storrs in the Municipal Gardens this afternoon, & triumphal arches in the streets, & to-night a big official dinner for heads of departments & notables at OETA, to which Norman goes, but ladies are not included.

There's been a horrid scandal this week – the Senior Judicial Officer's [i.e. Norman's] horse has been stolen from the Military Governor's stables where it lives, & the united efforts of the Law Courts & police fail to find it.

I went to a social service meeting at Mrs McInnes', the Bishop's wife, where were females from all sects & communities in Jerusalem, to talk over starting a Rescue Home, & sending in pledges & requests to the Governor to stop licensing bad houses. As usual here, it was mostly talk – I didn't do any, because nearly all the talk was done by Jewish women, & I wanted to show that one, at least, could keep quiet.

We were taken to a dance given by the officers of the Baluchistan Regiment, stationed here. It wasn't bad fun, because it was amusing to meet them all. But I can't dance – especially any of these new things – so I don't expect I'll be asked to any more. They have about one a week, usually at the Governorate [the Government offices] on Saturdays.

Sunday morning I cleaned my house out from top to bottom. I can do it so much better than my servants, & I'm sick of nagging them. It *is* rotten that just because you marry your whole atmosphere has to get bounded by a house & domestics. They monopolize one's life & interests – & I *hate* it all so. Food is a problem, too, as fish is impossible, & meat always gives one jaw-ache, it's so tough. We've been making a huge bonfire of accumulated rubbish – great fun in this climate, as you get such a lovely quick blaze, & the stone walls & houses make it so safe. Everything being stone, there are never any fires here – there's not even a hydrant or engine, because, I suppose, there is no water.

12.6.19: Two good things have happened this week – I've got my horse back & I've got an A1 pukka cook. First as to the horse. I never thought I was going to see him again, but, being the SJO's horse, the Public Prosecutor & the police made themselves very busy indeed about him, & traced the thief. Apparently a man in Hebron had seen me on him, & liked the look of him, so he promised a man in Jerusalem £8 if he'd steal him from the stables. I'm awfully glad to have him back – each of the thieves is getting a year ...

The Egyptian cook got off to a bad start. He was soon 'in the lock-up at Ramallah for trying to do a man in when he was very drunk'; but a few days later he was back, 'turning out more & more delicious foods every day'.

... On Tuesday last week there was the Garden Party given by Storrs in the Municipal Gardens, when we all dressed up in our very best, & started by being very mixed up & democratic, but soon sifted, in the inevitable way of the Orient, into the English in one tent, & the rest of the world outside it. How they must hate us!

Saturday we went to an awfully jolly dance at the Governorate where we jazzed & Bostoned till after midnight, to the strains of very excellent music provided by the British West Indian Band.

Apart from the garden party and the dance, that week's letter included an informal supper party, four dinner parties, four lunch parties, and two tea parties at their house; and they went out once to dinner and once to tea, and to a picnic. Helen need not have worried about there being 'not much chance of a social life'. And

so it went on – dinners, apricots and figs, meetings, exploring.
'Not one day since I've been here,' Helen wrote on 21 June, 'have
we been in alone for all meals.'

There was a major social duty for Helen when Norman had a
conference for the law officers and judges from all parts of
Palestine, and he held a large official reception at the law courts.

26.6.19: Tuesday was *very* strenuous. I was up very early getting
flowers, & had a car to take all my rugs, cushions, vases, small
tables & hangings to the Courts. There, I transformed 4 unused
rooms of the Russian buildings into quite civilized rooms for the
ladies, & about 7 into more or less civilized rooms for the men.
And decorated the window-sills along the long, bare passages
with shell-cases full of oleander & pepper-tree. Some criminal
took it into his head to cut off all the water-supply that day, & all
the water to wash things & for cleaning & flowers etc had to be
brought from the stables in everlasting petrol-tins. Then, the
chairs & tables never came till after lunch, & the cups & saucers
& glasses (200 of each) not till after 3, & every one had to be
thoroughly washed & dried. Some job! We had a few prisoners to
help with the big things ... By tea-time my temper had quite
gone, & I got bellowing Arabic to people who only talked German, & French to people who only talked English, & generally
getting very rabid. However, it all got cleared up & ready somehow. The Judge from Jaffa brought up the cakes – they have a
factory in Tel Aviv where they make lovely iced cakes & choco-
late cakes & macaroons. Miss Landau's school made 12 for us.
And we'd got chocolates from Cairo ... The show started at 8.30.
Very few Moslem ladies came – only about 6 – because I suppose
they won't go to parties, even harem. But I wanted to keep it
separate, even for those few, half of the time. Lady Money came
about 9, & after she had seen the ladies, & talked to them, she
went into the men's part, & then any others who liked trooped in
too. We had the American Colony band in the courtyard. There
must have been about 300 people altogether. I have a horrid
dread of receptions where we all sit on chairs and never move, so
I kept moving them on. We had heaps too much food – but alas,
it was *all* stolen in the night after, except the sandwiches.

Yesterday we dined with the Vesters, the American Colony
people, & had an awfully interesting time after dinner, going with

them to Solomon's quarries, some huge subterranean caves under the city, whence Solomon is supposed to have taken his stone for the temple. We walked miles & miles, with lanterns & candles. We were a very large party. The American Colony choir gave us songs – hymns & darkie jubilee songs – whilst we were in the caves, which was very effective & pleasant. It's a great place for Masons, as the keystone of an arch that was half cut out is the Masons' keystone, or something of the sort, & connected with Solomon.

In a story of life in Palestine at this time, something must be said about the Vesters and the 'American Colony'. In 1881, when she was three, Bertha Vester's parents had broken with the Orthodox Presbyterian church that had been the centre of their lives in Chicago and had come, with a small group of like-minded friends, as evangelist pilgrims to Jerusalem. They had lost four small daughters in a shipwreck and a baby son from scarlet fever, and could not accept a church that taught that such tragedies were punishment for sins and that the infants would suffer in hell. Others joined them over the years, from Palestine, America, and Sweden. Ronald Storrs wrote that 'they were cynically said to have come to Jerusalem to do good, and stayed to do well. The truth is that they did both.' They helped an assortment of down-and-outs, they ran soup kitchens and nursed the wounded in the war, and after the war they did relief work, and set up a clinic which still exists. They also successfully ran the American Colony Store and various business enterprises.[13] Hymn singing was a prominent feature of their life – they were friends of Moody and Sankey – and Helen's outing to Solomon's quarries was a typical American Colony experience.

Perhaps Helen's greatest pleasure during her years in Jerusalem was travelling over Palestine and the surrounding countries. The appalling state of the roads and the lack of reliable transport always brought a crop of mild adventures, with breakdowns and tyre-bursts part of the routine. 'Cars in Palestine,' she wrote in one letter, 'are first cousins to motor-bikes in Hertford.' The roads were particularly awful because they were repaired with large pieces of stone, which might lie around for months before a roller could come to break them up. Early in July she went touring for a

few days with Norman when, in spite of endless car troubles, they
had a wonderful trip:

6.7.19: Why we didn't go to Acre before when you were here, I
can't think. It's a perfect jewel of a place, about 12 miles from
Haifa & there is no road. And we drive slick along by the sea all
the way on the hard sand, with the wheels more or less in the sea
if the tide is up. There are two rivers to cross, which now have
pontoon bridges. There are quicksands there, & a lot of cars &
lorries have disappeared before they had bridges. With Carmel on
one side & the sea on the other, racing along this sandy track with
the spray in your face, it was about the finest drive imaginable.
But unfortunately the night before there had been an unpleasant
scrap between Tommies & natives, & the 2 native victims were
being buried then, so the Deputy Military Governor didn't think
it safe for us to see the town. They have a race-course at Acre, &
everyone goes from Haifa for the races. I should love to go by the
sea like that right up to Tyre & Sidon or Beyrouth [Beirut]. We
will one day – only unfortunately it is not our OETA,[14] so Norman hasn't to, & they are very down on joy-riding now.

15.7.19: This letter is rather late, but I wrote you one two days ago
which Norman said was too cross to be sent off. Due to the heat,
principally, which has been very trying here this last week, & always rumples my temper. I wasn't made for hot countries.
   We had tea with the Ashbees, & went with them to see a
derelict place in the Old City which Ashbee thinks might eventually be made into a children's playground by the Land Girls. But
he offers no funds, so it's not very likely. Tuesday I had a long
interview with Mrs MacInnes, the Bishop's wife. I'm taking over
her work among the bad young women of Jerusalem whilst she
goes home. We are hoping to open a rescue home quite soon –
undenominational, but all run kosher, with an English or American head. We are trying to collect funds from the population here,
by asking for a minimum of 2/- a month from everyone … We
know no more about coming home, except that we mean to do it
somehow, tho' probably it will only be for a month in England. It's
really very hard on Army of Occupation officers here. They have
been through 3, 4, or even 5 years war-strain without getting
home, & are now turned onto the thankless task of garrisoning or

administering Occupied Enemy Territory, & then only get a
month's leave, & it's very hard for some to get even that. The
men in Germany get an awfully cushy time.

Leave was a mirage, always retreating into the distance – Norman
had not been home for four years. The hot weather always made
Helen irritable and restless – as she was the first to admit – and
there was pleasure in planning what they might do:

> **23.7.19**: Norman wants to spend some time at Cambridge, & I
> want to pay a visit to Hertfordshire, & we want a bit of time on
> the river, & it would be much easier if we had a car, wouldn't it? I
> want to learn to drive a Ford somehow whilst I'm at home, if it's
> not too short a time. Because we are hoping to have one when we
> come back. And *lots* of theatres & other London joys – it's 5 years
> since Norman has been to a theatre ...

Norman always loved Cambridge. He had been an undergraduate
at Trinity, had many Cambridge friends, and had once hoped for a
fellowship. But in 1920, when there was a possibility of going back
to an academic post, he felt he could not leave Palestine; five years
later, when problems in Palestine led him to think of Cambridge
again, there was no opening.

> ... I'm getting rather bored with most of the people here – they
> are mostly very nice if you don't see too much of them, but they
> are very stereotyped & haven't many ideas. I am getting out a pe-
> tition to the Govt. from the society I'm running to stop all
> recognition of bad houses & licensed women, & am trying to get
> it signed by all the heads of the communities. And I'm trying to
> collect money for the Home. But I can't take a really deep interest
> in anything here – that's what's the matter with the place. No-
> body can. The future is so unsettled & everybody hates everybody
> else so, that it's not much good trying. We are slowly being ruined
> – living here is impossibly dear, & 6-course dinners aren't cheap,
> are they?
>   I'm glad to be out of all the 'Peace' Celebrations – with 23
> little wars going on, & surrounded by conscripts, & not being able
> to get leave, we don't feel much like 'Peace rejoicings'.

30.7.19: Thank the Lord it has got cooler again now, & I feel more civilized & liveable-with.

General Money is leaving tomorrow, & General Watson, from Cairo, is taking his place. Everyone is very grieved at the General's going – he is liked by everyone; but the worst result of this drawn-out temporary administration is that everybody gets sick to death of waiting for something permanent, & goes off home at the first opportunity. Norman is now the veteran at HQ here – & most of the changes are for the worse. It's a rotten situation for governors & governed.

We visited the Jerusalem water works. They haven't really got nearly enough water there to satisfy Jerusalem, & will have to make another one elsewhere. It's still worked by soldiers – the one we saw had the usual grouse that they weren't in the army, being paid army wages, to do skilled engineering work for civilians – which is the cause of most of the trouble here with the railways.

We are to have no Peace rejoicings till we make Peace with Turkey.

The Jerusalem water supply, which had been in crisis at the end of the war, had in fact been dramatically improved the previous year by the army engineers, following Storrs' initiative. 'Not since the days of the Romans,' wrote the historian of the Egyptian expeditionary force, 'has running water been so plentiful in the Holy City.'

9.8.19: We stayed the night with a colonist at Rosh Pina. The village is built on the side of a very steep hill, & like all the Jewish colonies, is very sordid & untidy & depressing to look at. I think colony life must be too depressing for anything – everyone is so very intense & 'political' & there are so few purposeless relaxations. And, except for a few, they all seem so very poor. And it's boring in the extreme – poor Nita[15] is utterly fed up at Zichron, she finds it so lonely. Next morning we went up to Safed. It's beautiful country to look at, & with a lovely soil – but a veritable plague-spot to live in, all round the Lakes & the Jordan Valley. The Colonists who try to live there die like flies of blackwater fever & malaria – the ones I saw in the Safed hospital were a terrible sight, & the only thing is to get them right out of those colonies, & scrap them altogether for the present, the doctors say.

I spent my time in the hospital at Safed, run by the American Zionist Unit – a wonderfully equipped place, built by the French
Jews years ago, who spent all their money on the building &
hadn't enough to run it after. I also visited an orphanage there
which had 50 children, & was in a scandalous state. The children
only had one lot of clothes, & had to be put to bed on Friday afternoons whilst those were washed. They also had no
nightclothes, & only 24 beds between them, most of which were
all broken, & the smaller children fell through in the night!

But back in Jerusalem things were looking up:

> We are getting very chic here – we have a restaurant, in between
> the Jaffa road & the City walls, very nicely got up & picturesque,
> where we dined one night with two of the medical officers, & had
> a very good dinner & *ices*. And we have a Jerusalem Sporting
> Club, with 2 tennis courts, for the social intercourse of the town –
> OETA & others.
>
> Did I ever tell you of an Arabic proclamation that appeared in
> Jaffa, announcing that the Law Courts would be closed on June
> 3rd (or some such date) because of the birthday of 'our noble
> king, Lloyd George'!

Now there was a sports club, Helen started to play tennis most
days, and tennis tournaments were soon to become increasingly
important in her life.

The letters often describe servant problems. For some time Ali
had been their very successful cook, but on one occasion 'Ali was
sick, but he had produced 3 other cooks, friends of his, to cook
the dinner for us instead. Mrs Popham's was one, as she was
supposed to be dining here too. In the end she didn't, & so she
didn't have any proper dinner, because Ali had summoned the
cook here. It's a good way,' Helen advised her mother, 'when you
have guests tell your cook who it is, & then he'll get their cook to
come & help.'

> **28.8.19**: I'm writing on my verandah, surrounded by flies, which I
> did capture a chameleon to kill yesterday, but I tied a string round
> its tail & it all swelled up so much that I had to let it go. Besides,

it was a fraud, & only went light & dark, & never went green, even tho' I carried it about in my smock pocket for ages.

The four Judges of the Court of Appeal & the Director of Public Prosecutions are dining here to-night, which is rather alarming, as only one out of the 5 talks English, 2 talk only Arabic, 1 French & 1 Hebrew. Tomorrow, some Bedouin chiefs are coming to tea, father & brother of one of Norman's men. And Saturday night Norman goes to Cairo, & I go too.

In spite of the heat I ride round the town most mornings till mid-day, & play tennis most afternoons. If all the cauliflowers I've sown come up, I shall have enough to feed all Palestine, to say nothing of the rest of Asia. I didn't know so many seeds went to a kilo.

The Bedouin tea party became 'unexpectedly enormous', when ten other assorted guests called, ranging from a Turkish Deputy to a missionary lady. Helen found the Bedouin and his four sons 'awfully interesting. They are a great family, & have 45 race-horses, & do no end of hunting with the British officers.'

Norman was over-working, and at this time often 'feeling rotten'. The visit to Cairo was happy, but left Helen even more restless when they got back:

7.9.19: What a barren desolate place this is compared to Cairo! I simply loved the shops – I didn't know I wanted things till I saw them in the windows, & then I went inside & bought them. And Groppi's ices & Shepheard's iced drinks & the fast buggies & the baths & electric lights & immaculate servants – I nearly wept to leave it all for *this* dreary, bathless, candle-greasy, un-iced, badly-servanted hole. So there! ... Ali is sick to-day, & Chaya & Max are fighting & scratching all day & smashing my china, & I *loathe*, loathe, *loathe* housekeeping, & don't mean to come back till I can bring someone to do it for me. So, for Norman's sake, *please* find me someone.

Helen's socialism never stopped her from wanting a comfortable house, well looked after by servants.

Meanwhile life, as she said, went on uneventfully, 'with no big issues or incidents, but plenty of trivial ones'. General and Lady Watson replaced the Moneys. There was more and more tennis,

and joy-rides, and dinners and dances, and there was land work
and charity bazaars – and still no news of leave. '*Perhaps* by Xmas.'
    Relations with OETA West (the French OETA) became a
worry:

24.9.19: Things seem to be very touchy between us and France –
due to our fascinating habit of playing with nations as if they were
pieces in a game, & disposing of them, as in the Sykes–Picot
agreement[16] as if they had no will of their own. And *then*, to win
the war & get in with America, to talk of self-determination & the
rights of small nations. We are in a very awkward hole out here, &
our worst enemy is France. I wish France would take the whole
rotten lot, & let us come home on leave! It's getting hot again, &
it won't rain, & one eats & drinks dust, & nothing really thrilling
ever happens. I think I've got the result of war-fever – unless I
get a new thrill once a week, I'm bored stiff.
    Friday was a great day here, because a Cardinal arrived from
Italy. There was nearly a war over him, as nobody could think
how to receive him, & Norman had to mug up a lot of International Law on the subject, & coach them. In the end we didn't
receive him, but we recognized him – a subtle difference!

19.10.19: I have been to 2 lectures by Professor Geddes[17] on the
University; they were very interesting in their way, but he gave
them especially to women, & talked 'down' to our level – telling
us how wonderful & important we were, etc, until I got so fed up
I rather told him I didn't like it at the end of the lecture yesterday.
He has a poor idea of women if he thinks they'll swallow that.
Some of these Jewish women here are violent feminists, bitten
with the 'difference' between men & women, & trying to empha-
size it. I'm an equalist, & can't agree with them at all. I just want
equal rights & education & chances, & then let individuals take
their own course.
    An Egyptian Moslem from the Courts, named Safoid, is being
sent to England to study at the London School of Economics. He
has been Legal Secretary here, under Norman, since the beginning, & Norman has given him your address, & told him to look
you up. He is very dingy & intense, but he is an interesting little
fellow. He is a keen Bahai – the new Persian world-religion,
whose prophet, Abbas Effendi, lives at Acre. I think you might

like to meet him because he can tell you lots of inside things about Egypt & the troubles there that you never get from the papers. And he knows nobody in London, so it would be nice for him to be able to talk to you.

The Committee of the YWCA bazaar had notices printed in English, French, Arabic & Hebrew, & gave me the Hebrew ones to distribute. Norman read them, & discovered many errors – the funniest of all was the English said the 'object of this association is to *help* girls of all nationalities & creeds', the translation said that the object was to 'lead them astray', the 2 words being very like in Hebrew. I told the General of it as a joke, but of course they took it frightfully seriously, Lady Watson's name appearing on the top, & sent the ADC post haste all over the town to trace the printer & translator & recall any stray copies.

We have seen the Weizmanns – we had tea with Mrs yesterday. She is elegant, but not pretty, & of course very foreign & fireworky ... I *can't* get on with people who don't laugh easily, & these Zionists seem to have lost the art, except in a scoffing, bitter spirit.

27.10.19: We went for an all-day trip to Kubabi (in the New Testament it is called Emmaus). We started off all on horses, & had a guide on a little black donkey. But we had not got very far outside the respectabilities of Jerusalem before I decided to try the little black donkey. It had an enormous red saddle, & was the comfiest thing I'd ever ridden, so I stuck to it until we reached respectability once again. No wonder the early inhabitants of this land wrote Bibles & things – a long journey on a donkey would be bound to make one a contemplative prophet.

I went to tea with Lady Watson, & told her a few plain truths about missionaries. She was very nice – but it's funny how all religious Christians seem to think missionizing incumbent on them. They don't think it such damned interfering cheek as we do.

We have funny afternoonless days now – breakfast at 7, lunch at 3.45, tea (very slight) at 4.30 & dinner at 8. It's a great squash to get them all in between 3 & 8, but OETA now works straight off from 8 till 2, & then no more. It's meant to make it nice for officers to take exercise after lunch, but they are all so dead tired there is less tennis played than before. We just walk out of the dining-room from lunch into the sitting-room for tea. And one is so hungry for lunch that one is often too hungry to eat much. Norman's inside is a rotten concern anyway, & a few meals more or less never seem to improve it. If *only* we could get home ...

8.11.19: The Weizmanns dined here. Mrs W. is very attractive to look at, isn't she, & has lovely clothes, so one can forgive her a lot. She doesn't like Palestine, either, & rather thinks the same about Zionism & living here as I do. He's very nice, I think. I don't envy him his job!

Vera Weizmann was not just agreeing politely with her hostess. Her involvement in Zionism, like Helen's, had come only as a result of her marriage. From an assimilated Russian background, she was by all accounts a difficult and ambitious character. Her clothes were bought in Paris, or in the dress shop run by her niece Eva Lutyens.

Helen was reluctant to get involved in bazaars – 'the silliest stunts extant' – 'But,' she wrote a bit sadly, 'out here, if one doesn't take part in a thing, & everyone else does, one is so lost & lonely. And when I *do* take part, I always like running it all, & it's so foolish.' So she did get thoroughly involved, organizing tickets, collecting contributions from the markets and from all friends and acquaintances – and enjoyed it.

At the end of November there was yet another Chief Administrator, General Bols, to replace General Watson. And Helen welcomed the arrival of an artist friend, Amy Drucker, 'very jolly, & different to most people here – those who are intellectual are intense & unhumorous; & those who are jolly & humorous are conventional & unintellectual'. Amy, Helen wrote the following year:

> is really living & painting in a native village on the coast, staying in a native hut, & thoroughly enjoying it all. She is a good sort to have here; it's nothing to her if the people are Jews or Arabs or Christians, or that this is a Holy Land – she treats them all the same. Such a relief after all the other people!

At last Helen wrote that they would be leaving for home soon –
particularly glad because her hand was in bandages for septic sores
which were not healing out there.

13.12.19: I can't write much yet – my hand is rather useless still ...
Storrs' sister, who is here now, a very energetic young woman
who lives in a settlement at Woolwich & goes to the School of
Economics & really is more congenial than most of the femininity
of these parts, is very keen on guides. So yesterday we inaugurated
a National Council, with Lady Bols as chairman, & with lions &
lambs lying quite peaceably side by side in the shape of Miss Landau, the ultra-Zionists, & the Missionaries. We are going to Mr
Ashbee this morning to ask him to design a really attractive &
suitable uniform for here.

Ali wants to stay with whoever we lend our house to, & be
with us when we come back. He really is a wonderful cook. I've
collected lots of bulbs – chiefly cyclamen, with a few iris, crocus
& tulip – to bring home.

They had a cold two-week journey home on a troop-ship, held up
for three days at Gibraltar by a dock strike, and checked for plague
on arrival at Liverpool.

---

[1] This oddly named hotel, owned by Mr Fast, was later renamed the Allenby.

[2] This dismissal of the Syrian & Palestine Relief Fund conflicts with Ronald
Storrs' description of the Fund's work for war refugees, with 'no thoughts of
national or sectarian propaganda'. See Ronald Storrs, *Orientations* (London:
Nicholson and Watson, 1945).

[3] In her manuscript memoir.

[4] Harold Nicolson in *The Spectator*, 16 May 1952.

[5] Lord Harlech, to Mandates Commission, 1937.

[6] Norman Bentwich, *Wanderer Between Two Worlds* (London: Kegan Paul, 1941).

[7] Quoted in Chaim Weizmann, *Trial and Error* (London: Hamish Hamilton, 1949).

[8] Bentwich: *Wanderer Between Two Worlds*, pp 97–8.

[9] F.H. Kisch, *Palestine Diary* (London: Gollancz, 1938), p 80.

[10] Ernest Richmond was the son of W.B. Richmond, and grandson of George
Richmond.

[11] Norman and Helen Bentwich, *Mandate Memories* (London: Hogarth Press,
1965).

[12] Redcliffe Salaman, authority on the genetics and history of the potato, a remote cousin of Helen's; in 1935 his son Arthur married Herbert Samuel's daughter Nancy.

[13] The American Colony Hotel, still owned by Vesters, was the site of the first direct talks between Israelis and Palestinians which led to the 1993 accord (*The Times*, 15 May 1997).

[14] It was OETA West, the French OETA.

[15] Nita Lange, Norman's first pioneering sister, had settled in Zichron with her husband in 1912. Her house is now a sad ruin (Amos Oz used it as the scene for his novel *The Black Box*), but 'Beth Daniel' (House of Daniel), built there by Lilian, Norman's eldest sister, as a memorial to her son, is a flourishing centre for art and a guest-house for artists and musicians.

[16] The Sykes–Picot Agreement (1916) was an agreement between Britain and France to split the post-war spheres of influence in the previously Turkish-held territories of the Middle East. Britain was to have authority in Southern Mesopotamia, together with Haifa and Acre on the Palestine coast; the area north of a line from Acre to Tiberias was to be under French influence; the rest of Palestine west of the Jordan would become an international zone.

[17] Patrick Geddes, scientist and town-planner, had been invited by the Zionist Commission to design the layout of the Hebrew University. 'His unused design for the main buildings seems today a wild fantasy.' Norman Bentwich in *My 77 Years* (London: Routledge & Kegan Paul, 1961).

1920

The High Commissioner's Niece

It was a happy leave, but marred by worries for Norman about his future. There was the possibility, which Helen would have loved, of a post in Cambridge, but, Helen wrote later, 'his conscience told him he must come back, as opposed to his inclination which hankered mostly after Cambridge & the English law.'[1]

The Bentwiches' life in 1920 was to be very different. First, domestically – when they returned to Palestine they brought with them as Norman's batman a half-Maltese demobilized soldier, John Rayner, who had been working for Helen's parents in London. For the rest of their time in Palestine, John ran their home, drove their car, took all the hated household worries off Helen's shoulders, and generally looked after them. 'He soon learned Arabic,' Helen wrote, 'and became a well-known figure in Jerusalem; in fact, after a time I was alluded to in the bazaars as "John's Missus".'[2]

Politically, 1920 brought the end of the Military Administration, and the establishment of a civil government under a High Commissioner. The High Commissioner was to be Herbert Samuel, the Liberal politician and philosopher, who in 1909 had become the first practising Jew to be a member of a British Cabinet, and whose enthusiasm for Zionism had grown during the war. Samuel had been active in events leading to the Balfour Declaration – in 1915 he had proposed the establishment of a British protectorate over a Palestine which would become a haven for Jews from all over the world. The appointment delighted the Bentwiches, both because of their respect for him as a statesman and because he was first cousin to Helen's father and married, in the way of the 'cousinhood' of Anglo-Jews, to her father's sister Beatrice (known in the family as Bee). In the new regime, Norman was to cease to be an OETA officer, and was to become Legal Secretary with general supervision over the administration of both the civil and the religious courts, and over the Land Registration and Survey Departments – much time was taken up in complicated disputes over land ownership going back to Turkish times – as well as being Legal Adviser to the Government, drafting the new laws.

On their return journey, the Bentwiches heard of a serious outbreak of violence, the first of many riots against Jewish immigration. The Arabs who had come to Jerusalem for the Nebi Musa procession on 4 April had been incited by Haj Amin Husseini (who was unfortunately appointed Mufti the following year) to attack the Jews in the Old City; there were about 250 casualties, nine-tenths of them Jews.

> **30.4.20**: We have arrived here safe & sound – really at rather a crucial moment; in fact, on the same day that the Mandate was announced. So far, it's all very quiet here; but we are fighting the Hedjaz people up by Tiberias. There's no end of intrigue & alarms about the row on Easter Sunday – enquiries & commissions & court-marshals [*sic*] without end ... It's impossible to say anything definite because things change so from day to day. One day Jabotinsky, a Zionist from the Jewish battalion, gets 15 years imprisonment for having arms, & many others 3 years each – & to-day we hear he's gone down to 1 year, & the others 6 months – & all will probably be commuted. It's undignified of the British to get the wind up in this way – but it's Ireland over again, only too plainly.

The riots, and the commission of enquiry that followed, added to Norman's burdens, and intensified the strained relationships:

> **9.5.20**: We've not seen much of the English people so far. It's all rather awkward, as most of them are so very outspokenly anti-

Jewish now, that it makes it rather difficult, altho' I think they are
all prepared to be very nice to us personally. The things they say
are too absurd. The Ashbees dined here, & he said that the Press
in England is entirely controlled by the Jews, & only express Jewish interests! They refused to listen to my accounts of the *Morning
Post* anti-semitism, & Northcliffe & Cadbury & Beaverbrook &
co. They can't believe that what they think isn't the right thing for
English people to think. And so when English papers have anti-
Administration & anti-Arab articles, they immediately proclaim
that these are paid for by the Jews. It's very difficult to get on
with people when they are like that – that's only an instance of
their purblind bigotry.

There were problems in their house as well as in the political
atmosphere – it was full of bugs, and they had to sleep on the
balcony until it had all been treated with formalin and whitewash.
But they soon moved a few doors away to a slightly larger house
with a bath, more room for guests and entertaining, and a larger
garden where they stabled their horse. Helen's letters home in
those days of shortages and primitive living often had a strange
mixture of requests – breakfast cereal, books, lampshades, inflat-
able frogs, sunhats, garden seeds – and thanks for an even longer
list, including such unlikely parcels, in those days of slow posts
and hot weather, as butter and chocolates.

'The same old round', as Helen said, started again, and the
same 'colitis' problems for Norman. There was more good music,
as Norman's cellist sister Thelma had come out with them to join
the other members of the family in Palestine – Helen described a
musical evening in the new house when '21 people came, &
Thelma & Norman & Tchaikov & Seale (our pros) played, & a
Miss Smith sang, very loud & high'. 'I've taken up dancing now,'
she writes in another letter, 'it's better than having to talk too
much to these very dull officers here,' but 'Norman finds these
dances very trying & boring.' On 10 June she said she had had an
evening with Norman on their own, for the first time since
coming back.

28.5.20: I'm always being pestered about Uncle Herbert, but I
know less than anyone. It's never been either confirmed or con-

tradicted if he's coming or not. I get *so* pumped about him and his family, & I *am* so discreet & guarded in my answers, & get so tired of giving the ages of his children and the list of all his previous political posts. Everyone is just about sick of the uncertainty & vagueness – one of the stock questions is '*will* Herbert Samuel bring his own administration out with him?'

It was a relief when Samuel's appointment was confirmed, and Helen looked forward to his arrival. Suddenly cheerful, she reports that she has no more sores & Norman is better. 'You *must* come out with Aunt Bee,' she told her mother, '& Father too, if he can possibly get off. But, if not, bring Alice – or as well.' Oddly, neither Helen's sister Alice nor any of her four brothers ever did visit her in Palestine, although they were a closely attached family.

17.6.20: As I expect you've heard, Norman's got the permanent law job here, & we can't yet say whether we're glad or sorry, because it depends so much on what other people come & general conditions. Storrs is a fixture here too. I don't know if any others are. However much one may dislike people politically, personally it's rather a wrench when those whom one likes as human beings go away.

I still think Cambridge was more our metier – but I suppose if we *had* taken that we would be feeling rather blue by now about missing *this*.

1.7.20: Well, he has come, & despite all the alarums & excursions he arrived quite safely. We have just been up there to tea – Uncle Herbert looks very well, & it makes the place seem so nice & friendly to go up there & pour out tea. Everyone had the wind up badly about his safety – armoured cars patrolling everywhere & aeroplanes up all the time skimming the houses, & guards & police everywhere.

Today we've been arranging for tomorrow's big stunt – the Law Courts' Reception to 400 people in the Municipal Gardens, in the evening by moonlight with the band. I'm arranging it – men & women *together* this year – & Herbert is making his debut, so to speak, there. I'm scared I've not got enough cakes – 1600 seems a lot, but John says it's 3 or 4 each *&* sandwiches at Porchester Terrace,[3] but I've no butter for sandwiches.

5.7.20: We both heave a huge sigh of relief that Saturday's show is over & nobody any the worse – except us, who are nearly suffering from nervous prostration. We didn't realize beforehand what a bold thing we were doing. We gave this Reception in the evening to between 300 & 400 people of all creeds & classes & nationalities & politics, in the public gardens in the middle of the town, on the Jaffa Road, surrounded by roads & houses, quite inadequately lit with a few Lux lights, & we ask Uncle Herbert to make his debut to Jerusalem under those conditions. It was jolly brave of him to come. The police & secret service were terrifically busy – confidential orders yards long being issued every hour or so; a cordon of gendarmes all round; detectives in the crowd to watch; the whole road closed except to people having invitations. All day I was helping – or rather, ordering others to help. There were 25 prisoners, dangerous ones in chains, to clean up & get things ready. Thanks to the invaluable John who took entire control of the catering arrangements, drilled the waiters, & supervised everything, there was no hitch at all. He *is* a marvel; & he never minds how much he does – when we ask if he's not tired he says it's 'a nice change'.

Yesterday we had the officials to dinner – we were 7 British officers, 7 local officials, Amy [Drucker] & me. Not much to you, with your big house & staff, but rather overwhelming to us. However, our dinner table spread out full just took the 16, tho' some of the native ones are awfully fat. Suddenly, at 4 in the afternoon, John & Ali decided to move the kitchen from where it always is, next to the hall & dining-room, down into the cellar, to make the house quieter & cleaner. So they moved it, stove & chimney & all, somehow, & we got an excellent dinner.

You would be revolted if you could see people's change of behaviour because I'm Uncle Herbert's niece – not nice people of course, but one or two others, which is very degrading ... Altho' circumstances are pleasanter now, it's not a *real* life for a wife – only for the men who are actually doing things. Petticoat influence in the Mrs Humphry Ward way is not much my line, is it? I hate not being something *myself* – only being it as Norman's wife.

Amy has gone off to her digs [in the Old City] today, & I'm having a quiet day in bed, whilst the house is all being put straight downstairs.

Every day now makes it safer for Uncle H. He has a big show
on Wednesday, asking all the notables from Southern Palestine –
& also, which rather makes me wonder if the above remarks may
also be amended under the new regime – he is asking English
women who do public work here, so I am going. If he gives us
women a status – not social, but public & national – apart from
our husbands, we will bless him for evermore. Tell Aunt Bee –
perhaps she can do that as well. After all, you're not 'Arthur
Franklin's wife' in Aylesbury, are you? I'm always 'Col. Bentwich's
wife' here.

9.7.20: You think we go out too much – but life's so expensive if
one is always entertaining at home, & never goes out. It's nice to
do it alternate nights, & then it about evens up. Besides, I've got
quite keen on dancing now, & Norman doesn't always come. I've
given up riding & going into the town in the morning more than I
can help, because the sun is so bad for me. Now that I have a
nice cool fly-less house, with a writing-room & fairly quiet servants & pretty well all the comforts I could have at home & heaps
& heaps of books, I don't seem to want to so much. I don't believe we shall have our own car yet, as long as Norman gets the
present one for business. Simply because we can't afford it. Pay
won't be much more, if any, than it is now, when allowances &
rations stop & we no longer have the canteen. Living here is terribly dear, & if we have to pay rent too, we'll perhaps be worse
off than we are now. Also, we'll have to save for leave, as fares
are so dear.

Norman is now plain Mr Bentwich, the Legal Secretary. There
will be 3 Secretaries to form an Executive Council with Herbert –
Deedes, the Civil one, Norman, the Legal one, & the Finance
one, yet to be found ...

They did, however, get a car the next month, which Helen drove
with much pleasure, claiming to be the first woman driver in
Palestine; in fact when Haile Selassie visited Jerusalem three years
later, he was so amazed at seeing a woman driving there that he
asked for the car to be stopped so that he could question her.
Often on long trips they would take a driver, but this was mainly
to deal with the inevitable punctures and breakdowns. Troubles
were generally expected – 'we went 100 miles & not one hitch,'

Helen once wrote triumphantly, 'which for a 19 months old Ford
is rather good.' Norman never drove or coped with cars.

This letter has the first mention of the entry of Wyndham
Deedes into the Bentwiches' life. Deedes, whose background of
Saltwood Castle,[4] Eton, and the army was combined with a
powerful social conscience, was to become their closest friend,
both in the following two years when he was Norman's colleague
in Palestine, and later when their paths again crossed over social
work and LCC affairs in London. He had served in Intelligence in
Turkey & the Middle East during the First World War, and was
working in Egypt for the Foreign Office when Herbert Samuel
offered him the post in Palestine. Samuel wrote in his autobiography that Deedes spoke Turkish perfectly, and 'was by profession a
soldier – not a bad thing in a country which might prove to be
turbulent. He had also great administrative capacity; and there was
in him a strong strain of idealism which drew him powerfully to
the Holy Land, and enabled him to understand and sympathize
with the spiritual essence of Zionism.'[5] He was equally trusted by
the Arabs. 'Every element in the country,' an Arab newspaper[6]
wrote, 'seems to think that he is their friend.'

> ... Wednesday was a great day, because Uncle H. made his & the
> King's pronouncement to all S. Palestine. About 300 were there,
> of all sorts – consuls & sheikhs & rabbis & Bedouins & commer-
> cial people & muftis & officers. And 10 righteous women, to
> show that Jerusalem was a saved city, I being one, much to every-
> one's amusement.[7] They chose 10 women to sit with the men, &
> the rest were in a gallery. Most of them were missionaries &
> school-teachers. Herbert wore a most gorgeous lace-covered
> white linen uniform with a purple sash & 2 orders & a helmet
> with a gold spike. It was in one of the great halls at OETA (now
> called Government House) & not half hot. The German eagles all
> round the room were outdone by the lion & the unicorn over the
> throne, & the picture of George & Mary. The band played the
> National Anthem a good many times, which always amuses me,
> as George *isn't* King over a mandate, or else it wouldn't be a
> mandate. The King's proclamation was read by H. in English, &
> then in Arabic & Hebrew. Then his own pronouncement – very
> definite & straight, in the same way. His remarks about bribery
> were particularly apt, & it was a very good thing to let out

Jabotinsky & all the other politicals … Life is certainly much
cheerier & better here than it has been before, now we are getting
settled in to a definite progress.

16.7.20: Last Friday we had a very enormous lunch with the
Mufti, where were also two Zionist doctors. He presented me
with his photograph signed after, as a memento. He is a very nice
enlightened sort of person, & always very interested in ideas &
movements everywhere. Sunday the Mayor & Mayoress & a lot of
other people came to tea. He is a very advanced Moslem, who has
married a very bright Spanish-French Christian, who means to
help emancipate the veiled women here. I hope she will. Monday
evening we had to go to Government House, to H.S.'s first official dinner. It was a very posh affair. It put 'decorations' on the
invite, but as Norman hadn't got any, I wore my white kid gloves
instead & looked no end of a lady in my blue satin dress & all
available diamonds.[8] I'm a great nut now, & sat between H.S. &
Dr Glazebrook,[9] who took me in. I'm a nut, not because H.S.
married father's sister, but because I married the Legal Secretary,
who is, at the moment, the only member of the highly exclusive
council of 3 who has a wife. Till Aunt Bee comes, H.S. will get
inflicted with his niece a good deal.

Tuesday evening H.S. came & dined here quite by himself. I
felt I feared his criticism much more as a relative than as a boss.
He admired the house, but I felt the dinner didn't go as smoothly
as usual because of the detectives. As we sat in the garden, in the
light of some lanterns I saw figures flitting about like pixies
among the trees – it was only 7 military policemen on guard, to
say nothing of two cars & two motorcycles as escort, & a special
man on a horse who guarded the road so effectively that even the
ADC couldn't get in. He is very nice, but I think so far we all find
it a little difficult to be natural. He is so much hedged round with
ceremony, & he never was very good at unbending.

I've been arranging this week about passing the land-girls on
to Ashbee. We will keep 25; 6 have got regular work, so we have
helped 31 girls in all. I want to start an Employment branch of
our Social Service – first to collect statistics about the number of
girls employable, & next to try & get capitalists to come & start
some industry for them. We are trying to get Vesters to run us a

library in connection with their American Colony Store. It's badly needed. One morning I went over 5 Jewish orphanages.

22.7.20: Norman has heard a horrid piece of news this week – it was published in our local paper that Israel Friedlander, Norman's brother-in-law, had been murdered by brigands in the Ukraine, whilst taking relief money through to the Jews there ...

Israel Friedlander, Zionist and scholar, had married Lilian, the eldest of Norman's sisters, in 1905. They lived in America with their six lively children, the eldest only twelve years old – 'there is no one to direct their animal spirits into quiet channels,' Friedlander had once written despairingly, unable to work except at night. After this tragedy Lilian moved back to England, and thought of joining her sister Nita who was already in Palestine at Zichron Jacob. Two years later tragedy was to hit again, with the sudden death of Nita at the age of 37, and Lilian took her family to make their home in Zichron, trying to carry on Nita's work in the settlement there. The problems of Lilian and her chaotic family appeared periodically in Helen's letters.

... Norman's friends the Goadbys are up, which is very nice – they are Cairo people, & he's in the Law School & is helping Norman draft new laws. They do about 3 a day – it's much easier when one hasn't got a Parliament to chip in with objections.

Frederick Goadby had been Norman's colleague both in the Law School in Cairo and in the Camel Corps. Later he was to be head of the Law School that Norman started in Jerusalem.

23.7.20: This morning I have been visiting the prison, & making arrangements for some of the female prisoners to be sent to our Home on release. There are about 500 males & 115 females here. They do shoemaking, tinkering, furniture-making, gardening, & lots of other things, & are awfully happy & well-looked after. But it's all rather Gilbertian, the care that is taken of anyone who has actually committed a crime, or got an illness, & the callous way in which they are treated both before & after. But I think the cheery, communal, useful life they lead in the prisons here is a great im-

provement on the hard labour, the solitary confinement, the useless labour & the general viciousness of our home system.

I've been having domestic trouble again – Ali beat the Armenian house-woman, &, when I remonstrated, said she had sworn
at him & he was too polite to swear back, so he beat her. He can't
understand my mentality at suggesting he had much better swear
back.

30.7.20: You ask about Uncle Herbert, & whether he's cordial or
official to us. Well, he is *official* – very kindly & considerately, but
most decidedly. Perhaps it's just as well, as I think he's very afraid
of people thinking he favours us for being relatives, & we are
equally afraid, & equally anxious to 'know our place'. But it has its
funny side. He can talk beautifully to strange wives about superfi-
cialities, & they flutter & are flattered & try to make a good
impression, whereas we stick horribly, & our efforts to be natural
are rather pathetic. However, we don't see much of each other, &
I'd much rather live my own life than be in any way an appendage
of his.

We are just applying for proper sanitation, & are getting it put
in. Hitherto we have been very primitive.

1.8.20: We've got another little war on now, as I daresay you've
seen. And our garrison regiment went off up north yesterday to
help the French – much to their disgust. There's rather an interesting story about Feisal's telegram in answer to France's
ultimatum. Feisal, after much heart-searching, agreed to the ultimatum, & sent off his cable which reached France about 6 hours
or so late. France wouldn't listen to it, & went on with the war
she had meant all along. Feisal said the cable was late because the
clerk didn't know how important it was, & went to sleep & left it
till the morning. But people here say the ultra-nationalists didn't
want him to send it, & so cut the wires. Whichever way it was, it's
fairly well done him in.

8.8.20: Yesterday I was playing tennis at Govt House with Herbert. He's not nearly as good as he used to be; but of course these
hard courts are different, & the light's very glary, & the wind up
there is terrific. I'd told people he was very good, & they must
think I'm one of the sycophantic flatterers that abound here.

20.8.20: I'm thinking of going off with the Goadbys to Cyprus, seeing Beyrouth, Alexandretta, Mersina & Smyrna en route – being away a month altogether. I need it. The worst thing here is the everlasting respectability & limelightness of the life. It's so *small* – any unusual remark one makes is repeated everywhere & comes back on every side. And if one only *dreams* of being natural & playing about just once, everyone notices & talks of it. Never to say what you think of politics, or you'll be called a Bolshevik; hardly ever to mention a good book or poem without being called an 'intellectual' or 'highbrow'; never to rag or you are called unconventional & undignified – it's all wrong, & yet it seems impossible to change. I'm having a meeting next week of all the 'ladies' (hateful word) in the town, to start a ladies' club. That ought to be better.

I am sending a group photo of all the OETA officers taken just before Bols left. It's rather good.

24.8.20: It's very sad about that Italian Commandante, Bianchini, who has been murdered in a train up at Damascus, because he was taken for a French officer. We knew him well last year – quite one of the most intelligent & attractive men I have ever met. He was on the Zionist Commission last year.

Uncle H. has just been over to Trans-Jordania, which we are 'peacefully annexing'. The Foreign Office wants it, & the War Office says it mustn't cost them anything. So it has to be done after all without troops, after they (including the camels) had been massed here for the purpose. It is done by a few political & intelligence officers. Uncle H. is reported to have said that it is so beautiful there – round Salt – that he can't think why the Children of Israel bothered about coming over to Palestine!

In his *Memoirs* Samuel quotes his letter to the King explaining how at least a hundred sheikhs had come to ask to be under British rather than French control, and the reply he received from the Private Secretary: 'His Majesty recognizes with satisfaction the significant attitude of the Sheikhs of the east of the Jordan towards the British Government, though I suppose we have to walk warily so as not to tread on the French corns! The presence of the British officers whom you have lent to assist in the administration of that country is, I should imagine, an original if not an unique arrangement. I hope they are safe.'

30.8.20: The great topic here, and bone of contention, is the ladies' club I am the prime mover in starting … It'll make all the difference to the women to have something in common, & after I've given them a few home truths at the next meeting, the lions & the lambs, I am sure, will never get up from lying together. Don't think I'm very conceited – but you should *see* the other females. I think we mix with quite abnormally intelligent folk at home, judging from here & Egypt.

I dined with the OETA Mess & danced there. Norman finds it bores him rather, so he stays at home, whilst I go with some other officer. As there are usually 5 or 6 women & 25–30 men, it's no wonder I enjoy it more than him. I can dance all right now.

I went for a lovely moonlight picnic – Norman had a touch of fever, so didn't come. We walked on the top of the walls nearly all round the city, where Ashbee has made a proper walk. We had supper on Herod's Gate, with a gorgeous moon-view of all Jerusalem. This morning I have been out to Ein Karem, where there is the first Girl Guide camp of about a dozen officers, in an empty Russian building. We took them out & set them going, & they will have great fun. I'm going again on Wednesday, to get up a paper-chase.

It would be easy, and wrong, to read too much into these dances and picnics and trips to Cyprus without Norman. Helen liked male company, and enjoyed behaving in a mildly shocking way in conventional society, but fundamentally she had a strong puritan morality. Although there was a determinedly 'modern' aspect to their marriage, so that they both always led unusually independent lives, it was a secure and devoted partnership.

3.9.20: I'm in rather a chaotic sort of condition, due to many causes. 1) I've a rotten cold in the head from the changeable weather. 2) The boat is due to leave for Cyprus tomorrow, & we can't find out whether it *will* go then or any time during the next week. 3) Ali has disappeared for the day – or longer – & 5 to lunch & 6 to dinner. 4) Thelma reappeared suddenly with a naughty girl on Wednesday – one of the worst – whom we have been chasing round Jerusalem ever since. 5) The Committee of the Ladies' Club expects me to do my work as chairman *before* I go, which is strenuous. 6) We were promised that if we stuck to this house we could have it all put in order & done up & servants' quarters built. Now they say it costs too much, so we may move after all – we don't know yet. Oh this *is* a lovely life!

I hope Norman has by now sent you a copy of his book – he's very sorry he didn't before, but, as usual, he is very reticent about it, & does all he can to discourage everyone from reading it.

I've just been interrupted to give exhaustive details to the Public Works official how I want my house done up. It's being all black & white, with green shutters – it suits my methods of decoration & dress!

Norman wrote nearly 30 books over the years, on law, or Palestine, or refugees. This one, because of the date, must have been *Palestine of the Jews, past, present & future.*

Helen did go on the Cyprus trip, though 'it's rotten Norman can't come'; he stayed at Government House to escape the smell of paint at home. She enjoyed the small boat that pottered up the Levant coast, taking nearly a week and allowing them to land frequently. Apart from her friends the Goadbys, the only other English person on board was 'a young man with long yellow hair & a dawning beard, who is called Baldwin, & says his father is Financial Secretary to the Treasury. He tries to be Socialist, but has Tory instincts. He is rather a Chelsea type, & quite interesting, & we sat very late last night talking politics & social reforms & religion. He frankly said he hated all Jews – I told him off for being a foolish youth with popular prejudices, & we thrashed it out till very late hours.' This was Stanley Baldwin's elder son Oliver, then aged 21, who became a Labour politician.

When she returned she found that some work had been done on the house – 'proper taps & sanitary arrangements' – the extra building work was under way, the garden was a mass of flowers, and Ali, after three days' absence had come back after all.

Rather self-consciously, Helen, like everyone else, started referring to Herbert Samuel as 'H.E.' (His Excellency):

6.10.20: Norman is working awfully hard, & I hardly ever see him. Today is the opening of the Legislative Assembly, at which he's rather a nut.

I went for an interview with H.E. (otherwise my uncle!) to talk about the Ladies' Club. They are calling it the 'Jerusalem Ladies' Club'. I object to the name – I hate being branded as a lady. But, as he said, somebody was sure to be offended by any name, & it's as well to be me that's offended as anyone else, & I quite agreed. There was the usual difficulty over languages, but we've decided to be officially tri-lingual. In the evening the Ashbees came to dine, & afterwards Norman practised with Mrs A. for a concert on Saturday night at Govt. House. Saturday, I played tennis, & then we – Norman & Thelma & I – dined with H.E., & after there was a big concert, by invitation, for most of Jerusalem, at which Norman & Thelma were the star turns, & after we danced. I sat next to Deedes at dinner; it was the first time I'd met him, & I think he's one of the nicest men I've ever met. He's most sympathetic to everything – extraordinarily clever, very keen Labour, & a real idealist. Norman thinks no end of him.

We dined with the Yellins. Thelma has got engaged to the eldest son.

Thelma became the third of Norman's sisters to settle in Palestine. 'It seems such a narrow life for a girl like her, to be stranded among this society for ever,' Helen wrote, 'However, it's her lookout.' She need not have worried. Thelma was a distinguished musician, a pupil of Casals; she had played the Brahms Double Concerto at the Proms with her sister Margery two years earlier, and had given recitals with Myra Hess. Margery (pupil of Kreisler and Leopold Auer) was soon to join her in Jerusalem, and together they started the Jerusalem String Quartet. Thelma helped run the Jerusalem Music Society, and later was involved in founding the Palestine Conservatoire and contributed enormously to the musical life of the country. Her architect husband Eleazar Yellin came from a family of Russian Jews who had settled in Jerusalem two generations back.

The next week the Royal Navy came for the first of their annual visits:

13.10.20: I've been having a terrifically gay week with the British Navy. A Super-Dreadnought, the *Emperor of India*, has been off Jaffa, with Admiral Webb on it. I tea-ed with him on it on Thursday; danced with the fleet at Tel Aviv to 2 am next morning; dined with them at Govt. House on Saturday & danced again till 1 am on Sunday; one officer lunched & joy-rode with me Sunday. And Monday I again was in Jaffa, & lunched in fine style with H.E. & lots of cinemas & photographers – on board again.

18.10.20: I have just decided to knock down a wall between the 2 sitting-rooms, to make one good-sized one, when we want to start weekly or bi-weekly musical evenings, & get all the most intelligent folk together, rather *à la* Chelsea. If you can't be smart, be modern – & I can't cope with dances & very large dinners, so I'll do this instead.

I have just sent Storrs [on leave in London] a letter of introduction to you. Don't believe a word he says about us – he has, as I always tell him, a delightfully picturesque habit of exaggerating things that haven't happened. He's good company & brilliantly clever. I believe he is going to get married – but when I asked him he said no. He said one couldn't marry unless one had money other than what one earned, in case one died or got ill. I said we'd risked it, so he said 'nonsense, you're known all through Jerusalem as the girl who has £25,000 of her own or more.' He wouldn't even believe me when I denied it! I think Miss Landau is responsible for those yarns, but it's rather fun to be thought so rich. Probably it excuses my many unconventionalities. I'm sure we don't splash – of course, the gold dress & fur coat look rich, & we make a habit of never talking about money, as so many do here, which also gives, as Daisy Ashford[10] says, a 'rich appearance'.

20.10.20: I'm feeling cross today – so would you if your house were full of yelling lunatics, ostensibly there to build, but who really destroy & steal for all they are worth (not much!). A blanket went yesterday – one of the best – & all sorts of things from the kitchen. And the other side, hoards of rowdy road-menders & a steam-roller. And builders in at the Club who won't go out; & builders in too at the bad girls' home, who won't go out. Everything has to be done this time of year before the rains, & a rottener sort of workman than you get here it would be hard to find.

One night we dined with the French Consul, where were also Storrs, & some big hats from Beyrouth. I sat between the Consul & Storrs, & felt that I was doing both the things my French governesses said I never would do – being quite a lady, & talking fairly good French. I did nearly *not* become a lady by dropping my ice-pudding on the floor, but as I had to have first cut, & it was very slippery, & served with a fish slice, it wasn't as unladylike as it sounds.

I'm supposed to be 1) chairman of the soon-to-be-opened club, & chief furnisher as I don't like anyone else's taste. 2) chairman of the social welfare society, whose new home is just opened, & where we are going to run a garden. 3) in charge of the garden girls, whom I visit & strafe at all free moments. 4) Honorary Commissioner of Girl Guides, at which I've done little. Thrown in, chauffeur & (long way down) housekeeper, & my life is full, to say the least.

Languages never came easily to Helen. A letter five years later showed her still struggling: 'I've just been having such a long French conversation with the new Italian Consul & his wife, who have been to tea. They're rather nice – I can't imagine what they think of me, as all my information & ideas vary according to what I know the French for.'

27.10.20: Norman has just started a Law School here. Quite a big affair, with 150 pupils, which takes place between 5 & 8 pm – this means, of course, that so far I see less of him than ever. He gets in at dinner-time only. We have been having quite a holiday this week – no entertaining or being entertained. We have moonlight evening walks which are very jolly instead.

31.10.20: I'm sitting on the very place where, when I last wrote, the wall was, in quite the most tastefully decorated room in Palestine. It looks *very* chic, all having been done in new black, with pale primrose walls with black dado & frieze, & lots of splashy silks. And 3 brass sconces on the walls with candles, & 2 long brass candlesticks which are being converted into lamps, & one 5-

branch candlestick for lighting, & a lovely new Bokhara rug, about 8 ft by 4, beautiful colouring, which we have just bought.
I've been tennis-tournamenting at Jaffa.

The following week she confessed that they had discovered 'the carpet we bought is *not* pukka Bokhara. It makes one feel such a fool – otherwise it doesn't matter much, as it looks very nice.'

At the beginning of November, Lady Samuel arrived 'with family & entourage complete'. Helen enjoyed seeing and organizing them, 'finding her domestics & dressmakers & telling her what's "done" & what's *not*'. Nancy (age 14) and Godfrey (age 16) had a flat with a schoolroom at the top of the house, next to a private detective with his wife and baby. The eldest son, Edwin, had been in Palestine with the Zionist Commission since 1917, and was to be married in December at Government House to Hadassah Grasovsky, of Tel Aviv.

> **16.11.20**: Yesterday there was a tea-party at our club given for Aunt Bee to meet all the members. She came first to see my house, which she quite approved of, & I took her there. About 50 members were there – one Moslem lady, & lots of Jewish ones & Greek & French & Italian & Spanish & American besides all of us & many missionaries & locals.
>
> Many thanks for Norman's wig & gown, which arrived safely. I was putting them away when Freda, my small maid, saw them. 'What's that?' she asked. I couldn't explain, other than by saying the wig was a 'sheitel'.[11] 'Oh, sheitel for the master to wear at the office,' she said in Arabic.

In a letter on 25 November, Helen refers to an 'unpleasant cutting from the *Morning Post*'. This was an article published on 5 November, one of a series called *Palestine To-day*, which, without mentioning Norman by name, said the Department of Justice should not be in the charge of a Jew. The article said they understood he had given up 'a more lucrative position in Egypt' (where he was paid in fact, £600 a year) for lower pay in Palestine (in fact £2000 a year), and that it is 'immaterial how much he multiplies proofs of his fairness ... to be a Jew in office in Palestine is to be dubbed an instrument of a Zionist conspiracy to drive the Arabs from their homes and Holy Places'. The article also criticized, among other things, the closing of the brothels in Jerusalem (which had been done after a campaign supported by both Norman and Helen), saying it led to an increase in venereal disease. It is not surprising that Helen was irritated.

It was better to think about the excitement of a planned visit from her parents in the New Year. 'You must stay here at least 2 months – I'm going to take you everywhere over Palestine & show it you all from Safed to Beersheba.'

1.12.20: I hope you will like the house; it's rather cottage & simple, & a bit chilly, especially the stone floors. Through driving the car my feet get too hot from the engine, & get cold on the stone floors, & the result is they are so sore from chilblains I can hardly walk. Like they were from the motorbike. You *are* going to stay here the whole time you are in Jerusalem, & the only other place I will allow you to stay at would be Government House. Norman will draft an ordinance to that effect if we have any trouble about it. So you see how powerless you are. The reasons you must stay here are: 1) Because we both want you to, & have been looking forward to it all the year, & have been built on to with that in view, & have heaps of room. 2) The hotels are *impossible*. Full of bugs & fleas & dirt, bad food, noisy, cold, uncomfortable, no sitting-rooms, & ruinously dear. 3) We are even asked to put up quite strangers, because the hotels are so uncomfortable & dear. So we must put you up too. 4) John would give notice, I know, if you didn't stay here. All the servants know about your coming, & are excited to see you, & would be most hurt if you went elsewhere. So that's settled. You can have two rooms leading out of each other, fairly good size; & Heal beds. About clothes. Bring all the warm things you can – jerseys & furs & thick stockings & strong shoes etc. And they dress a fair amount here in the evening – tail coats & white waistcoats for men at Government House dinners. And low evening dresses for ladies; and some quite smart afternoon functions, too.

I was up at Govt House for tea-parties on Wednesday, Thursday & Saturday, & doing things there for Aunt Bee on Friday. It takes up a lot of time, & the tea-parties are rather dull.

Later she tells her Father to bring his fur-lined coat – 'All lucky enough to have them wear them here. Norman is buying a sheep-skin one.'

6.12.20: I have just come in from Edwin's wedding.[12] There were hundreds there, over 500 I should think [the next letter corrects this to 1100]. They had it in the large Assembly Hall. There were three rabbis, & both lots of parents & 2 people to sign, all under the Chupa.[13] The contract was read, & the rest was mumble, with stage directions in between. They missed a good chance, having no singing or good chanting except the unimportant contract. They had been previously married by the governor in the morning at the governorate in a civil marriage, which had given Norman much labour as they wanted it there, & Norman thought it wouldn't be legal except at the governorate – which the Foreign Office agreed when cabled to. After the ceremony there was some squash over tea, & a reception in the large mess-room, & a huge cake designed by Edwin & made by the American Colony. Then Edwin was invested as honorary head of the Beersheba Sheikhs – a little bit of play-acting which seemed unworthy, & which he much enjoyed. He was dressed up as a Sheikh by them & marched about in front of the cinema folk. Aunt Bee looked very swell in pale grey. There were no bridesmaids, but Nancy & Hadassah's sister both wore pink dresses which suited neither.

In the same letter Helen talks of the first of their musical 'at homes', all evening dress and full of generals and administrators. Thelma and Norman and the local professionals played. 'I don't think there had been such good music heard here before. It's funny me coming out as the giver of *the* musical receptions. But it's an inevitable consequence of marrying Norman, I suppose.'

9.12.20: Today is the 3rd anniversary of the taking of Jerusalem, & there are great dos on, starting with a review of the troops by Uncle Herbert & the General – that takes place in the Russian Compound by the Law Courts. There were Indians & Lanca-shires, & it was very smart & well-attended. Then he took the salute at the Jaffa Gate, where Allenby had entered. And at 11.30 there was a most impressive service in the Cathedral. Everyone was there – H.E. & family in the front, with the Bishop's wife &

sisters & the Moslem mayor & mayoress; flanked by the consuls
in front on one side, & the secretaries & wives on the other –
secretaries being Norman, Deedes & Smallwood. The part where
the singing goes on was full of patriarchs & priests, choir-boys,
the band, & clergymen. And the rest of the church was packed
with men and women, Moslems, Jews & Christians. The Greek
Patriarch read some of the service in Greek, the Bishop in Arabic,
& the Church Mission Society clergyman in Hebrew. What a tragedy it all is that we can't live up to that pitch, & that the brotherly
love feeling is all jarred at the end by the 'Confound their knavish
tricks, Frustrate their politics' of our national anthem.

Wednesday I had driven to Hebron to inspect a place for a
women's prison. The Administration is getting very good about
calling in women's help for these things now. We have a meeting
this afternoon where Aunt Bee is in the chair, to talk about
forming a proper women's council to advise the government on
these things. Mr Deedes is attending. I'm taking Deedes round
some more places on Sunday, including Miss Landau's school &
the Alliance Israélite.

Helen was delighted to find how genuinely Deedes shared her
interest in social problems. She took him, at his request, to see the
worst as well as the best of the Jewish charitable institutions:

14.12.20: I went with Deedes & Miss Berger over the Hadassah
hospital, then to their nurses' home, then to the Alliance workshops & orphanage; the workshops are ill-run, & a great waste of
plant & opportunity. He is writing to Jimmy Rothschild about it.
The orphanage reminded him of Nicholas Nickleby, it was so
uncomfortable & ugly. So we took him to the girls' orphanage run
by Miss Berger & Norman's orphan committee, which is a real
model. They have girls from nothing upwards, & a matron & a
cook & a kitchenmaid. None are over 13, but they do everything
themselves, & the place is beautifully kept. They have self-
government – their own parliament & law-courts & punishments,
& look very fat & healthy & happy. Then he came home to lunch,
& after took me to see some ex-Sherrifian officers from Mespot,
who had been stranded in Syria & come over here, & were living
in quarters with their families in some intricate area of the Old
City. He talked to them in Turkish, & sent me in to the women &

children meanwhile, where I struggled along in Arabic. Some
were Indians, some Circassians, some Baghdadis, & some Egyptian. I had to pass off as his wife for the afternoon, as he said they
wouldn't understand his going about with a lady who wasn't.

They are forming a Women's Council of 8 to advise the Administration – my scheme, & he & Aunt Bee have taken it up. We
are having it elected democratically, tho', as he says, we'll have to
'work' the elections to get the right people in! Don't tell anyone
that here, tho', whatever you do.

The Club is giving a New Year's Children's party; it is opening
a library of 200 books from the American Red X – an excellent
selection – & starting a debating society.

20.12.20: Norman has achieved a 'kawass' [an armed servant] –
very beautiful in blue & gold lace & baggy trousers & a sword &
whip, to go about in front of him. He is very dignified. We took
him with us to Salt to create an atmosphere. The sword was useful for cutting rushes on the way back, to decorate my hall. As
Norman walks much faster than he does, they are always collid-
ing. Still, it looks very rich & aristocratic to have one.

This was written with amusement, but there are signs of increasing
concern for appearances. A list of clothes for her mother to bring
out – the first of many such requests – includes a new evening
dress, because she only has the gold tunic and the blue satin '& we
do go out such heaps', and stockings to match, a black or grey or
white tea-set to go with her black & Bokhara room; also her
hockey-stick, because mixed hockey is starting.

---

[1] Helen's manuscript memoir.

[2] Helen's manuscript memoir.

[3] Helen's parents' London home.

[4] Later the home of Kenneth Clark, the art historian, and of his son Alan Clark.

[5] Viscount Samuel, *Memoirs* (London: Cresset Press, 1945), p 154.

[6] Quoted in the *Dictionary of National Biography*.

[7] cf God's promise to Abraham to save Sodom if there were ten righteous men in
the city.

[8] Norman actually had an OBE and an MC and three campaign medals, but had
not yet got the insignia.

[9] American Consul and, amazingly, Civil War veteran.

[10] Daisy Ashford's *Young Visiters* had been published in 1919.

[11] A wig worn by orthodox married Jewish women, who must not show their hair.

[12] Edwin Samuel to Hadassah Grasovsky.

[13] The canopy held over bride and bridegroom at a Jewish wedding.

1921

Parents and Riots

Helen's chief excitement, at the beginning of 1921, was the prospect and planning of her parents' visit. Not all their ideas could work out as they had hoped – 'I'm afraid Petra or anywhere there is entirely out of the question; they shoot at sight in all that district now. We can do Salt, & possibly Amman, but otherwise only Palestine.'

After a bout of flu at Christmas, she was full of irritable energy:

4.1.21: I was perfectly wild this morning when I came down, to find that a wretched army lorry, trying to turn outside my house, had knocked down my wall in *2* distinct places, & crushed all the viola & wallflower plants that were coming on so nicely from the seeds you sent me. I sent for the Staff Captain, & told him just what I thought of the army & its drunken ways & carelessness & noise. I'm *very* fed up over it. *And* they've imported 8 hounds or so, which run riot everywhere!

14.1.21: We lunched at Nablus with the Moslem member of the Legislative Assembly, a very rich man who has a soap factory, which we saw. The Christian member was there too. Both are very pro-Arab nationalist, &, rather amusingly, we had struck the very day when Nablus was having an anti-Jewish demonstration. I think they were a little embarrassed – it was over before we arrived. But we said nothing, & had an enormous lunch – 8 or 9 courses again – & in the Harem to talk after.

Monday we had the first meeting of the Palestine Association of Women which I had called, to elect a Council of 8 women to advise the government & act as an intermediary & progressive body, between the government & charities etc. The women were all supposed to represent some organization, & organizations all over Palestine as far as I knew had been asked. But, inevitably (the governors had never answered our letters) some in the outlying districts were left out. And, what with that, & the usual language question, we had rather a lively meeting. Aunt Bee was in the chair, & weathered it well. Most fortunately, we elected 4 Jews & 4 others, & next day the Council met & started work – prison reform is our first go – so it's not so bad. I'm secretary – rather a stiffer job than I bargained for.

21.1.21: Monday I lunched up at Government House, & met Mond[1] who is *not* prepossessing. He's so exactly like the caricature of a profiteer, one can't help laughing. In the afternoon, there was a talk at our Club on the 'Local Colour of the New Testament'. There is a talk or debate each week, & I do it next week on the 'Economic Questions of Today' – all cribbed from Keynes & Russell of course. About 30 turn up – all ladies – & we think ourselves very highbrow.

There are no more letters till May, because her parents were with her. But all the family were compulsive diary-writers, and we have Caroline's diary of the visit. They arrived on 18 February. They had been much disappointed in Cairo, because they heard that Helen had problems with her ear, and was unable to meet them as planned. Then Norman and John met them at Ludd to tell them that Helen was in hospital with an abscess, and to take them after all to start their stay at Government House – it was nearly two weeks before they could move to the Bentwiches. Caroline found Helen comfortable in a private ward, bandaged, with 'heaps of visitors'. The day after she arrived, Caroline, as well as spending half the day at the hospital, was seeing women from the American Zionist Mission and discussing Jewish organizations. Helen was allowed out after three days, and meanwhile Caroline was busily sightseeing, meeting people, visiting the Evelina School, going to lectures at the Ladies' Club and at the Bishop's and to hear Herbert Samuel lecture on Keats. The weather was startling, with a foot of snow on the 25th – 'Hadassah & Ruth[2] snowballed H.S.'

At Government House Caroline was well aware of local political problems. 'There is great nervousness in the Admin.,' she wrote, 'on account of movements of Abdullah brother of Feisal in the districts beyond the Jordan – he is said to be moving against the French – this may cause grave complications as the Salt Arabs & possibly the Nablus ones will join in. This is the cause of so many military coming to see H.'

She was not dazzled by Government House entertaining. 'An official dinner of 22 at Government House; particularly dull,' she noted. 'Dinner simple. H. & B. come in after the guests are assembled – they do not mix with them but send for those they wish to talk to.' She found the next one 'much brighter', though with a 'poor dinner'. Storrs gave them a bad dinner too, but Helen's, on the other hand, were rated 'excellent'.

She was also complimentary about Helen's driving, and was very happy sightseeing and flower-hunting with her. They both took their flowers quite seriously – Caroline mentions finding over 60 varieties on one expedition. On a flower-hunt from Jericho, 'we called at the Governorate for a guide – they gave us a prisoner who was in for stealing, & kept the head of his tribe as hostage for his return.'

15 March was a busy day:

Mamie [as Helen was known by her family] left home early to help in the arrangements for Thelma's wedding. I did some shopping with Arthur & then to Miss Landau's school. Thelma's wedding in afternoon in St John's Hotel in Old City. Large hotel but poor in quality – about 600 people including H. & B. & Mr Storrs, many members of the Administration, many Arabs, Dominicans etc. Bride looked charming – refreshments well managed by Bentwiches. Home by 4.30. Dinner party of Yellins & Bentwiches in evening so Arthur & I dined at New Grant Hotel – met Mrs Fawcett & Miss Garrett – to station to see H. & B. off to Egypt to meet Churchill. Home in time to hear some Hebrew speeches at the dinner.

Millicent Fawcett, the campaigner for women's votes, and her sister Agnes Garrett, were great travellers in their old age, visiting Palestine four times.

The Mandated Territories in the Middle East were now under the Colonial Office, not the Foreign Office, and Winston Churchill was visiting as Colonial Secretary. Caroline and Arthur watched him open a sports club, review the troops, and plant a tree in the grounds of the future Hebrew University. They met him at a big reception at Government House, which Caroline found very entertaining because every section of the community and every race was represented, but 'the refreshments were awfully bad'. 'In the evening,' the diary continues, 'dined at Government House at official dinner. Taken in by French Consul, an awful bore, with Churchill on the other side; he was quite pleasant and we chatted occasionally, but nothing of much interest was said.' A reported conversation with Lawrence, who was in Churchill's party and who became friendly with the Franklins on the boat home, was more surprising: 'Col. Lawrence told Arthur he did not much like his work with the Arabs – he had to pretend so much all the time.'

Parties were getting ever bigger and grander. Miss Landau again gave a large fancy dress ball, '500 present including H. & B. – they did not go in fancy dress nor did Norman. Mamie as Alice in Wonderland. Edwin [Samuel] as water-carrier gained prize. All excellently & not extravagantly done.'

The last days of their visit were overshadowed by news of serious riots in Jaffa. Here is Caroline's account of Norman's report:

Being May-day the Labour Party were allowed to hold a meeting & have a procession, but the Workers of the World, the Bolshevists, were forbidden to hold a meeting. Apparently they held an informal one & came in conflict with the labour people, without doing damage to one another, but it was the spark that set the Arab people going – others said they knocked an Arab mason down for working on May-day – anyhow the Arabs seem to have been glad of the opportunity & attacked the Jews with great cruelty beating them to death with sticks. They broke into the Halutzim hostel & there massacred 11 men & 2 women. In all 30 Jews & 10 Arabs were killed & about 180 wounded … The Arabs looted the shops badly. This morning it broke out again, but this time the Jews of Tel Aviv seem to have started it in revenge. There were some deaths, but it did not last long.

Helen sent news of the aftermath:

> **6.5.21**: You left, really, at the psychological moment, because there could be no more trips to Salt or even to nearer places now, & Jerusalem itself is very panicky. Norman has gone to Jaffa again today, in khaki this time. It was troublesome again during the week, & is now under strict martial law. There have been small disturbances round about in a colony or two, & fears for trouble at Tul Keram & Nablus – Deedes has gone up there today. But, so far, no further north, & not in Jerusalem. It's *very* gunpowdery, & one feels it needs very careful handling to keep it under. It's terribly sad, & I think Uncle Herbert must feel it very deeply. Jerusalem is very jumpy. They had a big panic on Tuesday – everyone rushing through the streets out of the City, cars & carriages & all, simply because they saw a Jew running through the bazaar to fetch something. The troops parade the Old City in full marching order, to keep them quieted.
>
> Despite this, we go on the same as ever. Yesterday I went to Jericho, the Dead Sea & the Jordan with Baxter & Mrs Goadby. It's quiet there, but we took a gendarme to please Norman, & were in great danger from his loaded gun when the car bumped. Last night the Society of Advocates gave a very pleasant al-fresco dinner-party, & Norman made a very good speech. Tuesday, our Women's Union meeting went off very well indeed – surprisingly well. Two Moslems came. Lots of others didn't, I suppose because of the trouble, so we are sending out voting papers ... We so *loved* having you, & we *must* have you again.

The troubles came close to the Bentwiches when Eleazar Yellin's colleague was killed, at Petach Tikvah, 'where the Jews kept the Arabs off till the army came, & then bombs were dropped & over 30 Arabs killed'. Norman of course was deeply involved in trying to keep the peace:

> **13.5.21**: Norman went to Jaffa again, with Richmond. It's quiet at the moment, but may bust up at any time. One feels it's very deep & bitter. I believe the only point on which the Jews & Arabs

agree is that neither of them wants Norman here – a good tribute
to his impartiality! The Arabs say *of course* he favours the Jews, &
the Jews say they expect him to but he doesn't! It's all rather black
otherwise. The Jews are very critical of the Administration, as well
as the Arabs. I think H.E. must be having the hell of a time. As
you know, *all* the Administration are not as high-minded as Norman & Deedes, & there is still a good deal of intrigue & place-
hunting going on. The average Englishman here is instinctively
anti-Semitic.

Norman gets later & later – nearly 9 the last 2 nights. So I've
bought a lovely new carpet to look at whilst waiting for him. It's a
very good Seraband – 150 years old – pink with a lovely blue border.

21.5.21: Monday we heard a lecture by Storrs on Dante. Everyone
went, & there was a great crowd, at the governorate. It was very
well done, & I learnt quite a lot, as I knew nothing before. He
gave a lot of Italian interjections to please the monks & people
there, & H.E. made a speech after & gave some Italian too, which
he pronounced well, tho' I don't think he understood it. Tuesday
afternoon there was the much-talked-of party given by Deedes to
all his clerks. There were 50 or so there – & H.E. & the family &
us. It really was great fun – out there on their terrace. First we had
a most excellent tea; the Allenby [Hotel] band was there. Then we
danced, all together – Uncle Herbert & Mrs Deedes leading off.
Then they played musical chairs – H.E. being left till nearly the
end, because nobody liked to turn him out; & Deedes cheating &
putting in another chair when *he* was out, to go on playing; &
Aunt Bee being very dignified over it. The next day I took Mrs
Deedes out in my car to the Reformatory & the Jewish girls' orphanage, to distribute the remains of her cakes ...

This was all very jolly, but the troubles were still with them. The
same letter continues:

... The Arab press is starting to go for Norman very strongly,
calling him a 'Militant Zionist'. Poor Norman being a militant
anything! He can't go to Jaffa or Nablus or Tul Kera, because the
people are so opposed to him interfering in anything. It'll be interesting to see if he & H.E. go to the ship at Jaffa or whether the

Arabs will think *that* is 'Zionist interference'. They have to be very
pampered at present, as we've not enough troops to do anything
else. It's rather undignified, but it's better than a general massacre.
They've stopped the immigration for a time, too. People say 'take
a strong hand', but it's not so easy when they *have* the strong hand
& we *haven't*; & when they know fairly exactly our strength or
weakness. The worst thing we have to contend against is the
'military mind', which is following the scent of Bolshevism to the
exclusion of everything else, & who arrest the most respectable
Jews & threaten to hang them for just having fire-arms in self-
defence.

By the next letter, full of the Royal Navy visit, things had calmed
down. The only frightening event was a ride with Storrs – 'We
galloped all over the polo ground, & I was terrified & hated it, &
told him so. I don't enjoy it a bit, & don't like going fast on things
I can't stop with well-regulated brakes & levers. However, I shall
take him out in my car & make *him* frightened, in revenge.'

4.6.21: Yesterday was a busy day, being the King's birthday.
Norman got his two war decorations. And Deedes was knighted,
which pleases everybody in Palestine except him, as you may
imagine. Then H.E.'s speech which, to me personally, seemed
very sad. Such a climb-down from the hopefulness of the last
year's one when he came. The Jews all felt as if they'd been at a
funeral, & received it without a sound. The moderate Arabs & the
English were very pleased, but the ultra-Arabs were disappointed.
I'm not a keen Zionist – but I did feel sorry for them. And it was
a bitter moment to see the triumphant looks of the Arabs all
round, & not least the expression on Storrs' face the blackguard!
Actually what he said wasn't so bad – but mentioning Bolshies by
name and *not* the Arabs who had committed the murders, & the
whole tone of apology about it, was most sad, from Britain's
point of view too. I daresay he could do no more.

A sad thing happened here this week – do you remember Miss
Lomax, the funny little lady with short grey hair who lived at the
Garden Tomb, & who taught the boy-apprentices down Ashbee's
bazaar? She was missing for 3 days, & now has been found in the
well in her garden. Opinion is divided as to whether she killed
herself – she was very eccentric – or whether she was murdered

by an Arab gardener she had who has disappeared, apparently along with her horse. She was such a harmless old soul, it seems very sad.

Helen was suffering badly from a wisdom tooth, and Palestine had not yet become flooded with doctors and dentists:

12.6.21 Cairo: I have come down here partly because I was so fed up with Palestine I couldn't bear it any longer & partly – this is the reason I chose here instead of anywhere else – I thought I'd better come down to a proper dentist & doctor. Talk of Trades Unionism – not one of the 5 doctors I'd had in Jerusalem would look in my mouth as that was a dentist's job, until I asked Biskind last week as a favour, when he at once said it was septic there & would account for the glands & pain behind my ears! That's *much* worse than a bricklayer refusing to sharpen a pencil as it's a carpenter's job. I don't expect I'll stay long – but it's a huge relief to be away from the politics & turmoils of Jerusalem.

I don't see any immediate leave, because if we did come whilst the country is like this, Norman would be so worried & anxious he'd spend all his time telegraphing & seeing officials, & it would be worse than last time. But it's sure to be settled some way soon – *I* shouldn't mind if we came home for good & all!

I had quite a good train-journey down; Mrs Deedes & Ruth [Franklin] & Rutenberg were there, & an awfully nice artist called Kennington, out to illustrate Lawrence's book, who is a friend of Amy's. Amy was on the train too – 3rd class – & I travelled part of the way with her. It wasn't as bad as the wagon-lits, which are *full* of bugs. To see Kennington trying to catch them around Mrs Deedes' feet was a funny sight, as she *did* so disapprove. Rutenberg was governor of Petrograd in the Kerensky regime, & is very powerful & rather exhausting, but most interesting. He's going home to see Churchill about his concessions.

This was an impressive train-load. Mrs Deedes, Wyndham's mother, is credited with writing a letter to Weizmann which dissuaded him from resigning the Zionist leadership (one of his many threats of resignation) in the crisis of 1922;[3] Eric Kennington drew 30 of the fine portraits in *Seven Pillars of Wisdom*; Pinchas Rutenberg, the dynamic Russian-Jewish engineer, was planning the

Jordan hydro-electric scheme, which was destined to make a fundamental change in the economy of Palestine.

19.6.21: I returned here on Friday. I had another tooth stopped, & the ear-man said it was all right now in my ears. So it should give me no more trouble, & it's a great blessing not to have an incessant pain in my head.

Yesterday we dined with a lawyer from Beyrouth and his wife. I asked him if he were much interested in Women's rights. 'Yes,' he said – &, after a pause: 'I am also interested in the Society for Prevention of Cruelty to Animals!' I found afterwards that he connected them in his mind as both being typically English. He told us how, during the war, he used to have to play bridge with the Turkish governor of Beyrouth, who was an awful tyrant. If he put down an ace, & the governor a king, the governor would take the trick. And if he commented that aces were superior to kings, the governor would reply 'Not if I wish it otherwise.'

I'm rather busy at present, as I am helping in a garden fête for the Blind Institute, collecting & selling flowers; & this 'Welfare of Immigrants' of Deedes' takes some time, & then there's always the Women's Council.

I bought some lovely pieces of Bokhara silk embroidery quite cheap in Cairo.

26.6.21: Miss Nixon, the English woman who was called into being by the Women's Council & is going to be sort of Welfare Officer, Prison Visitor, Probation Officer, Juvenile Offenders' Officer, etc, all in one, has arrived, & is staying with me for a few days. She is quite nice, &, I should say, *very* good at her job, but she is so capable she terrifies Norman, & he runs miles to avoid being left alone with her.

Mrs Garstang is my latest effort as an enemy – she resigns the Club Committee under the plea that criticisms are made that the club is 'too Jewish', & so she wishes to give up her position of responsibility on the Committee. Cat! It's all because I was elected chairman & she wasn't last year. We are too Jewish because we had a Hebrew lecture (they forgot about the Moslem one too) & because so many Jewish people & not 'British' ones come to them. There are such a lot of English people one can't meet on equal terms now, because of their anti-semitism. [Friendships came and went; the following year she was to write 'I get on really *very* well with Mrs Garstang.']

10.7.21: Domestics are rather troublesome this week, but John has seen me through all right, more marvellous than ever. I tried a woman this week who called in over the garden wall to learn if I wanted a cook. I said yes, come along in, & she came, a Roman Catholic from Warsaw. First thing, she boiled all the dessert, including a melon; then in the evening John said 'I don't know if it's drink or drugs, madam, but I've locked her in the cellar.' Next evening she boiled the potatoes in paraffin & yesterday Norman & I both had bad pains so we sent her off. Norman keeps nagging at me for taking people without characters, but I really thought she was heaven-sent when I was just saying I wanted a cook & she stuck her head in & offered. But she was obviously from the other place instead.

17.7.21 Tel Aviv: I am staying down here with Hadassah [Edwin Samuel's wife] & Nancy [Samuel] for a week, with Hadassah's people. We bathe at 5 am – come home & breakfast – lie on the terrace & read or sleep – lunch – sleep – tea – bathe again – stroll around – dinner – & then talk & bed. Tel Aviv is very proper – they have a gendarme to prevent mixed bathing & undressing on the beach (I'm afraid we circumvent both laws somehow) & get quite shocked at one's walking through it, even at 5 am, in bathing dresses & towels. It needs educating.
Mrs Garstang still tries to spoil the Club, by trying to make it entirely Jewish, & then forming a British one of her own after. But I wouldn't let her ... Norman & Deedes are doing a tour of the colonies, & we went over to join them at Rishon.

Now that Caroline had met many of the people involved, the letters tend to become over-full of personal gossip. Another change is that games of various sorts feature more and more – tennis of course, and hockey, and now mixed cricket. A more surprising game was to be added the following year – mixed football on Storrs' tennis court. Norman played tennis and hockey too, and in football matches between the departments. But the Sports Club, where games were played seriously, and which was meant to draw different sections of the community together, became increasingly British and exclusive. Helen was often torn between her enjoyment of the games and her hatred of the atmosphere, particularly at times of political tension.

Thinking there would be no home leave, the Bentwiches planned a two-week break in Crete. But the day before they were to go, Norman was summoned to England to work at the Colonial Office on the drafting of the Palestine Constitution. To add to his problems, while in England he was also involved in two long-drawn cases of litigation: the first concerned a Greek, who claimed that the Turks had given him the concession for waterworks and electric supply to Jaffa and Jerusalem and that the British had no right to grant the electric concession to Rutenberg; the second was a complicated land claim by Mrs Rosamond Owen Oliphant Templeton, granddaughter of the socialist Robert Owen, and widow of both Laurence Oliphant (writer and friend of early Jewish settlement in Palestine) and of an English naval officer drowned at Haifa.

Helen stayed in England until November, though Norman returned earlier. After such a long absence Helen seems calmer, happier with Jerusalem life, socially and philanthropically busy – and with a new Aberdeen puppy.

17.12.21: We *have* had a week of it. Out to dinner 6 nights out of 7. One Shakespeare-reading, one musical evening, one with hilarious games, two with excellent recitations or imitations (notably of Ashbee in a temper at the pro-Jerusalem Exhibition, which Ashbee appreciated as much as we did), one public dinner with first-rate speeches; two lectures – one from the custodian of the King's pictures at Windsor, & the other from a well-read, literary woman; one sale of work; one wedding & reception; one tea-party for social workers; one afternoon of mixed hockey for me, football for Norman; two ordinary tea-parties, one Women's Council meeting; one P.N.E.U. [Parents' National Educational Union] meeting; & two club committee meetings, & a social work meeting.

Tuesday, I & Miss Storrs & Miss Nixon lunched with the girl clerks at Govt. House, to talk about starting a club for all the govt. girl clerks – about 100 in all Jerusalem.

23.12.21: Norman rang up Sunday morning to say that Abdullah & Philby[4] were coming to tea. So I had to get a good tea, & a party to meet them – & we had a dinner-party of 12 in the evening. The Corries [the senior British judge and his wife], & the 4 judges of the Court of Appeal all turned up. Abdullah was quite nice & friendly – rather simple & childish; it's a farce to think of him as royalty! He's just a puppet chieftain, with less intelligence than any of the judges, for instance. Far less. [It's hard to know, at times, whether Helen is really guilty of under-estimating character, or is simply writing to amuse.] Norman, in desperation, played the fiddle for him, which he appreciated very much. He liked the simple, lively things best; & it really was rather absurd to hear all these people absolutely entranced by the 'Beggars' Opera' – they liked 'Over the Hills & Far Away' better than anything else. Abdullah invited Norman to go to stay with him in Amman, & bring the fiddle. Norman said, might he bring me too. Abdullah shrugged his shoulders, & said yes, if you like. But be *sure* to bring the fiddle!

---

[1] Alfred Mond, Liberal MP and industrialist; founder in 1926 of ICI.

[2] Ruth Franklin, Helen's 29-year-old cousin, later married to Fred Kisch.

[3] Christopher Sykes, *Cross Roads to Israel* (London: Collins, 1965), p 90.

[4] St John Philby, explorer, orientalist and father of Kim Philby, the future spy, was then British representative in Transjordan.

1922

White Paper and Black Moods

1922 was to be an unsettling year in many ways – Norman described it as 'a year of obstruction'.[1] Uncertainty over the future government in Palestine was reflected in Helen's personal uncertainty. Her resentment that she had no role other than as Norman's wife, while he was thoroughly absorbed and fulfilled in his work, led to an independent pursuit of pleasure in visits to friends and travel and tennis which, though enjoyable on the surface, worried her. When Caroline accused her of being self-centred, she said that she was pouring out her problems in letters because, apart from a couple of friends who had visited and left, there was no one she really talked to. She was restless, feeling there was no scope for her ability.

The main political events in Palestine were Churchill's White Paper in June, followed by the endorsement of the Mandate by the League of Nations in July. The White Paper, which followed the 1921 riots, attempted to clarify the Balfour Declaration, confirming that the Jews were in Palestine 'as of right and not on sufferance' and that 'the existence of a Jewish National Home in Palestine should be internationally guaranteed', while at the same time reassuring the Arabs by limiting the immigration of Jewish workers who had no capital, trying to tie them to an estimate of jobs available – 'Immigration will not exceed the economic capacity of the country to absorb new arrivals.' And the idea of a Jewish National Home would apply only to Palestine west of the Jordan. The Mandate, which had been entrusted to Great Britain by the Allied Powers when Palestine changed from military to civil

government in 1920, was not ratified until after the acceptance of
the White Paper by the Zionist Organization. In the summer, the
British Government issued a constitution for Palestine on the
principles of the Mandate, defining the powers of the High
Commissioner and an Executive Council and laying down the
judicial system. Hebrew, English and Arabic would all be official
languages, and everyone would have freedom of worship. Also as
a result of the riots, a British gendarmerie of 500 men was brought
in from Ireland instead of the planned combined Jewish and Arab
defence force.

To relax the atmosphere, Deedes had written to the Women's
Council asking, Helen said, for 'a humanizing influence for government institutions'. Her first letter, full of accounts of Christmas
and Chanukah parties and pantomimes for children – regimental
children, reformatory children, Palestine Judiciary children, Jewish
orphans – explains that these are the result. Jerusalem was also
being humanized by the first concerts of the new Musical Society,
with Thelma much to the fore.

Deedes worked hard in many ways to improve the spirit of the
Administration:

8.1.22: Mrs Deedes had a very cheery dance, with games too & a
sit-down supper, given to all the people who worked up at Govt.
House, 112 in all, & it was a great success. Sir Wyndham made an
excellent speech, about the democratic relations which should
exist between Junior & Senior Service, & Palestinians & English,
which the Junior Service appreciated far more than the Senior,
who don't quite follow his good lead in all that.

15.1.22: Norman gave a lecture at St George's on 'Philo-Judaeus',[2]
which was very good & much appreciated. He is giving one at our
Club tomorrow on the 'Legal Rights & Wrongs of Women in Palestine', & another next week at St George's again. His International Law book is at last finished.

We are going to hunt a fox on foot at Kataman this afternoon
– as I'm confident we won't get it, I don't mind joining in; I hate
hunting if one *does* get anything. But to hunt a fox with Aberdeens
on these mountains seems quite a safe way of taking exercise.[3]

22.1.22: We lunched with Abdullah, at Shooni, in his winter camp. The Philbys were there – she with a baby of 2 months & another of 2 & an English nurse, living in the camp. We had to wait over an hour for lunch, in Abdullah's tent; he was very friendly. Many of the party – including Philby – ate with their fingers, but Abdullah used forks, so I copied him.

29.1.22: I think Mrs Deedes is a little shocked at my methods of housekeeping – the fact that we don't keep accounts rather appals her, & she made Norman put out half the candles in the room because she says I'm so extravagant! I think you & she have a lot in common, & you needn't be afraid of my being spoilt or uncriticized in this life here. No more is known definitely of our future. In a few months Norman descends to Attorney-General[4] – & our pay decreases considerably. But whether we stay on after the summer or not is no more fixed than before. Most people seem to want Norman to – I mean H.E., Aunt Bee, Deedes & people like that. Deedes offers us occasional free meals if we find the pay a starvation wage. Mrs Deedes says I have extravagant tastes, but the car & John are all I really need.

Northcliffe is due next week – I hope he'll get lost on the way! We have a cinema company here at present – the Fox Company from America – doing David & Goliath with a girl as David, à la Principal Boy in a pantomime. Ramsay MacDonald[5] is due – I hope he'll come, & that I'll meet him.

Both Norman & I keep getting septic – his arm won't heal, & I've got a bad finger, due to a cut which has got poisoned.

A series of relations came on visits too – a fair proportion of Helen's aunts and of her 35 first cousins – some more welcome than others. 'Aunt Henrietta[6] is coming here, as you know! And Jeanette.[7] Aunt Bee has given me a talk (as a deputy for you, I expect) on being nice to them. I'm sure I shall, most conscientiously.' But Evelyn Waley, second cousin and school-friend, was a kindred spirit, later to be involved with the League of Nations Union and the Women's International League for Peace and Freedom. She arrived loaded with very welcome books and chocolates and clothes from Caroline, and Helen was happy showing her round.

12.2.22: Firstly, Evelyn has arrived quite safely, with a lovely lot of presents for us – for which, very many thanks.

We have been having two of the world's personalities here, & the contrast between them is illuminating. Northcliffe & Ramsay MacDonald! And they are so absolutely clear-cut, & true to type, that it has been like a play. I half expected to find Northcliffe disarmingly charming, interesting, damnably clever, & to find myself fascinated by the man, instead of hating him as his doings warrant. I half expected to find MacDonald domineering, dogmatic, uncouth, & to find him uncongenial & aggressive in spite of my desire to like him. But results have killed these thoughts, & more than justified all my hopes to the contrary. And not only mine – *everyone* is of the same opinion, especially about Northcliffe. MacDonald they haven't seen much ... Northcliffe is obsessed with the fear of Islam, especially in India, & would do anything to placate them. At an official dinner at Government House (Uncle Herbert is still ill, & Aunt Bee didn't come in till after) Northcliffe was treated like royalty – all getting up when he came in, & being introduced singly, & he having 10 minutes with each administration. He never took any interest in Uncle Herbert or in Aunt Bee's health, but merely went off all about Zionism & Palestine. He kept stating his views without being asked, & dogmatizing, & telling everybody about Palestine, instead of learning. Tuesday he did a very unfortunate thing – which I expect you've seen in the foul-mouthed press by now. Storrs gave a Pro-Jerusalem Society dinner for him, & he got up & made a most offensive speech, against Zionism, & sneering at everything. Considering he is Uncle Herbert's guest, & that the Pro-Jerusalem Society is a non-political show it aroused the ire of everyone – even Storrs *says* he is very upset about it. Then we found the hidden hand. Gabriel [a strong anti-Zionist who had been in the Military Administration] is in Cairo, & had interviewed Northcliffe there, & given him a dinner at which was present also Gustaki, the ex-public prosecutor who was turned out of the Law Courts for intrigues & misdemeanours, & turned out of the country as a nuisance last month. No wonder Northcliffe was prejudiced, with those two behind him, working on his fears of a pan-Islam rising ...

England, Northcliffe told the settlers at Rishon-le-Zion, had 60 million Moslems in her Empire, and 500,000 Jews; she would not upset her Empire for them. They must go slow, work for good relations with the Arabs, and teach the immigrants to be modest.

... MacDonald, to turn to a pleasanter subject, arrived on Friday. He talks to us of everything, in a human way, & only politics if we lead up to it. He is very fond of the right things in the Mosque & the odd bits of the town & the views – & looks at everything here just as you did, in the right way. He is very nice-looking, & has a fascinating Scotch accent – but that's *not* the reason I like him, as we have heaps of fascinating good-looking men here, & I *don't* like them. But he's so congenial & human & humorous, & I know you'd like him too. Norman does, very much.

Disasters came sadly often in Palestine in those days. Norman's sister Nita, who had settled with her husband Michael Lange in the colony at Zichron, died that February after less than twelve hours' illness. They had no children. In the same week a neighbouring army officer died, leaving a widow and small baby. And Herbert Samuel was still weak – he was suffering from rheumatic fever and was ill for three months.

19.2.22: There is very sad news this week, as you already know. It was a dreadful shock to Norman ... Nita was taken ill quite suddenly after a sort of fête day in the colony. Michael was at Haifa, & she had only with her little Joy Friedlander [her niece], & another child about 10 who lived there, & a German cook-person. They sent for the doctor, who gave her something, & said it was colic, & went away. He was sent for again at 11, & did the same. And at 5 am, when the servant went to fetch him again, Nita died ... General opinion seems to be that it was acute appendicitis, which led to peritonitis. She had had occasional pains, &, as you know, that family never fusses about health, so she never bothered. One doesn't know if she had been elsewhere if an operation might not have saved her. The doctor there was undoubtedly incompetent – but it would have been the same in a small isolated village in England, wouldn't it? Everyone has been as nice as they could be about it.

25.2.22: One gets depressed here by all sorts of exterior things – when politics go wrong, or the papers here say particularly unpleasant things about us. And one sits on Committees & meets socially all the people who inspire these things. You wouldn't like it, I know, if the Bucks papers made a dead set against you & Father for being Jewish, & gave twisted motives for everything you did, & if you knew that half your Committee agreed, & were rather pleased. That's our position at times, so it's no wonder we dislike it.

Jeanette arrives Monday! How utterly *awful*. If she tries to come here, Evelyn & I are going away, & she would have to go too, to make it proper, as she couldn't be left with Norman.

About my accounts. It's not that I don't know what I spend that matters – it's the thought that one doesn't see, in our standard of life, where to spend less. For instance, fuel is a great extravagance. Yet one *must* be warm here to be comfortable, & Norman really does appreciate comfort as much as I do. Again, Norman will say – only us two for dinner. Then, two more, or three or four, will turn up. It either means we always have to have enough for more, or else get it at the last moment, which is always extravagant. That's not once or twice, but two or three days a week. And I have no room for anything at all in the way of stores. It makes for un-economy. But, as everyone knows one's income, one is rather supposed to live up to it. And don't worry, I can meet all my liabilities, even to dress, I'm sure.

We did not go to Miss Landau's Fancy Dress, but Evelyn did, in my Bethlehem peasant's dress. She borrowed the head-dress from the cook next door, & we had to pay £5 deposit on it because it had all the dowry on. It was so heavy she couldn't wear it to dance.

4.3.22: On Tuesday the Ochs family came to dine. He[8] is very keen on Reform Synagogues & things, & desperately afraid of Zionism interfering in any way with his nationality. He is so typical of newspaper magnates in pictures, that one felt one had met him often before. Rather a bounder – he said of course he believed in Zionism if Hadassah [Samuel] was a product, & rather went on that tack with her.

17.3.22: We had the most *heavenly* picnic by moonlight on the walls – what you have to return to Jerusalem especially to do. We picnicked on Herod's Gate, & then walked round the walls to St

Stephen's Gate, & back to Herod's Gate through the middle of the Old City. It was a very warm still night with a brilliant moon, & it was grand.

Yesterday, more football with Storrs. Norman played, & Mr & Mrs Richmond & the two girls & Mrs Vester & family. In the evening we dined up at Government House to meet Lord & Lady Milner. He was so impressed with the country the few days he had here in 1920 that he brought his wife to see it. Their visit is quite non-political. They are coming to dinner on Sunday, which rather impresses John. I'm not very much looking forward to it, as I feel that people like that who meet all the most interesting people of the civilized world must find us rather boring – that's not modesty, but cold fact. Because, if we were in England we'd never be seeing people like that, & the mere fact of being here doesn't really alter us. However, I suppose it'll be all right, & they are much too nice to show how bored they are. If they weren't so nice, I wouldn't mind what they thought of us. H.E. being away [convalescing after 8 weeks' illness], we come in for rather more of the celebrities than we otherwise should, as we help Mrs Deedes & Sir Wyndham.

Today we have done an orphanage & the Alliance school – the latter is as slack & rotten as ever.

The dinner, with music after, went well – 'Lady Milner is quite one of the most charming women imaginable; they are absurdly fond of each other, for such old people.' Milner said that 'if you worked in the Colonies you had to be prepared for giving & breaking your back with hard work, & then finding out that nobody backed you from home'. Helen readily agreed.

11.4.22: So far, everything has gone off very peaceably as regards Nebi Musa. We have been to watch most of it, & have been down at the Jewish quarters of the Old City every day, helping Mrs Solomon at her milk station there. The procession on Friday, that goes past the tent on the Jericho road was so whittled away & submerged by the Police, that there were literally more gendarmes than processors. On Sunday, when the Hebron crowd came in, it was a little more thrilling, but they didn't stand a chance with machine guns pointing straight at them in every direction, police & soldiers on all the roofs, & a triple lining of

police, gendarmes & soldiers, three deep all along the route. The
Jews were feeling quite safe, & kept their shops open in the most
sporting manner, to give confidence to the district.

We all go up to Govt. House to stay tomorrow night for the
Seder,[9] which Norman gives.

21.4.22: Relatives have loomed large on the horizon, but, D.V.,
there will be a close season from tomorrow onwards. I really have
been a model niece to Aunt Lucy. Last week Evelyn & I chaper-
oned each other with, by, for, or against, Storrs, up to the
Samaritan Passover at Nablus. It was very interesting, & well
worth going to. Norman gave the morning service after the Seder
at G.H., & then we walked down. Uncle Herbert wasn't able to
walk to Synagogue & back.

We watched a large Moslem procession go by, welcoming the
returning Nebi Musa flags. In front of the flags were three enormous red mouths – which turned out to be gramophones, carried
on the heads of men. The funnels were painted red, & each one
played a different tune. Every few minutes the men carrying them
were stopped, to wind up the machines.

26.4.22: Norman gave a lecture at the Y.M.C.A. hut on 'Ideals of
Judaism'. The hut was more than packed to overflowing, & it was
a good talk – altho' the Arab papers naturally were very rude
about it.

There was an extraordinarily good dance given by the military
at their Club here – a farewell dance, as they leave next month &
are replaced by Indians. We danced in the open, on greased tar-
paulins spread over the tennis-court.

3.5.22: It's very hot here at the moment, & I've been living in a
plethora of meetings, of all of which I am secretary. So the minutes get rather muddled, & the Ladies' Club gets information
about Immigrants, & the Immigrants about Rescue Homes, &
everyone is unpleased. The Women's Council went off all right, &
they quite approved my report. Wednesday I went to a lecture at
the Y.M.C.A. on Christianity, given by a missionary. Deedes was
in the Chair, & Norman on the platform, & he went soundly
asleep. It was translated sentence by sentence into Arabic, & went
on for 1½ hours.

10.5.22: Sunday we had a birthday picnic for Evelyn, out to Emmaus on donkeys, with Norman & Nancy. Nancy, you might tell her parents,[10] has missed her vocation. She is a wonderful donkey-boy, & made the donkeys gallop all the way home, with the use of a big stick & a lot of bazaar Arabic. It's a pity to send her to Oxford when she's so useful here.

Yesterday to tea to meet 'the famous Gertrude Bell'! I hate meeting tame lions shown off so obviously. Anyway, she seemed very pleased & gracious, but everyone was allotted 10 minutes with her, & I didn't appreciate it properly. She's very rabid anti-Zionist.

24.5.22: I'm knocked out of 2 of my 3 contests in the tennis tournament, which, with the Mandate, forms our entire conversation at present. It will probably prove one of the most tragic turning-points in the history of this country, not having signed the Mandate now.

Yesterday Mrs Deedes had a party for the Jewish blind people, which was very pathetic; but they did enjoy it. I'm taking Deedes out this afternoon to some bad Jewish orphanages, as most people only show him the good ones; & over the prison, & to tea with Miss Nixon. It's awfully good of him to find time for all this.

There's a vague chance that we may go to Buenos Aires on our 4 months' leave, in September. There is an International Law Conference, & they'll pay part of our fare & put us up. And we do so feel that they won't care a bit about Palestine, & it will be so good & refreshing. We are making all sorts of plans & enquiries, which are always attractive even if they don't come off.

Our Irish Constabulary [brought in after the 1921 riots] have arrived – we met some of them at a police show the other afternoon, & a rough-looking lot they are. The Colonel *doesn't* look our sort – horses & dogs are his interests. And already they are painting Jaffa red, people say. They don't seem to fit in with one's scheme for a moral Utopia, which we were rather aiming at here.

I want a new evening dress, badly. I want a shot mauve & silver silk, with silver tissue girdles & thick silvery fringes of silk – like the afternoon one of beige colour with the bright green sashes you sent me last year in shape & design only low, & with sleeves half open at the sides.

To the Bentwiches' distress, Deedes had said that he was leaving
Palestine. He had 'set his heart & ambition on home politics'. This
added to their own restlessness.

6.6.22: We are *so* tired of Jerusalem, Norman & I. We have no
quiet, & not a moment of private life together. I have quiet myself, of course, in the mornings when there aren't meetings or
inspections. But Norman never has – when he comes home in
the evening the house is as littered up with people as a dentist's
waiting-room, four or five deep, & he has 'em in one by one till
dinner time. And on the rare occasions when we are alone, there
are usually some after too. It's chiefly because Government
House is so far away, he won't ask people to go & see him there,
as it is so much trouble.

Our lunch party to Abdullah went quite all right, although
there was rather a heterogeneous selection of company – Abdullah speaking not a word of anything but Arabic on one side;
Tommy Haycraft [the Chief Justice], babbling delightfully of Cyprus & green fields in Devonshire on the other, not talking a *word*
of Arabic. Norman miles away the other end of the table, flanked
by Lady Haycraft & D'Avigdor Goldsmith. And the Corries &
two others & Evelyn in between. After lunch, Norman & Abdullah played chess, & each won a game, & then he went. And we all
met again at a garden-party at the Bishop's. And we dined at
Government House – a nice dinner, because Deedes took me in,
& was very cheerful. And after, we had music – Norman played –
& games & dancing in the Assembly hall. Abdullah played pilidex,
a sort of badminton with air-balloons which Deedes loves, &
which is very rowdy.[11] And said it was the nicest party he had
ever had at Government House – only *don't* tell your guests [the
Samuels] this, as it might be thought tactless.

Monday there were parades & receptions for the King's birthday, but as usual there were 'incidents'. The Moslems, for the
most part, refused to take part, as it was not held on the proper
birthday (Saturday) & was changed to please the Jews, the minority. So the Mufti & his friends sulked, including Richmond, who
absented himself from everything too, which seemed extraordinary bad form. Oh, how I loathe all this squabbling & discord
here.

21.6.22: I have the large meeting of the Union of Women Workers, to elect the Women's Council, tomorrow, & it's a tough
proposition. We have got the Catholics in this year – the nuns
have voted for the vice-consul's wife as their representative, & an
Italian doctor's wife, & an Armenian doctor's wife. And a German. And we are hoping that Mousa Kazim Pasha's wife will turn
up. So it won't be just Jews & missionaries, as heretofore. Still, it's
lots of work.

Evelyn, I suppose, has told you all my news & everything. I
miss her badly. Thanks most awfully for the books. The Huxley
one is most entertaining – too revolting for anything, really, but
good reading.

This week I've visited various institutions with Miss Nixon;
went to the Nablus Agricultural Show; played a mixed cricket
match – the Club against the Army – which was awful fun. I took
7 wickets, & made 13 not out. And played tennis.

Mrs Deedes gave a party to 150 Post Office employees; we
always have to go, & do get a little bored. The Fleet arrives Friday.

The annual visit of the Fleet brought the usual round of gaieties
and guests. Afterwards Norman and Helen went to Amman,
staying with Philby, and paid a return visit to Abdullah, in his
camp just outside:

3.7.22: Abdullah was very pleased to see us, & gave us 6 meat
courses, which were rather an effort in the heat. He has a well-
caparisoned tent – but has just replaced his divans with bamboo
chairs from Haifa of which he is very proud, & which are hideous
& uncomfortable. Abdullah & I can't say much, as my Arabic is
all in the imperative mood & not fit for his ears, but he has very
big dark eyes, which he suddenly slews up at you in the most ex-
pressive manner. He remembered everything he had had to eat at
my house. He is extraordinarily lazy – never walks & seldom
rides, & goes everywhere, when he does go out, by car. He was
told that Uncle Herbert was walking in France. 'Why,' he said, &
when told he was doing it for pleasure, 'why walking – are there
no trains or motor-cars?' He tells us long stories in the Arabian

Nights manner, through an interpreter, about Kings of Persia & woodmen & Kings of Mesopotamia & courtiers etc.

Sunday morning early we went out to Madaba, about 15 miles off, to see the 3rd century mosaic map in the church there ... We passed some deserted Roman villages & remains of a temple. And lots of Bedouin tents & thousands of grazing camels. The chief of the most important tribe of that part – the Beni Sakker – stopped us, & insisted that we should go into his tent & have coffee. So we went – a large shelter, 3-sided, of black goats-skin, with part screened off for the women. A smouldering fire of dried cow-dung in the centre, with shining brass coffee-pots of all sizes – some 3 feet high – with large beak-like spouts. And copper implements of good workmanship for grinding & roasting the coffee – but a blue enamel kettle for boiling the water. We drove the car right into the tent, it was so big. We were made to lie on divans of cotton mattresses & camel-saddles & sheep-skin rugs, covered with carpets – & simply bristling with fleas. Arab coffee is particularly nasty – it is all spices, & you can't taste any coffee. They only pour out a sip at a time in little bowls, which, when you have drunk, you hand back. To pour out a full cup would be extremely rude, as it would mean it was a hint for you to go. The little bowls are never washed. There were 20 or 30 men in the tent, all squatting round, dressed in proper Bedouin clothes. But Bedouins aren't what they were – the head one goes everywhere in a Dodge car, which was standing in the encampment with an Egyptian driver; his young son had on a Boy Scout belt, & both wore American boots. I think the Bedouin life is all that I dislike most in the world accumulated – dirt, vermin, suppression of women, convention outpassing everything else (i.e. the coffee, & their laborious salutations & good-byes & ceremonials over guests & meals); the clan traditions; the lack of any initiative or hope in the young people; the lack of any thought or originality or ideals; their patriarchal habits; the utter futility of their whole existence; & their love of murder & killing.

12.7.22: If this letter comes to a sudden & abrupt termination, it won't be due to a sudden raid or attack – although they are expected this week-end – but to a mouse which keeps running over the table where I'm writing, & getting in my way.

The next few days are rather anxious, because of the Mandate. Deedes & Norman have taken every possible human precaution, & it won't be their fault if any trouble does arise after all.

H.E. arrived back last night, looking extraordinarily fit & well. The great excitement is the new baby [Edwin & Hadassah's son, David] – weighing 8 pounds & as ugly as most of that age. They have queer ways with him – they oil him all over, hair & all, & hardly ever wash him. And they fold up all his limbs so that he can't move. It makes him look very queer.

16.7.22: The whole country is undergoing bad nerve-storms & has been expecting things for 4 days which haven't happened & which probably won't. Above all, we are waiting more than anxiously to hear the result of the Mandate – if it goes through, Norman & Deedes will have to stay to see things straight – if it doesn't, we will probably get home in a few weeks. That would be very nice – but there would always be the prospect of trouble hanging over us when it *did* get passed. Whenever the atmosphere gets at high pressure like this, & lots of bad feeling is rife, I feel ill & miserable. Norman brightens up at the difficulties, but Deedes is like me & can't stand the atmosphere of discord. I can very easily give up all the good things of this life, if I can give up that everlasting jarring & discord which underlies it, at the same time. It's worse for us than for anyone else here – Norman is the scapegoat of so much.

I'm sorry you think my letters scanty. It's chiefly owing to the heat, if they are, & to the feeling of rapid living which we have here. Nothing is of any importance – & if I write as I feel today, I've changed entirely by tomorrow, & yet again by next week. It's a bad life – very enjoyable at times, but with no background.

Most mothers would not criticize these weekly letters – usually at least four closely written sides – as 'scanty'. They always include full diaries for the week, besides the flow of thoughts and views.

19.7.22: There has been a sort of expectation of trouble all the time. The Moslem & most of the Christian shops shut all Thursday & Friday as a protest. It fell rather flat, because all the shop-people treated it like a Bank Holiday & went off for picnics & joy-rides; & the Jews made more money than on any other day.

About 50% of the Old City population moved out – Jews &
Christians & Arabs, they were each so scared of the other. The
Government were very noisy about their force – the new gendarmerie very much in evidence, & lots of armoured cars. We
keep wondering what will happen after – & if – the Mandate is
really signed.

I have been to the dentist a lot of times lately, to have teeth
stopped, but I still get a bit of ache. I go to quite the best here –
Dr Weizmann's sister.

26.7.22: The Mandate has come on us, in the end, like a thief in
the night. And the army & gendarmerie here have been so much
in evidence this week that nobody has dared to express any great
opinion about it – either side. Everyone is very thankful that it is
at last finally settled somehow. Leave is off, definitely, because of
the new Constitution & preparing things for the Legislative
Council. Which is damnable!

Uncle Herbert read us a lecture on Einstein given at Oxford,
the other night; Norman was the only one who really took it in.
Also, another evening, some modern verse. And Aunt Bee is an
ardent Couéist.[12]

Visiting Zichron, Helen was distressed to see the state of Norman's widowed sister Lilian Friedlander and her children – 'all
have had fever, & are covered with septic sores, & altogether have
been having a rotten time'; in Zichron they had 'no friends, no
proper school, & no interests'. She took two girls, Joy aged seven
& Judy aged nine (later changing with other members of the
family), back with her to recuperate in Jerusalem – not such hard
work as that might sound as there was plenty of domestic help
around: 'Sophie [her Armenian maid] is admirable in looking after
them, & her daughter of 13 who is here having school holidays is
invaluable in playing with them, & makes dolls' dresses all day
long with great skill.' Helen did her best, equipping herself with
toys and asking other families round to play, but was not used to
coping with children, finding them 'infinitely more exhausting
than 3 dinner-parties a day'. 'They won't have baths when I tell
them, & suddenly want them other times. They won't get up, they
won't go to bed, they won't put on the right sort of clothes, they

ask for things & won't eat them, & generally give themselves a
very difficult time, to say nothing of those in charge.'

Since there was to be no leave, Helen relaxed with escapist
visits to friends in other parts of the country, playing tennis,
reading & swimming at Mount Carmel, and touring in Lebanon
and Syria. Norman was not always able to come, but joined her
when he could – for weekends, and for a week in Lebanon.

> **26.8.22**: I rather tremble to tell you, but I'm going on alone with
> Dennis [Dennis Cohen, who had just resigned from the Immigra-
> tion Department and was 'like a brother'], to Damascus &
> Baalbek & other interesting places, motoring & riding. My two
> arbiters of conduct here – Norman & Mrs Deedes – most entirely
> approve of this trip, so it must be all right. It was really Norman
> who urged me to go; & Mrs Deedes says 'Honi soit qui mal y
> pense, and if a man can't go away with a nice married woman
> friend alone it's a poor look-out.' So *you* mustn't mind, if she so
> heartily approves. I asked her this time – & before going on
> Carmel alone [as a guest of Colonel Sawer, the middle-aged
> bachelor Director of Agriculture] – & she urged it both times.

A letter from her mother now warned her that she was writing
only of tours, parties, tennis, and picnics, and that she ought to be
less frivolous and get back to social work. Instead of being irritated, Helen accepted the criticism. She was herself guiltily aware
that dislike of official life had made her too detached – 'day by day
& in every respect I am getting worse & worse' (see note 12). Mrs
Deedes had told her she was 'aimless & drifting', and Helen did
not deny it – 'it's better,' she wrote, 'than being purposeful &
stodgy.' So, although she put up a rather unconvincing defence, it
was a timely reminder.

> **14.10.22**: Your letter has arrived with your indictment of me as
> the typical society butterfly. I will defend that charge with an ex-
> haustive summary of my life during the last week. As to my
> leaving my home – tell me how many of your friends in England
> stay in London by the sides of their husbands all the summer
> through, if the husband can't get away for a holiday? Why should
> we have different standards here – & the fact that my holiday
> sounded more by being taken in different bits, was only because I

arranged it so that Norman & I were never more than a fortnight without seeing each other. Ask anyone who has a husband in government service in London whether they do not go away for the summer without them, & often don't see them for a fortnight at a time. I don't quite see why I shouldn't have the same standards as regards holidays here as you do at home – this year it has been 10 days' holiday at Easter & 7 weeks in the summer; & only, I think, two week-ends not with Norman, all through the year, I don't think that is so very much 'being on my own', do you? – especially when the man is like Norman, tied to his work as much by choice as necessity. I'm afraid I see nothing wrong there; probably we have quite different points of view on that, but neither I nor Norman see that wrong *at all* ... One can't help being on one's own when one marries a Government official who takes his work so seriously. Besides, I'm getting to be a personality here apart from Norman, & am wanted for work, & even pleasures, not always as his wife but as *myself* ...

The other excuse offered is that because Aunt Bee was so serious, and good only at 'the Good Works business', it was:

... less necessary for *me* to concentrate on the Good Works, & more necessary not to cut the Jewish life off entirely from all the social pleasures ... There's not a Jewish woman besides myself who plays tennis, or takes part in the more frivolous social life at all.

As to taking an interest in individuals – in a position like this, one's life gets so absolutely diffused, that one cannot concentrate on any one piece of work, let alone families. One's money & one's interest has to be divided between Jewish & other interests – & again between girls & infant welfare & medical work & orphans etc. One must keep a little aloof & take an interest in a lot of things, so I am told. After all, with the Women's Council, the Social Service, the Welfare of Immigrants, the Infant Welfare, the Ladies' Club, the social work among the girl clerks, & all the other things for which I'm on committees & *do* work, you can't say that I have no interests. Too many, & too superficial, if you like – but I'm the only official's wife here who does anything like as much.

After a diary to prove how purposeful and busy she was really, Helen added, 'I don't say it's the life I like – I admit I enjoyed it 100% more on Carmel. But that only makes me more virtuous.'

To add to her frustrations, Helen periodically tried, and failed, to get some writings published. Ever since her childhood efforts at stories and family magazines, Helen had experimented with writing. It was to be another 40 years before she achieved books (histories of Sandwich, Kent, and of the Vale of Health, Hampstead, where she lived, and her first volume of autobiography), but she always had ambitions that way.

> **21.10.22** You suggest I should write up my account of Mount Hermon – but what's the good? It's not possible from here to get things into papers casually, & I don't think anybody can do it for me at home. Evelyn has two things I gave her to try with, & you have the Samaritan one, & unless they can be got in, I don't see much point in writing any more. Accounts of travels & things are rather overdone these days, & it's only professional writers or personal friends whom editors publish. And I'm not either – unfortunately.

The next frivolity was amateur dramatics. The Jerusalem Dramatic Society was a new feature; Helen had not been in their first production, but was tempted to join now.

> **29.10.22**: My time this week has been divided between bed & rehearsing – I've had slight fever & pains, the same as everybody else has this time of year, & have been staying in bed, or going about the house in pyjamas, till lunch-time, & then rehearsing 'Midsummer Night's Dream' in the afternoons. The rehearsing is great fun, tho' I'm afraid I won't be a very great success as Hermia.
>
> We are *very* disappointed that you won't come out again – it's no good preaching to you, I suppose, as you say it's no good preaching to me. If it were me, I'd have come out with Uncle Ernest, & taken Father for a holiday elsewhere later on. But I believe that is a point of view on which we will never see eye to eye, so we must accept our differences.

She dyed & painted white cotton for the stage costumes, and enjoyed the classless atmosphere of the rehearsals:

5.11.22: It's so nice in this play *not* being the wife of the Attorney-General, but to be bullied & teased like any ordinary mortal, & mixed up anyhow with the junior service – the only other times this happens is at mixed hockey.

Norman sends a request – could you please send a little cheerful literature for him? Friday night he couldn't sleep, so started the 'Garden Party'. I heard him walking about at 3 am & asked why. 'I'm looking for a Bible,' he said. 'It's the only thing to take the unpleasant taste of these modern books out of my mouth.' I like them, except when I'm not feeling well, but he likes funny or instructive things. Could you please send me as soon as possible 12 table-napkins – French linen with hemstitched borders like I had before. And 12 large bath towels.

22.11.22: I've had – & still have – five children & Lilian staying here; I've been acting; I've had to dye, paint & sew my own costumes & 2 for the children; I've got a new car, & have been learning to drive it; & I've had electric light put into the house. The electric light was a necessary evil, as the lamps always smoked, & got worse & worse. But I think it so ugly, that I've not got it in the drawing- or dining-rooms. It only comes on about 5, & is off about 11.30.

The play went off splendidly …

We had the silver-wedding dinner at GH on Friday – Aunt Bee wore her wedding-dress, the original! – what a waste of good material to keep it like that all the time.

Aunt Bee's wedding-dress, far from being wasted, was to have periodical outings at anniversaries. I remember her wearing it at her diamond wedding.

26.11.22: I feel I can ill spare a moment to write to you tonight, because all my time is so badly needed for my latest craze – painting my bedroom furniture. Having got rid of the family this morning, & feeling that their finger-marks rather obtruded on things, I've decided to paint my spare-room furniture a light blue

& dark blue, with medium blue curtains; & my own room white, with a green stencil, & new green curtains; & the bathroom green. Fred Kisch turned up yesterday. He has come out to run the Zionist Executive, & is a great asset. I think we'll like him very much. He'll go down well with the English people, being regular Army, & knowing India & the War Office things.

'It's a good thing to have an ex-military man at the head of Zionist affairs,' Helen wrote later. 'It does make their shows punctual & well-organized.' But Fred Kisch's abilities and qualifications went far beyond that. With a Zionist family background, and a distinguished career in the war and at the Peace Conference, he successfully bridged the Jewish and British cultures and was ideally suited to his new job; the Bentwiches did indeed come to like him very much. In 1927 he married Helen's cousin Ruth Franklin. He was killed by a land mine in 1943 when, as Brigadier Kisch, he was Chief Engineer with the Eighth Army in Tripoli.

3.12.22: I'm rather depressed as I've got very bad earache & neuralgia again. I just sit by the fire in the little room all day. I have painted the spare-room furniture, which looks nice, only the ceiling is all falling down & the rain pours in in bucket-fulls, which rather spoils the look of it. Altogether, it's rather a bad week.

I'm sorry you are incredulous about my having made my own acting clothes. As a matter of fact, so were lots of people here, & asked if I'd done it with a hoe, or a hammer & nails. But it was quite genuine.

11.12.22: I enclose a notice of the general meeting of the Ladies' Club, from our Daily, the 'New Jerusalem' which comes out in all 3 languages. I wrote the article, as I didn't know what the editress, who was at the meeting, might say otherwise. And people keep saying 'what nice things the paper says of the Club,' & I just say yes, & pretend I didn't write it. Last Monday Storrs read some plays and over 40 people turned up; today there is music, including Norman; Uncle Herbert has promised to give us a poetry reading later; & we hope to do more play-readings among ourselves.

30.12.22: I've never kept Xmas at home like I keep it in the National Homeland. Out 10 nights out of 11, & eating more plum pudding & pulling more crackers than ever in my life before.

The year ended with Helen giving a New Year's party for 50, with music, dancing, games, and singing choruses – 'I expect it'll be rowdy, but as all the neighbours will be here, it won't matter' – and with dreams of a spring holiday in Italy, to be followed by a tour of England, and a League of Nations conference in Geneva.

---

[1] Norman Bentwich, *Wanderer Between Two Worlds* (London: Kegan Paul, 1941), p 122.

[2] First-century Jewish philosopher in Alexandria.

[3] At the age of eight Helen had carried out her own hunt protest on her parents' land, by sitting on a gate and refusing to let the huntsmen pass.

[4] Under the new constitution.

[5] Ramsay MacDonald was to become, two years later, Britain's first Labour Prime Minister.

[6] Henrietta Joseph, sister of Arthur Franklin and of Aunt Bee.

[7] Jeanette Franklin, sister of Ruth and a cousin of Helen's.

[8] Adolf S. Ochs was proprietor of the *New York Times*.

[9] Service on the eve of Passover, normally held as a family service at home.

[10] Herbert and Beatrice Samuel, Nancy's parents, were convalescing in Buckinghamshire with Helen's parents.

[11] Deedes was still standing in for the convalescent Samuel.

[12] Couéism, then fashionable, is defined as 'a system of using optimistic auto-suggestion as psychotherapy'. It was reckoned helpful to repeat 'Every day and in every way I get better and better'.

1923

Einstein, Petra and London

This time some of those dreams of leave and travel did come true. Wyndham Deedes, to their great sorrow, returned permanently to London that April, so Helen and Norman stayed till he left, then travelled with him, visiting Venice on the way. Norman returned to Palestine in July, but Helen remained with her parents till September – Caroline's criticisms of her for going away without Norman seem not to have applied to visits home.

So many members of the family were in or visiting Jerusalem, that at Helen's birthday dinner in January there were not only Herbert and Bee, but also another aunt, three girl first cousins and two of Norman's sisters.

Helen seems to have become increasingly interested in new settlements:

> **27.1.23**: Can you please let me have as soon as possible all available information & prospectuses about schools for Colony training for girls? They are going to start one near Haifa. Six months' intensified training in domestic & farm-work is the most they can afford to give at present, as there are so many needing it. So could I have some syllabus about similar schools in England? And would you ask Alice[1] if she knows of such training for immigrants arriving in British Colonies, & if so if I could have particulars of those too.

> **3.2.23**: I went with Mrs Solomon by train to Benjamina, a new Jewish village on the railway near Zichron. It was the opening day of the village, & they had a great ceremony there. Unfortunately,

it poured hard, so the speechifying was done in a large new cow-shed. Crowds of people from the neighbouring colonies were there, also some Arabs … In the evening we had supper with the group, and they sang the most delightful songs after – Hassidic songs, & Russian Volga songs, & German folk songs, & comic Yiddish songs, & new songs written for the Chalutzim[2] here. Some of them had beautiful voices; & then they all did an old Palestinian dance – about 20 of them in the little hut. Visitors kept coming in & out, & they were all very lively & young & full of good spirits, & most of them unusually good-looking. One was a Russian – got up as a Bolshevik, with a large beard, long curly hair & a black worker's blouse. He is a builder, but was an engineer from a University. He had perfect manners, which kept peeping through his Bolshevik make-up, like rather a bad actor on the stage … It makes life much more ordinary & less narrowing to get away often for the week-ends, like one does at home.

Flora Solomon, Helen's companion on that expedition, was the daughter of a Russian Jew who had made a fortune from oil in Baku. She was not kind to Helen – or to anyone else – in her colourful memoirs.[3] Although she seems to have got on well with Helen – they were often guests at each other's dinners, and she and her sister stayed with the Bentwiches when visiting Jerusalem in 1925 – she wrote, with retrospective cattiness, that Helen 'had a Bedford College diploma in social studies and let no-one forget it … She might have been Britannia rising on her chariot from the azure main. When she entertained she organized a tolerable version of a Buckingham Palace garden party.' More fairly, she added that Helen was 'married to a saint'.

Standing out from the general round of dinners and meetings is an account of a visit from Einstein. His *General Theory of Relativity* had been published in 1915, and he was to give the first lecture at the planned but not yet functioning Hebrew University on Mount Scopus.

11.2.23: The great event has been Einstein. Monday evening we went to an 'At Home' at Ussishkin's to meet him. He is very simple & rather bored by the people but very interested in the music provided for him. Mrs Einstein is a mixture between a Hausfrau & a Madonna. Tuesday evening they came to dine, & there was

music. Margery, Thelma, Norman, a man Feingold & Einstein
played a Mozart quintet; Norman on the viola & Einstein on
Norman's violin. He looked very happy whilst he was playing, &
played extraordinarily well. He told some interesting things about
Japan & his visit there, & talked of music, but not of his theories.
He said of some man – 'he is not worth reading, he writes just
like a professor' – which was rather nice. He only talks French &
German, but his wife talks English. She said they got so tired of
continual receptions & lectures, & longed to see the interesting
places they visit alone & simply. Wednesday afternoon he gave a
lecture. About 250 people were there, including government officials, Dominican Fathers, missionaries, & of course lots of Jews.
He gave it in French, which of course was a handicap to me to
start with. But, although I understood more or less every con-
secutive argument, the fitting them together was the trouble ...
After he had been here to dinner, John said 'Is that the Einstein
that works with theories?'!

18.2.23: The wife of the Director of Education died on Tuesday
quite suddenly from meningitis. She was younger than I am & had
two small children. It's terrible the number of deaths of young
people under 40 there have been among the small English community here during one year. Nita just a year ago, & Major Drew,
Captain Mackenzie, Mr Broatch of Tiberias, Doris Badcock from
Nazareth, & the wife of a post office official, of typhoid in Haifa.
Also, three English children within the year – one of blood poisoning, one from convulsions, & one from being run over by a
government car last month. The suddenness of it all here seems
to unnerve everybody.

25.2.23: Evelyn [Waley] and her mother have arrived and are
staying at G.H.; we are just off for a donkey picnic.
 Philby is very anti-Jewish now. I had his wife in for four days
– she's so much nicer than he is. He's such an intriguer & boaster,
I don't like him much any more. She came with the two children
of 1½ & 3, who were very amusing, & an English nurse. One
baby had bad eyes, so she came to see the doctor.

12.3.23 [to her father]: The Mauritania came into Haifa this
week, with hundreds of bloated American sightseers aboard. It

was a good picture, to see this huge ship in the bay. Beaverbrook
was among the passengers, but nobody takes much notice of him.
After the trouble they took over Northcliffe last year, & the way
he repaid it, I don't think anyone wants to do anything for newspaper proprietors any more.

19.3.23: Norman & I haven't any money left, which is a pity just
when leave is due after 3 years. But they've cut our pay rather
more than I thought they would – we've dropped about £500 a
year [out of £2000] – & heaven knows how we'll get on for the
next few months. We'll have to spend our hard-earned war sav-
ings – & I suppose Keyser's[4] is always ready to be borrowed
from. But it's rather worrying, & irritating, & Norman gets depressed over it. Of course, we can economize, & sell the car, &
live like poor people – but it's difficult in our position, & there *is*
such a lot of entertaining to do, & charities to be supported. We
aren't as badly off as some people, but it's a pity, & I still think it
a mistake to consent to have our salary cut like that, as Norman
did, without a murmur protesting, when we are supposed to go
on living the same sort of life. It's irritating to be in debt to anybody, but it's better to Keyser's than anyone else, I suppose.

Before the leave, they were guests in a party of 20 on a grand and
wonderful visit to Petra, where they indulged in rather casual
amateur archaeology. Even after all Helen's other tours and
excitements, she was so deeply impressed she could hardly describe it – 'it took one's breath away' – 'more marvellous than
words can convey'. Philby was there to greet them at a camp at the
end of the gorge.

26.3.23: We were most frightfully comfortable – we had a bell-
tent, & I had a camp-bed, & Norman was on the ground; and a
sentry walking up & down outside all night, of the Transjordan
police. It was very cold. We ate in a large Bedouin tent, 22 of us at
one long table. The first morning, we walked & climbed to another temple, seeing all sorts of tombs on the way, & one large
cave full of maidenhair & trickles of water, with an old Roman
bath. In one tomb, we found bones & sarcophagi & mummy-
cloths – Dr Dolbie is an anatomist from Cairo & got very excited
over these, saying they were from a Western race, either crusaders

or early Macedonians, & took some back to Cairo to examine. The other temple, to look at, was just like St Pancras Church where the buses stop ... In the afternoon we pottered around a large hill at the back of the camp, covered with remains of pottery – some of them found exciting things there, but I only got odd bits. In the evening, a climb to a Crusader castle; after dinner, Norman gave us a concert in a tent ... It *was* lucky to be able to do it.

That is the last letter until September.

In a country full of rabies, leaving Jock, the Aberdeen terrier, for some months, was a problem, but he was taken by kind friends on Mount Carmel. 'They are poisoning stray dogs in Jerusalem, & if I were away & he wandered about looking for me, they'd be sure to kill him.'

Helen kept a diary of the leave. She was busy meeting friends and relations, and also compensating for the lack of theatres and art galleries in Palestine. She went to ten art exhibitions in London, apart from gallery-hopping in Italy on the way, and altogether to 18 plays, with a special mention of Capek's *R.U.R.* – 'very thrilled, even Norman'.

Norman returned two months before Helen, and some of the letters she wrote to him at that time have survived. They show how unsettled she felt, searching uncertainly for her role in life, feeling she was not fulfilling herself or using her abilities in her bits and pieces as a colonial official's wife. Helen and Norman had a close relationship, but sometimes she needed to get away from the claustrophobic atmosphere of their Palestine life – and she felt guilty at doing so. She seems to have written almost daily, opening her first letter with the revealing sentence: 'By the time you get this you'll be once again in the land of your ancestors' – thus, whether consciously or not, still dissociating herself from the homeland by the use of 'your' not 'our', in the manner of the 'wicked son' in the traditional Passover service.

29.6.23 [to N.B.]: In thinking over in bed last night the specially special bits of our leave [the letter continues] what stood out best of all was the same as you said – the times with Wyndham, &, above all, the times just us two alone.

I went to Wimbledon with your father, but I *didn't* find it thrilling. I'm never very good at watching games, & it wasn't nearly as much better than ordinary tennis as I had expected – women were even serving underarm!

Today I spent the morning buying clothes. Don't be angry, but they are *very* nice ones, not dear, in the sales. They're not as smart as Mrs Snowden's,[5] so you mustn't preach Labour to me! I can't help enjoying myself, even without you. Do you mind? It *has* been such a lovely leave – but I don't expect it'll be very long before I join you, as it's always only half a life when you are away.

2.7.23 [to N.B.]: Well, so Ronnie [Storrs] is safely married, in case Jerusalem has any doubts about it. Mother & I went in a car with H.E. & Bee, & so sat near the front. The Dean officiated, & Ronnie really looked a bit nervous.

Talk with Fred [Kisch] of my idea of an English kibbutz. Mrs Solomon thinks it good, & it might be started while I'm home. An English group to work on the land, or any other job, financed by the Zionist Organization in the same way as the Russian ones, & recruited here in England. If they said there was an opening for so many men to do some sort of work & so many girls to look after them, & they must each have certain qualifications, it would be a great publicity catch, I believe, as people would think of Palestine as something actually relieving our labour market, & removing those 'undesirable' aliens. And it would prevent all this talk of only Bolshevist Jews going there.

6.7.23 [to N.B.]: I lunched with Mrs Snowden & I talked all about myself. I think she was bored at the end of it! She was awfully nice about my speaking – says I'm a born orator, & that having an official husband mustn't be allowed to spoil my natural gifts! She seemed to think I only wanted to talk on Palestine, but we got on to Labour things, & she said I ought to get in with Margaret Bondfield,[6] or go round like Deedes is going to, to Labour meetings. But she says a year or two's time won't be too late to start.

22.7.23 [to N.B.]: It sounds foolish, but I *would* so like to do some more speaking, now that I know I can. When one *knows* one can do a thing, it's so thwarting to have no chance. The only thing is, that all the time I'm getting experience on what to speak about.

30.7.23 [to N.B.]: Two such jolly letters from you, telling of all your doings. It all sounds so terribly strenuous – don't overdo it, & do keep plenty of leisure time for doing the book & any other reading & writing. I do think that's what's wrong with our life, we try to do too much & see too many people & have too little intellectual leisure. Here endeth the first lesson.

I tore up the novel. But I may try again later. I've bought lots of nice shiny foolscap, which makes writing so easy.

The problem with the novel, she explained, was that it was hard to write something that passed her own critical standards. It was to be full of morality, 'with a man of Deedes's & Mrs Snowden's Christianity as hero'. She realized that she was unlikely to achieve it.

13.8.23 [to N.B.]: I feel awful at having suggested returning on Oct 4th. What about it? Of course a broad-minded, much-travelled wife is always a social asset – on the other hand, I hate your being lonely. Do cable strong-mindedly – be the dominating male for once! – & tell me what to do.

14.8.23 Chawton House[7] [to N.B.]: I've just been for a long tramp with Wyndham all round the most beautiful lanes & through wonderfully green woods, & we've talked & talked & talked … He says that your one & only failing is the one I always tell you of – diffidence & depreciation of yourself. For the rest, he has never met, in Palestine or out of it, anyone approaching you. So there!

16.8.23 [to N.B.]: My conscience is giving me nearly as much trouble as your inside is giving you! Because every letter you write me you say come back soon, & I *want* not to, which is rather dreadful, isn't it? But, you know, I have got attracted by the Danube idea … But I'll still come at once if you *really* feel you want me to, & cable. I don't think the Club or *Julius Caesar* or things like that are worth coming back for, do you? Which brings me again to my talks with Wyndham, who has made me more than ever realize the danger of thinking those things important ... He told me I had no idea how selfish he was, & that it was your un-selfishness that appealed to him so enormously. And I believe it's right, & that his morose moments are rather like mine when I won't take the trouble to be nice to people I don't want to be nice to.

25.8.23 [to N.B.]: It's funny how you always win out in the end, making me feel mean by letting me have my own way. And how I'm always selfish & take it. Evelyn [who had just been on a walking tour in the Cotswolds with Helen] said just the same as you say – 'You never give way one inch – you are thoroughly selfish' when she got peeved with me the other day.

As to the revenue – you know my constant criticism that so long as you tax what should be encouraged – agriculture – & don't tax what should be discouraged – profiteers like hotel-keepers, land transacters, traders etc – the country is bound to be bankrupt ... Why you can bring in ordinances & laws on any giddy subject you like, & leave the one subject which will bring prosperity to the country because you consider it 'unconstitu-tional' to tamper with it, I'm not the only one who fails to understand. Still – as Wyndham told his sister of me – I'm a rebel & agin all governments. But *do* try & see sense & act on it – in this matter. Indirect taxation – customs – kills trade & is unsocial & damnable. It sends up the cost of living, & reacts in direct pro-portion to income. I mean, the poor feel it intensely, & pay all out of proportion on their food & necessities. And it hardly touches the rich. And in Palestine, delightful Alice-in-Wonderland home of farcical finance, luxuries are cheaper than anywhere else & ne-cessities are dearer.

29.8.23 [to N.B.]: This should arrive just about the 8th anniver-sary of our great gamble – the 8th year is supposed by novelists to be the most precarious, & we seem to have weathered it satisfac-torily so all is well. I never can write all I feel – but you know it too well. And, like Coué, year by year it gets better & better doesn't it? It *has* been a successful gamble, hasn't it?

7.9.23 [to N.B.]: Our day again – eight years after. I was a queer unformed thing when you married me, wasn't I? I hardly seem to myself to have existed properly in those days. Life is a very full & wide affair for both of us now, isn't it? Anyway, it was damned clever of you to suggest our taking it on together.

All my love on this day of days, & three weeks tonight we'll be beginning our next honeymoon.

She was back at the end of September, and soon fully and cheerfully taking part in her old activities on her return. The long break seems to have been successful in clearing many of her irritations, and it left her more ready to co-operate with Jerusalem life:

28.9.23: I'm back once more in the whirl & gaiety of the Holy City, after the quiet of Chartridge[8] & a London season.

I went to lunch at Government House, where Aunt Bee was very pleased to see me. I realize that a short absence of a few weeks makes one be treated as a delinquent or defaulter on one's return. But, after 6 months, the fatted calf is killed in true Biblical style. After lunch we went to see some sports got up by the young Jewish people, & met all the Jewish crowd. And then to see the finals of a tennis tournament, where we met all the English crowd. And then to see Thelma, who had a new daughter on Wednesday, much to everybody's surprise; Norman looked in on her yesterday morning knowing nothing about it, & found it there. Then in the evening to a dance at the Sports Club, which served a useful purpose of meeting the rest of the world I'd not already seen. Next day I went to call on Miss Landau to get *all* the gossip & talk of Jerusalem. A few grains amid much chaff, & I'm quite well up in it all.

Nieces and nephews accumulated, among both the Franklins and the Bentwiches, but there is no clue in Helen's letters, either to her mother or to Norman, about whether they themselves wanted children. Possibly the lack might have contributed to Helen's recurring feelings of vague dissatisfaction. It is clear that she worried about the dangers of illnesses and inadequate medical care for small children in Palestine, so possibly – and again this is guessing – she had decided to wait until they were back in England. But by then she was nearly 40.

5.10.23: One *does* live at a pace here – I have been roped in to be
Commissioner for the Jewish Girl Guides; to be chairman of a
children's playground; I have attended a meeting (in German &
Hebrew) to decide what to do with illegitimate babies; various
talks & interviews about the Ladies' Club; two official dinner-
parties & two lunches; many rehearsals of Macbeth, in which, if
you please, I am 2nd Witch – the other two are men. [The following month she wrote 'I'm out of Macbeth. I may just walk on,
but being a witch is *not* my metier.'] I have organized a mixed
cricket-match for tomorrow, when I captain the ladies' side. I've
played tennis. I've called with Aunt Bee on Moslem women. I've
paid calls. And I've had Thelma's eldest girl down here for the
day. I've lunched with the Magneses & had a long talk about the
new congregation on Western lines he & Norman mean to get up,
& attended a meeting between them & some very orthodox
young men who are English & American but don't believe in the
equality of the sexes which Norman & Magnes insist on …

Judah Magnes had recently arrived from America, with his wife
and three sons, and was to devote the rest of his life to the Hebrew University. He had, Norman wrote, 'been in turn Reform
Rabbi, Conservative Rabbi, lay leader of the Jewish community of
New York, and during the World War a pugnacious pacifist'.[9]
Helen said that he began to fill the gap in Norman's life left by the
departure of Wyndham Deedes. They lunched with his family
every Friday, and he and Norman started modernized Saturday
morning religious services. Helen did not share Norman's religious feelings, but she went to the services, happy to be making
new friends in the Jewish, as well as the English, community.

… I have been to a very entertaining Hassidic service the last day
of Tabernacles, when they do real Arabic songs & dances & proc-
ess through the streets in real Arab fashion on each other's
shoulders. We struck two such processions when we were returning from the service with Storrs & his Mrs, when they tried to
lift Ronnie [Storrs] on their shoulders, & his wife clutched at his
coat tails, & it was a funny sight.

In her next letter, Helen wrote, 'I'm looking forward to seeing
what's said about me in the Mrs Humphry Ward book.' In her

Land Army days Helen had sometimes, to her great pleasure, been
billeted on Mrs Ward, and now Mrs Ward's daughter had just
published a biography of her mother. 'Mrs Ward,' the book said,
'had many an absorbing conversation with one of the "gang-
leaders", Mrs Bentwich, who made Stocks [Mrs Ward's house] her
headquarters for a time and delighted her hostess by her many-
sided ability and by the picturesqueness of her attire. All this gave
her many ideas for her four war novels.'[10]

12.10.23: I'm getting my new little room ready. I've just been
enamelling furniture – the room has pale green walls, mauve di-
van cover, mauve & silver curtains (I'm awfully tempted to cut up
my mauve tissue evening dress for these!), black shelves & chair,
an old wood desk, silver framed pictures of what we saw in Flor-
ence. My house *does* look so nice.

19.10.23; I should very much like you to send me 'Jacob's Room'
by Virginia Woolf, which is supposed to be very original & modern.

Saturday we went to the prayer-meeting, played tennis, had 4
people to dine, & about 24 in after to dance – I think they all enjoyed themselves very much & I had forcibly to stop the
gramophone at midnight & tell them – especially the Bishop's
secretary – that I didn't approve of Sunday dancing! The only
misfortune was that the powder we put on the floor left the
whole house white, especially the black curtains & covers, & the
next day we had a lunch party & there wasn't a drop of water in
the house! However, I went out early & came back for lunch & it
was all perfect. I *have* rather a wonderful staff!

Tuesday I had a tea-party – one of the most hateful things
ever invented. Aunt Bee came, which was very nice of her, & was
very charming, & Margery came to play. The rest were 2 English
women, 4 Jewish women, & 10 Moslems, & 2 other very junior
English women who came to call by accident & whom I com-
mandeered to help. It seemed so slow & immoveable & chill, that
I went outside & sat in the hall for a bit, pretending to order tea,
because it depressed me so much. Of course neither Norman nor
John could be there. I believe those sort of things are always depressing – Aunt Bee said it was all right, but no more for me.

My new sitting-room, where I now write, looks *so* nice. I think
mine is quite the most artistic house in Jerusalem – I'm not conceited, as I'm sure it's an inherited trait! The bathroom specially is
nice now – blue & white, with rhyme-sheets of modern poetry
framed in black on the wall – & some from the 'Beggars' Opera'
too.

26.10.23: I'm sorry you find my letters too much of a chronicle –
my life is so much 'doing' & so little 'being' that I've little else
except events to tell. One interesting thing about myself, though
– I find that, partly as a result of being 6 months in England &
being able to think things more clearly there than I can here;
partly, I think, as a result of Wyndham's influence; partly as a reaction against the unfair & pro-Arab partiality of all the British
officials & Army here; & mostly as a result of getting so bored
with the English people, & partly also perhaps Fred's influence –
anyway, I find I have got much more sympathy with, & desire for
friendship towards, the Jewish people here than before. It's
largely, too, due to their attitude towards me. Formerly, it was
Hebrew or nothing; now they are all prepared to talk to me in
English, or apologize if they can't. Formerly, because of the language difficulty, they debarred me from their institutions; now
they are asking me to be on their things, & to be chairman &
president of their things; & now that I am reconstructing the Ladies' Club they are all flocking to join, & say they want to learn
English & meet the English people. When we first came here, the
Jews were exclusive & kept to themselves – now it's the English
that do that, & are narrow & bigotted, & the Jews are liberal &
progressive. They are, too, the persecuted & downtrodden here in
every way, & I feel I like to champion them in the same way as I
would Labour at home. They *are* the most interesting people here;
it's a real joy to talk to men like Rutenberg or Joshua Gordon[11] or
Dr Magnes or Ben Zvi[12] – or Fred [Kisch] & Nurock[13] & Sacher[14]
– instead of the ordinary British official & his inanities.

Tel Aviv is enormous now, with 19,000 inhabitants – only
about 2000 less than Jaffa itself. Of course, it's hideous, but it's
very alive & modern & free, & for those three reasons I feel at
home in it. It's the one place in Palestine where I feel safe alone at
night, just like in England, & where one needn't lock up anything.

3.11.23: I lost everything in the Jaffa tennis tournament with great skill & dignity – but I enjoyed myself very much, & had some lovely bathes.

Tuesday, 2 hours of Social Service Committee in the morning – we are going to start a *men's* branch, for prison visiting & probation work & social service generally. It's amazing here, the go-aheadness of the women, & the way the men are prepared to follow them when they have broken the ground successfully. Rutenburg & Edwin [Samuel] to lunch; & a meeting of the Immigrants Welfare for 2 hours in the afternoon. *Rigoletto* after dinner. There is quite a successful opera company from Tel Aviv; but opera is bad art.

10.11.23: H.E. gave an excellent reading of poetry at the Club, to an audience of well over 60. It was the inauguration of our new session. In the evening we all went to the first concert of the season of the Musical Society, held at the governorate, with Margery & Thelma playing. Jerusalem seems to gain a lot from our family, one way & another. I don't think they're half grateful enough!

Yesterday I lunched with Fred, & took him round the Old City in the afternoon. He knew nothing of it.

Since Fred Kisch had been in Jerusalem for a year, and wrote later of his 'constant joy of living in Jerusalem'[15] that might seem odd. However, it was in character, for when his sister and a friend visited in March 1924 he wrote in his diary: 'resigned myself reluctantly to a few days' sight-seeing at which I am no good at all.'

To celebrate their silver wedding, the Samuels had bought and furnished a house in Jericho, 'Beth Miriam', and had given it for the use of members of the Administration and other residents of Jerusalem needing rest or convalescence. Similarly, a house was built as a holiday home for the Junior Service with money given when Wyndham Deedes left:

23.11.23: I'm just off to Jericho for the week-end, to shake off the remains of the very foul cold I've been having for the last 3 weeks. It leaves one so weak & rotten that I'm looking forward to the quiet there. Aunt Bee, H.E. & Ruth [Franklin] go to their little house, & Norman & I stay in the hotel opposite & meal with them.

8.12.23: We've just come in from a very delightful – very strenuous – game of mixed hockey. We have taken the bull by the horns, the women of the Club, & decided to play in drill-tunics, instead of long, awkward skirts.

Scouts and guides, on the other hand, according to Baden-Powell's rules, were not to be mixed. But not even Helen could persuade the existing Jewish Boy Scouts to let the girls be separate, so she gave up the idea of being Commissioner. She had run guide companies enthusiastically in London, and was determined to do it properly or not at all.

14.12.23: I'm revelling in a glut – or would you say wallowing in a mire? – of modern literature. I enjoy the *Mercury* & the *Adelphi* very much. But I can't think that Huxley's new book is in any way modern – it's rather like Fielding or Smollett. And he writes for the would-be fast – the jazz-jumpered young people who live on their own & are most respectable & yet want everyone to think they aren't – just as Ethel Dell writes for the servant girls who always hope they're going to marry lords, but know there's not a chance. This vicarious experience is very old-fashioned in books, & I can't see why he should be such a cult. I like the Virginia Woolf one because of its style, & the Rose Macaulay because of its satire. But however did *you* get through 'Antic Hay'? Didn't it bore you very much? Anyway, I'm always very glad to read these new books which everyone talks of.

We *are* so bucked with the election results;[16] it's quite a new experience to be on a side that's fast getting a majority, & not always to be a rebel.

Helen was in good spirits, her break in England having made this a rather more cheerful year.

---

[1] Helen's sister.
[2] The 'pioneers' – the early Jewish settlers on the land.
[3] Flora Solomon, *Baku to Baker Street* (London: Collins, 1984).

[4] The merchant bank where her father was a director.

[5] Ethel Snowden, wife of Philip Snowden, the Chancellor of the Exchequer in the first Labour government, 1924.

[6] Margaret Bondfield was to be, in 1929, the first woman Cabinet minister.

[7] Helen was staying with Wyndham Deedes' sister, Mrs Knight, in her house with its Jane Austen connections.

[8] Her parents' Buckinghamshire home.

[9] Norman Bentwich, *Wanderer Between Two Worlds* (London: Kegan Paul, 1941), p 34.

[10] Janet Trevelyan, *The Life of Mrs Humphry Ward* (London: Constable, 1923), p 289.

[11] Zionist official, looking after immigration.

[12] Labour leader, later to be President of Israel.

[13] Max Nurock, Herbert Samuel's Private Secretary.

[14] Harry Sacher, of the Jewish Agency; formerly leader-writer for the *Manchester Guardian*.

[15] F.H. Kisch, *Palestine Diary* (London: Gollancz, 1938), p 363.

[16] 191 Labour MPs and 159 Liberals made Ramsay MacDonald the first Labour Prime Minister.

1924

The Social Round

'1924,' Norman wrote, 'was a year of consolidation. The Mandate was at last in operation, and the Administration was responsible for its doings to the Council of the League of Nations. The High Commissioner went to Geneva to render the first annual account, and passed the examination, both oral and written, as the Germans say, "summa cum laude".'[1]

Norman and Helen did not feel so secure themselves. They were already worrying about life under the next High Commissioner, whoever it might be; Norman was missing Deedes, and Helen was feeling that they must surely soon come home.

The previous year had ended with a cheerful celebration of Christmas. Jews are often rather ambivalent about Christmas – perhaps particularly so in Jerusalem – and Helen of course was often ambivalent in her feelings towards Palestinian Jews:

1.1.24: On Christmas Eve we asked all our Jewish friends to dinner – Dr & Mrs Magnes, Thelma & Eleazer, Fred, & four or five others. After dinner – they were a little sniffy about Xmas at first, so it had to be all very ordinary, & no special food or decorations – Mrs Magnes suggested a game. So we played the balloon game strenuously, men v. women, & they all got terribly rowdy & excited. And then we danced what they call the Virginia reel, & we call Sir Roger de Coverly; & then Dr Magnes insisted on teaching us all poker, so we sat in a ring on the floor & played for matches till midnight, being instructed by a Rabbi & the head of the Zionist Executive. It's upsetting all my preconceived notions that the two nicest men here should be a Rabbi & a Regular Indian Army soldier.

In spite of her social round of dinners, weekends away, dances and dramatics, Helen was still uncomfortable about the divisions in this strange society:

12.1.24: One misses friends so here – one has such heaps of nice acquaintances, but few *real* friends. All the English Christians are so awfully nice in not telling us what they *really* feel about Jews; & all Jewish non-English are so nice in not telling us all they feel about the English. But one knows so well what it is, & that it's there – on both sides. Often it is only with the English Jews, like Fred, that we can feel really at ease. I've had two days with the army at Bir Salem, in their camp. I stayed with the Copes – he is the son of the artist and is the Staff Captain there. I saw crowds of the army & gendarmerie, & had a very jolly time – but I knew they were all being awfully careful to say nice things about Jews, & listened most politely to my views. They make no attempt to understand things here, &, while lumping all Palestinians as natives, expect the same standards of conduct from the Jew as from an Englishman, & yet treat him the same as an Arab. They *will* always call everything 'Jew' instead of 'Jewish' – it doesn't matter really, but it jars. Jew-boys, Jew Government, Jew villages etc. However, I enjoyed it very much, & it's a jolly place this time of year. We rehearsed three plays in which I'm to take part – I think it's a great thing to have more contact with the army. I'm the only woman in the government circles the Copes have ever spoken to, except Aunt Bee! And they've been here three and a half years …

A few months later we find Helen performing in the three plays – 'the rest of the cast are the jolliest people imaginable' – going to the Ludd Hunt Ball and feeling 'quite at home' with the army people.

… One point about our life here – it brings us in contact with all sorts & conditions of people whom otherwise we shouldn't meet. At the moment, John is a happy man! Mr Bill Hunter is staying with us. Mr Bill Hunter used to be a crack player for the Bolton Wanderers & is, at present, the trainer of the Vienna Jewish team,

the Hakoah, who beat West Ham last year. Jerusalem has gone
football-mad. Yesterday there was a great match when the
Hakoah played Palestine (Army, Air Force & Gendarmerie) &
beat them 3–0. There were about 5000, or more, to watch, at the
Sports Club. They are being very fêted here. They beat the army
in Cairo. They are all under 25, & amateurs. But I wish the Jews
wouldn't be as intense about their football as they are about
everything else! Bill Hunter says the Hakoah are the best piece of
Jewish propaganda going today.

As a set-off to Bill Hunter, we meet Prince Arthur of Con-
naught at a dinner at Government House next Monday.

19.1.24: We had our Princeling here this week – & he hasn't done
much to impress us with the divine rights & powers of royalty.
He is a snob of the first water, continually alluding to the 'middle
class people' whom he had to meet in South Africa, & saying that
nothing could persuade him to stay out his time there, as he
hadn't met a 'real lady & gentleman for three years'. At the small
reception they had for him, he made no effort to talk to the notables who were introduced to him, & frankly made no attempt to
hide how bored he was. He said 'These people must be jolly glad
to have us Britishers here, what?' in front of all sorts of people
who aren't always particularly glad.

9.2.24: It's been horribly wet & cold this week, so we've avoided
going out in the evenings, but we've enjoyed our tête à têtes at
home, & have been playing mah jong & patience. We had a dinner party here to meet a Miss Annie Baker, the League of Nations
Investigator for the Abolition of Traffic in Women & Children, &
rather a big personage in all these societies & things in England. I
took her to see a Milk Station, the Rothschild Hospital, the
Nurses' Home, an Orphanage, & Miss Landau.

A milk station and infant welfare centre had been started in the
Old City by Flora Solomon, with £3000 from her father, run by a
nurse and providing clean milk.

This is Helen's first mention of playing mah jong. It had been
introduced to Europe and America only the previous year; always
keen to be up with the latest trends, Helen had asked her mother
to send out a set.

16.2.24: I've got a very nice fancy dress. An artist friend staying here has painted me a mah jong costume – ivory-coloured satin coat, with the figures & patterns off the blocks painted on in red & green ink, & all bound with bright green satin. And green satin straight trousers with figures painted round the bottom, & the 'Great Wall' in black down the side-seams. And a tight-fitting satin cap, with the compass painted on it. And mah jong written in the three official languages round the part that fits on to my head. Norman again refuses to wear one.

We motored out to Nablus, where the most anti-Zionist, anti-British Arabs wanted to give a banquet to Norman. I kept being afraid they'd knife him – or anyway that he'd have a pain after. But he was quite all right. I was the only female with 24 men. Ten courses, & dinner in two rooms, Norman & the arch-antis in one on their own.

'We' usually means me & Norman – in reply to your letter. But I thought husband & wife were meant to be one, & so it seems supererogation to write of us as two people. Also, Norman's desire for work leaves a lot of my time free to be entertained by people whom he provides for the purpose. It's all very select & correct, & he's only too glad to get me amused gratis by other people, I assure you.

I'm just going up to town, as we are going to look at the pictures of the man Bomberg, a protégé of Alice Waley-Cohen's, who has settled here. Will you examine the picture she gave us for a wedding-present – a huge futuristic atrocity – & see if it's his?

Helen later became an admirer of Bomberg. She mentions visiting him the following year and having 'a long discussion on art', and at different times she bought several of his pictures.

23.2.24: Miss Landau has been the heroine of this week – an enormous dinner, with 140 or so guests, Storrs in the Chair & H.E. making a speech, given in honour of her twenty-fifth anniversary. And her inevitable fancy-dress party. It was overdone – food from Cairo, including strawberries & cream; about 500 people – including a lot of the tradespeople, the station master etc (for which I admire her), but there wasn't room for all that number & it made everybody's head ache.

In answer to Caroline's criticism that she was keeping 'out of things', Helen sent a formidable list of her week's activities – 'I really haven't missed one thing of interest – or even of boredom – worse luck. This is our *one* night at home alone out of *twenty-five*.' The social duties often included having guests to stay whom they had not previously met, and this March brought them the Magnes's friends Felix and Freda Warburg, an immensely rich but (Helen felt it was 'but') entirely charming pair of Americans, who became their life-long friends. 'They are most awfully nice people,' she wrote, '& one quite forgot how rich they were.' She took them round 'institutions etc' and to Bethlehem and on a tour of the Jewish settlements. They gave her $300 when they left, to be used anonymously for her charities, and they endowed the Institute of Hebrew Studies, the first research institute of the Hebrew University. Helen wrote[2] that they were so impressed with John that they told him to look them up if ever he was out of a job; some years later, in New York, John did so and they promptly employed him.

Helen took one trip after another that spring, unsure how much longer they would be there, and anxious to see as much as she could in that period of calm. She went on three major tours; the later ones were with Norman, but the first was with Mr Abramson (Commissioner for Southern Palestine) and his wife:

21.3.24: Sitting is rather difficult after my long rides of last week, but it was well worth it. I met the Abramsons at Hebron & from there we went a few miles by car to a village called Dura – famous as the home of the highwaymen. The bandits came from there who murdered a tax-collector last summer; also those who murdered the British sergeants a few months back. They have been severely punished by the Government, & have been in disgrace. And this occasion was a reconciliation. We had our own tents, but fed in the evenings with the people ... We started off at 8.30 next morning. I hadn't really been on a horse for 3 years, & was feeling distinctly nervous, especially as the Arab mare I was given to ride was quite lively at first. But she soon quieted, & we rode on & on till 6.30, with an hour for lunch. The first part was full of flowers – sheets & sheets of red anemones & wild virginia stock & yellow daisies & tulips, & lots of miniature anemones, red & orange & yellow. But later the country got wilder & the going

more difficult – & the Bedouins with whom we were to spend the
night had moved, & we went on & on, over hill after hill, always
expecting to see them. At last, after dark, we came to some tents,
& were so tired we stopped there, tho' it wasn't the main part of
the tribe. However, we sent for the Sheikh, & he came there to
talk to us. *Our* camp had got lost, too, & didn't appear till 11. We
flopped down on the rugs in the very primitive goat-skin tent, by
a small furze fire, & were *very* thankful for the food they gave us.
They killed a sheep, & gave us sour milk & bread like soft mat-
zahs, & we all ate avidly out of the common pot. This Sheikh had
been the one who captured the murderers of the two soldiers. He
had discovered all about them & suggested that he & three of his
tribe should join them in a gang. They agreed, & all found a cave
together. Then the Sheikh went to Hebron & fetched the police,
& they went to the cave ... The Sheikh got £100 which Dura had
had to pay as a fine for harbouring the bandits, & £70 from the
government. He kept asking us to tell the Catholics what he'd
done, in case they'd give him some more – the soldiers were
Catholics. It was a brave thing of him to have done, because of
blood feuds. The natives don't know he did it, or they'd kill him.

The tours with Norman were in the north of the country, very
beautiful, but less eventful. An outing to the Dead Sea shortly
after they got back included some irresponsible archaeology:

7.5.24: Benton Fletcher – the originator of the party, couldn't
swim, & relied on my information about a certain cartouche
which he claimed to have seen before, of some Pharaoh's period,
& which he said was *most* important. Only Nancy & I swam to it –
the object of the expedition was to identify it. However, I don't
know much about these things, & not wishing to disappoint him,
I said yes to all his questions about it. It *might* have been a cartouche – on the other hand it *might* have been – & looked much
more like – a natural marking. Imagine my horror when, in a most
serious lecture by an American at the Dominican Monastery, on
Moab, this was referred to, & its authenticity claimed to have
been established by Major Fletcher on the strength of this last
expedition. If you hear that a Pharaoh was proved to have
marched to the Dead Sea – don't believe it too thoroughly.

Our leave plans are a little vague, but roughly are to leave here the end of July & return to England quite slowly, possibly taking a month over it. Norman never gets really let alone by officials etc in London – he has too much law & Zionism & Colonial Office – & he isn't awfully good in the country, as he *does* nothing. So I think we'll try this instead, getting home the latter part of August, & I shall stay as long as I like after he goes back.

28.5.24: A mad dog ran amok in the German Colony two days ago, & is alleged to have bitten Jock & Bob – my dog & John's. We can't find any marks, nor can the vet – & at the moment they are willing to let us leave them in the Animal Hospital for *6 months* – paying! I'm perfectly prepared to leave Jock – he's a valuable dog, & worth quite a lot here – apart from all sentimental feelings. But Bob is my problem. Being a democrat, I can't object to his mixed ancestry. Nor can I expect John to pay. Nor can I say I have *any* affection for him. However, I suppose they'll both have to be treated alike. It's a dreadful plague here. Budge [Norman's sister Muriel, who had settled in Palestine to do social work in 1919], & one of Lilian's children & one of Thelma's have all been bitten, by non-mad dogs, but have had to have the injections.

18.6.24: I'm having a really successful party, of 4 small girls, from 8–12, who came at 11.30 & haven't gone yet – 5.30. At the moment, they are Red Indians, eating dough-nuts under a wigwam of the car-tarpaulin & the washing line, painted crimson with my theatrical make-up, bristling with chicken-feathers, & with their skirts tucked inside their knickers, & bare thighs, legs & feet. There isn't a tree or wall they haven't been up – & they've had all the pillows off the beds for a pillow-fight, & sacks for sack-races; & they've trussed up Sophie [the maid], & knocked down John, & eaten any amount of ice-cream & chocolates, & really had a good day.

Definitely a party only to be given by someone with Sophies and Johns about to cope and clear up, while the hostess writes her letters.

Although there is always the undercurrent of 'good works meetings', Helen seems to be in a particularly frivolous state at this time, over-occupied with her theatricals, with entertaining & being entertained by the naval officers on the fleet's annual visit, and with her tennis. And the plans for leave were developing – 'Will you send us any introductions if you know any people in any of the following places: Constantinople, Constanzia, Bucharest, Belgrade, Sophia, Buda-Pesth, Vienna, Linz, Salzburg, Munich, Luxembourg, Cologne?' They would then have about four weeks in England together – although Norman hoped to spend one of the weeks on a walking tour with Wyndham Deedes – 'I shall certainly stay longer. What about coming back with me?'

2.7.24: We are awfully like home here. We've had a murder & a strike here this week. The strike is rather pathetic. The government suddenly increased the tax on cars, making the hired cars pay more than double – £36 a year for a big car. Poor things, they'll suffer in the end, as they have nobody to back them up, & no money – the one awkward thing is that they keep putting nails & tacks on all the roads, & those of us who do use our cars keep getting punctured. However – we must be up-to-date.

The murder is unpleasant – a Dutch fellow, correspondent for the *Daily Express*, was shot & killed by an unknown hand the night before last. He was rather mad – a most unpleasant fellow – a thorough bad hat, people said – who posed as the leader of the most intensely orthodox Jewish party, although he had a Christian wife! However, his defence on that score was that he no longer lived with her because he was too orthodox! He was the man who caused all the trouble among the Jews when Northcliffe was here, & poisoned the minds of all the political visitors, including Astor. He was violently in with the Arabs – dressing up as one, & staying with Hussein when he was over – & a hanger-on of the Latin Patriarchate. He had a lot of money dealings with Arabs, so quite likely it was one who shot him. Tho' he betrayed the Jews so often, it may have led to some quarrel. He may do more harm dead than living, because of the *Daily Express*, & being a martyr always pays. How I hate violence & bloodshed in *any* form – it's never justified, not even capital punishment.

I've had a long letter from Amy [Drucker] from Peking. She's quite 'it' in China, painting all sorts of celebrities, & being run by all the advanced European crowd, with shows & things.

It was not until 1970 that the truth came out about the case of the Dutch-born Jew Jacob De Haan. Contemporary horrified suspicion that the murder was committed by Zionists turned out to be right. Because he had tried to politicize the ultra-Orthodox, and to establish a movement opposed to secular Zionists, De Haan had been shot by Haganah, the Zionist self-defence group that had been set up to combat Arab terrorism.[3]

Helen and Norman journeyed to England across Europe as planned, ending by flying, for the first time, from Holland to England. There are no more letters – and no surviving diary or letters to Norman – until November, when once again Helen was back from leave fully ready to join the bustle.

1.11.24: Life here seems as crowded as ever – for besides the bazaar, I've been rushed straight into organizing a Health Week – lectures & pamphlets & demonstrations all over the country, through schools & all organizations. Today I struck, & have been working 6 hours solidly in the garden. And the Storrs are behaving abominably about my gardener he wants to come back to me, & Storrs threatens him with a road-gang (misusing his power of conscripting villagers for road-making shamefully) & not to give him any money for the 6 weeks he's worked there. [It was two years before Helen got him back.]

Clayton,[4] who is acting H.E., is ill, & Norman had to give a legal decision as to whether he or Storrs should take it on – being Norman he elected that Storrs should. What *is* the use of a husband like that? However, better Norman with a clear conscience & Ronald radiant, than Norman sleepless & depressed, & Ronald ditto – for opposite reasons.

Aunt Bee, & all the haute monde, are crazy on cross-word puzzles.

Like mah jong, crossword puzzles were the latest fashion. They had appeared in 1924 for the first time, with immediate success. Helen planned a crossword costume for Miss Landau's next fancy-dress party, but Miss Landau was ill and the party was cancelled.

8.11.24: Lady Storrs told the Jewish woman who is organizing health week that she could take no interest in it, as it was no good trying to promote good feeling among Jews & Arabs as long as the Balfour Declaration existed. From the wife of the Acting High Commissioner, that is, to say the least, tactless.

15.11.24: Wednesday evening there was a big banquet at G.H. for General & Madame Weygand of Syria, who seem very nice. Norman, I, John & all our silver were at the banquet. It's very English the way we treat Weygand as such a frightfully honoured guest, & let him have all his flags everywhere, & all the French places decorated up like anything – I don't suppose they'd do that for H.E. in Syria!

You say you wonder if Norman will agree with me as to its being our last year in Palestine. He does – & he even told H.E. so the other day, when he went to Ludd to meet him. H.E. gave all the reasons why he had refused a longer term of office – not good to stay in a job too long, good for the country to have a change, you don't always want a Jew in the same position, etc. So Norman, seeing that those were just *his* reasons for wishing to go, said so – & H.E. was horrified at having them used back on him, & couldn't see the application at all. I think it will be Xmas next year – 6 months after H.E. has gone. As to feeling bored at home, we neither of us have any fear of that. It's so funny that you all should! We won't live in London – we're rather thinking at the moment of Seer Green, the Quaker garden village near Gerrards X. We'll do Labour work in the district. And we're hoping that something on the lecturing way will turn up to give Norman a beginning, & provide a modest income. We're so full of plans & ideas, that it'll take us a few years to try them all successively, even if the first few fail. Gradually all our friends are leaving here, so we'll see them at home anyway. We know so exactly what we want, & have no illusions as to our income, & no desire for the 'smart life', & have such a variety of friends, of all different religions, classes & nationalities, that it should be quite entertaining. If we can manage a spare room, we'll always be sure of Palestine friends when on leave, in shoals.

There was hardly a year in all their time in Palestine when Helen and Norman did not think their time there was nearly over and that they should plan a new life – though they always felt the pull of their 'shoals of Palestine friends'. Helen found it perpetually

unsettling. They were wrong again this time of course, and that
vision of the future did not materialize. In 1924 Helen was less
than halfway through her time in Palestine.

29.11.24: I've been putting in a lot of time gardening. It's such a
good way of spending one's time – I think I like it better than
anything else. Four to six hours a day solid work on it isn't bad, is
it? I do that whenever I've nothing else to do. Hockey was to start
today, but it was too warm – I'm all off tennis, & haven't played
since I came back.

We've been seeing Asquith[5] this week, dining up at Government House both Monday & Wednesday to meet him, one
proper official dinner, and one with the family. He was amusing
& told some good stories. One was how Winston became Chancellor of the Exchequer. Baldwin sent for him, meaning to offer
him the job of Chancellor of the Duchy – but he'd got no further
than the first word when Winston accepted, saying he'd always
hoped for that job. Meanwhile the man who was waiting in the
lobby to be offered the Exchequer, only got the Ministry of Labour when he came in, which he indignantly refused.[6] After
dinner, we all did cross-word puzzles for a bit – Asquith & H.E.
snorting at them, but unable to tear themselves away for quite a
time.

In his *Memoirs*, Samuel wrote of the Asquith visit: 'I took him to
some of the more interesting places, but he did not seem to be
impressed. As to the striking Jewish constructive effort that was
going on all around he only wrote in his record: "The talk of
making Palestine into a Jewish 'National Home' seems to me as
fantastic as it has always done".'[7]

Helen and her mother thought alike on so many things, that
arguments are rare in their letters. Politically, however, they
disagreed – Caroline was a Liberal, and Helen, like her sister and
her brother Hugh, was passionately Labour:

5.12.24: Why do you call Wheatley more real Labour than Ramsay
MacDonald? It's always the way with Conservatives to disparage
any fine Labour man by saying – 'Oh, he's not Labour'. Just like
anti-semites always say – 'Oh, but not a Jew like you!' Ramsay's
good enough for us – his only equal is Snowden – & we'll follow

them all right, & you needn't fear a revolution, but will have to be
wary of a wholesale conversion.

You're quite wrong about my clothes – one of the objects of
the Labour people is to make the world more beautiful, as well as
better. And really, pretty clothes cost no more than ugly ones! But
I expect I'll stick to breeches, so long as I live in the country. I
wear them a good deal here still, for gardening & long walks.

Now, 70 years on, it is hard to see any conflict between holding
Labour principles and having an interest in clothes and interior
decoration. More bothering from that point of view is Helen's
assumption of privilege, a secure feeling that her energetic life of
Good Works and frivolities would always be properly backed by
servants who would enable her to live in comfort.

A new friend, whom they were to see a great deal while he was
in Palestine for the next three years, was Gaston Maugras, the new
French Consul. He was greatly liked – Storrs called him charming
and distinguished, and said he was 'welcomed by the Administration as a colleague rather than a foreigner'.[8] Writing to her mother
the following year, Helen described him as 'one of the most
interesting men I know – full of knowledge of the Bible & all
religion & history, serious-minded, but with a great sense of
humour'.

13.12.24: Monsieur Maugras is a most entertaining person – tall &
very good-looking; speaks perfect English; unmarried, between 35
& 40; & one of the keenest senses of humour I've ever struck. I
seem to see him every day, as he plays football & hockey with us.
On Liberation Day he sat opposite me in Church, & had on *the*
most fascinating costume, all gold lace, with a velvet cloak which
he flung over one shoulder. As I told him – I felt I was at the
'Scarlet Pimpernel' & the 'Prisoner of Zenda' rolled into one,
rather than at Church.

Could you let me have, some time, the Burnham scale for
teachers – especially kindergarten teachers? Or any scale which is
paid in Bucks would do. They expect such very high pay here – &
are so bad! I do wish they'd someone like you to advise them! The
Zionist education is very bad indeed; do you know, they haven't a
woman inspector anywhere – not even for kindergartens – & the
girls' schools are staffed & controlled by men.

1. Helen's parents, Arthur and Caroline Franklin.

2. Helen in her parent's house in Buckinghamshire, about the time of her marriage.

3. Officers of OETA with General Bols, 2 June 1920.

4. Norman as Senior Judicial Officer in the military administration, 1919-20.

5. Norman as Attorney General, with the law officers.

6. Herbert Samuel with ecclesiastical dignitaries. Norman is standing, fifth from the right, with Ronald Storrs in uniform on his left.

7. Picnic for Herbert Samuel's 50th birthday (1920). Norman is on the extreme right with Nancy Samuel next to him; Wyndham Deedes is in a grey suit without a hat.

8. Tennis in times of trouble (1929). Helen is fourth from the right in the second seated row.

We have at last shut up our Ladies' Club. There seemed no demand for it any longer – the members had to be galvanized all the time, & I got rather sick of being the one to do the galvanizing. And those Monday lectures were an awful effort to arrange, & increasingly difficult.

The British women had deserted the Ladies' Club because they preferred the new Sports Club. And Helen found a new interest in a poorly run kindergarten in the Jewish Quarter of the Old City. 'The children,' she wrote later, 'came from the poorest homes at the age of three, sometimes so swaddled in rags that they had to be undressed before we could determine their sex.'

This year's letters end as they began, with an account of a 'Jewish Xmas dinner' – 12 guests, with crackers, balloon games, tug-of-war, skipping with the clothes line ('you should have seen Miss Landau, in a shimmery evening dress, very seriously counting how many she could keep up'), poker & animal grab. 'Dr Magnes was the rowdiest, with Norman a close second.'

---

[1] Norman Bentwich, *Wanderer Between Two Worlds* (London: Kegan Paul, 1941), p 130.

[2] In her manuscript memoir.

[3] See Martin Gilbert, *Jerusalem* (London: Chatto & Windus, 1996), pp 108–9. In 1998 yet another side of De Haan's complex character came to light – an exhibition in Amsterdam's Jewish Historical Museum celebrated him as a homosexual poet.

[4] Gilbert Clayton, Chief Secretary 1923–25, was acting High Commissioner because Samuel was in Geneva reporting to the Mandates Commission.

[5] Herbert Asquith, then aged 70, was still active in the House of Commons.

[6] This is a more entertaining version of the story told in G.M. Young's *Stanley Baldwin*, which has Churchill, expecting to be Chancellor of the Duchy, overwhelmed at being offered the Exchequer.

[7] Viscount Samuel, *Memoirs* (London: Cresset Press, 1945), p 175.

[8] Ronald Storrs, *Orientations* (London: Nicholson and Watson, 1945), p 427.

1925

Uncle Herbert's Last Year

1925 was notable in Palestinian history for the opening of the Hebrew University by Balfour,[1] and for the appointment of Lord Plumer as the new High Commissioner. Both these events deeply affected Helen and Norman. The University was to take an ever increasing part in their lives, and there was no longer to be the cosy family relationship with Government House.

The government of Palestine had become, incidentally, something of a family business for Storrs as well as for the Bentwiches. Archer Cust, Storrs' cousin, was Samuel's Private Secretary, and Storrs' stepson was an ADC.

For Helen, 1925 was also notable for the second visit from her parents. Before that, there was the usual mixture of activities – meetings, visitors, kindergarten, twenty-mile walks, gardening, weekends away, moonlight picnics, tennis, basket-ball & even baseball.

9.1.25: We went to Bethlehem to see the Greek Xmas, which we'd never seen. It was beastly! Crowds of irreverent people, & all the processing done by government officials & consuls, carrying candles, & the Greek Christians quite left out of it.

There's a vague chance that I might go to America! The Women's Council has joined the International Council of Women, & they have a conference in Washington in May. They want our President (Aunt Bee) or Secretary (me) to go, & are willing to send £100 for the passage. It would be fun – but I feel frightened of meeting so many earnest-minded women en masse alone. Would you come? & Alice or Jack?[2] It seems tame not to, & I can't make up my mind. Norman's keen for me to go, but I'm thinking I won't. It's all those women, & their horrible efficiency, that puts me off.

16.1.25: Monday there was the famous 'Hakoah' match – about 5000 people present, to see the Jewish team from Vienna play against the English team from Palestine. Vienna won, 4–2, but it's not a pleasant thing to watch, as feeling – Jew v. non-Jew – runs so high. And any bad behaviour on either side – which seems inevitably connected with soccer – is always magnified into an 'incident'. We longed for it to be a draw.

23.1.25: I had a painful tea-party with Miss Newton,[3] who told such outrageous lies against Jews that in the end I told her she was telling 'absolute lies', & walked out. It's awfully absurd to lose one's temper with her, but she goads & goads you till you are quite worn out.

I am quite determined now not to go to America with all those women, but to go to Teheran & Isfahan with Norman instead. *Much* more fun.

13.2.25: I went to Tel Aviv & ran into the Monds there, & committed the faux pas of disapproving of it. As he'd just put £10,000 into it, as a loan, it annoyed her that I shouldn't like it. She got very angry, & said to him, 'Just like your Jews, always criticizing & never sticking together.' She may be right, but he took me aside & was very charming about the possibilities & hopes of Tel Aviv, & how we wouldn't like it, but it was all right for 'them that did'. I'd said something about Tel Aviv finance being involved, & she rounded on me & said 'How dare you mention finance in front of my husband.' I didn't know financiers were like Bishops – that it was profane to talk their shop before them.

But the following month Helen wrote that she and Lady Mond were 'quite friendly, in spite of Tel Aviv'.

20.2.25: I'm playing base-ball with the American Colony. We have played twice – it's great fun learning a new game, & I'm getting on well at it. And netball twice this week & hockey once.

We are rationed for water as if it were August – the poor people are already buying it. We had an alarm the other night – they'd given us no warning that they'd cut it off, & when the geyser was lit (a primus one) for my bath, there was a little there. But it soon ran out, & when I went in for my bath, the bottom of my £10 geyser was melted right through, & the fumes & smell appalling. I'm very lucky it didn't explode – they sometimes do.

I've been reading a lot of quite serious books lately – on various religions, & the Crusades – & even the Bible. I've been talking a lot of these things with Magnes & the French Consul & other people here, & we talk about it all on our Sunday walks – folklore & religion & the origins of the Bible etc – & get very critical & destructive, & then I come home & read it up for a new spurt for the next week. So it's not all frivol – even the Sunday walks.

Helen was excited to hear that her parents were planning a spring visit:

13.3.25: I should advise, both for you & Father, tussore dust-cloaks for motoring. A topee isn't necessary for women, but veils & scarves are best, & felt hats better than thin straw ones, & linen dresses that you won't feel the sun too much through are preferable to muslin ones for travelling around, tho' for afternoons any sort are all right. We'll do our best to give you baths – but there'll always be heaps of water at Carmel & in Jaffa when you feel too dirty in Jerusalem.

Serious illness was always a worry. That March, for the first time, they had typhoid inoculations, and Helen recommended her parents to do the same. Later that year one of their friends was ill with typhoid, and Weizmann's sister died suddenly of tetanus.

Helen wrote of one journey from Haifa to Jerusalem with a visiting friend, when an unreliable car and total mechanical ignorance combined with the rough roads to bring even more chaos than usual:

20.3.25: Laura & I & my small boy Mahomed & Jock [the dog] left Haifa at 10 – without watches. Somewhere between Jenin & Nablus – after our insides had told us it was lunchtime – the car refused to go on, the engine being overheated. We waited by it – there was a thick white mist & we could see nothing & had no idea of the time. First, a car with an Arab Jerusalem driver came along, & he tinkered with the oil-feed; then a Sephardic Jew came along, & tried the plugs. Then a Damascus Syrian came along, & tore bits from my nice linen handkerchief to repair rubber that had melted round the wires. Then a Jewish boy, driving some English clergy people staying with the Bishop here came along, & finished doing that, taking about half-an-hour over it. Then a British officer came along, & gave a hand too; lastly, a Hindu driver also assisted. Finally, the clergy-people's driver made it go, & they insisted on us driving ahead of them, in case we needed help again. We got to within 5 miles of Nablus, & again it overheated. We then left Mahomed & Jock in the car, & went with the clergy folk into Nablus, & threw ourselves once again on the British gendarmerie. The officer & his wife gave us tea, & sent out their fitter, who found (what these 6 pros hadn't guessed at even) that the bottom of the radiator had come out, & that was why the car was overheating. They plugged it, & brought the car in; & I drove down here with a British gendarme with a loaded rifle as escort, arriving here at 10 pm. I was rather tired – but it's nice how kind & helpful people are, & my car ran excellently, despite the handkerchief.

For Judah Magnes and for Norman, the opening of the Hebrew University was, Helen said, an event of 'almost mystical quality'; the University was 'the symbol of their vision of Jerusalem as the cultural centre of the world'. The site on Mount Scopus had been bought during the war, and the foundation stones had been laid in a ceremony in the early days of the Military Administration, in July 1918. That same morning the law courts had been reopened; 'The pursuit of justice and the search for knowledge,' Norman wrote, 'were to mark a new era in Palestine.'[4] Balfour, as signatory of the Declaration and as Chancellor of the University of Cambridge, was doubly qualified to add distinction to the formal opening. Here is Helen's account of his visit, and her view of the official celebrations:

10.4.25: Well, don't believe a word you have seen in the papers, because everything went off splendidly, & not *half* the fuss &

bother that there is every year to keep Christians from cutting each other's throats at the Holy Fire. And not a tenth of the Nebi Musa show of force.

Personally, I thought, & still think, it was a great mistake to rouse ill-feeling in the press & among propagandists by bringing Balfour here. We are all appalled by the dishonesty of the press – so shocked that nobody seems to be able to take it seriously, or to know how to combat it. *The Times* is undoubtedly England's only decent paper.

Balfour arrived on 24th, but we didn't meet him till the 31st, at a dinner at Government House, when I sat next to him, & found him one of the most interesting & fascinating people I'd ever come across. One of those *really* nice people who make you seem a brilliant talker by wanting to hear all you have to say. We talked all the time – of Jews & Arabs & Palestine, & of the University, as well as of things at home.

The following afternoon was the opening of the University. The amphitheatre they have made is wonderful in its site & position, & full of people it was a most impressive sight. There were 12,000 people there – & a more orderly crowd you couldn't conceive. Not a scuffle or push anywhere – a child alone was quite safe in it (the little Magnes boy, left at home, ran away & found his way into the crowd, got to the front, & saw all he wanted, unknown to his parents). All the English, & quite a number of non-Jewish Palestinians were there, including a number of of Bedouin sheikhs from Beisan. The ceremonies themselves failed to impress me. The Chief Rabbi – Kuk – began, & wouldn't stop. He was told to speak 5 minutes, & promised to. Despite every effort to stop him by Weizmann (who presided) & Magnes, he went on 30 minutes, quite upsetting everything & everybody. Then Weizmann spoke in Hebrew & English – inadequately. H.E. spoke next – better than he ever had before, everyone thinks. Then Balfour – & frankly, I was awfully disappointed. He had told me the night before he was afraid we would be, as he never wrote his speeches, but relied entirely on the inspiration of the moment. And he felt that, with an audience the majority of which didn't understand English, the inspiration wouldn't come. And it didn't. Then Bialik, a Hebrew poet, emulated Kuk & wouldn't stop, which made an anti-climax. And then Hertz,[5] with his common voice, gave a prayer, & made one feel ashamed of having him to

represent England. He seemed so shoddy. There was some ade-
quate music, by children. And the robes & gowns of the
representatives of universities, & other officials on the platform
were quite impressive. It got very cold before the end. The banquet in the evening was followed by 16 speeches, in all languages,
by consuls & rabbis.

Monday, we went up to the Colony Balfouria – Norman is
chairman of a children's colony of orphans there, which Balfour
visited. We lunched with all the crowd at the Colony – the impressive part there was Balfour's entry, escorted first by Bedouin
sheikhs, beautifully dressed, with lovely horses, chanting their
war-cries & waving swords, & then by Colony boys & girls on
horseback. Not much ill-feeling in *that* part of the world, anyway.
Only you won't read of that in your rotten old press! ...

So, what was the 'rotten old press' saying? Philby, in an article in
the *Nineteenth Century*,[6] wrote scathingly of the 'Anglo-Zionist
administration of Palestine'. The *Daily Mail*, then bitterly hostile to
Zionism, never lost an opportunity to attack Balfour's visit and his
'connection with the Zionist scandal' (31 March). 'While Lord
Balfour and his Zionist friends are making festival amid an outraged nation the moment seems fit to make known the scheme by
which, under cover of the British flag, the Zionists propose to
obtain control of the government of the soil of Palestine' (2
April). The paper talked of the unfair results of 'so many Jews
holding high positions in the Palestine Government' (30 March) –
meaning the British Jews, Herbert Samuel, Norman Bentwich,
Max Nurock, Albert Hyamson and Edwin Samuel, all of whom
were in fact scrupulously, perhaps even obsessively, fair.[7] Palestinian Jews, like the Arabs, held only lesser positions.

Storrs thought Balfour's visit had 'put the clock of reconciliation back by at least a year', but Fred Kisch, who had a lot of
responsibility for taking Balfour around, was enthusiastic: 'Looking back upon the University ceremonies and upon Balfour's visit,'
he wrote in his diary, 'I feel that they have in a fortnight advanced
our movement in a manner that might have demanded a century
of work. Thank God everything went well.'

Meanwhile Helen was busy planning her parents' visit, and the
same letter continues:

... I don't think I'll come to Alex. to meet you, but we'll ask Bar-
ron (who used to live next to us, & now runs the Bonded
Warehouses there) to have you met & looked after. The government official at Kantara is to look after you there, & I propose to
meet you at Ludd, & motor you up. Would you care for going to
Syria with us & Aunt Bee & the girls [cousins] on May 3rd?

Caroline and Arthur arrived at the end of April, and for the
next month we turn once again to Caroline's diary. Having been
duly met at Ludd, they thought Helen an excellent driver, the
country looking more prosperous, and Helen's house 'very cheery
& comfy & pretty'. Following their usual quaint ideas of a holiday,
on the first afternoon Caroline accompanied Helen to the annual
meeting of the Women's Council and heard her read her report.
Next day to the Evelina School, then social calls, and a dinner
party where there was music, Norman playing and Storrs whis-
tling. There was much conscientious sightseeing and fact-finding,
conscientiously documented, together with visits to institutions
such as the Infant Welfare Centre and Helen's kindergarten.
Caroline did not fall for Maugras' charm at his dinner party: 'I
doubt whether he is trustworthy where the English are concerned.
A private cinematograph was shown after dinner – a rather dull
evening & chilly.' Helen was aware of those doubts, as a letter that
November showed: 'I know you & Aunt Bee think Maugras a
Dangerous Diplomat, & all that. But he's the next best thing to a
modern play in Jerusalem, & so long as I can't have a theatre here,
an evening spent with him is the best substitute.'
    They went for a fortnight's tour north, starting without Nor-
man (who joined them in Damascus), but with the Samuels and
their daughter Nancy, and the two girl cousins – a convoy of three
chauffeur-driven cars with an ADC and a guard of soldiers. At
first there were official deputations wherever they went, but then
Herbert Samuel left them, to start his ten days' farewell horseback
ride through all the villages of Palestine, from north to south. Bee
was to have stayed with them as far as Damascus, but the consul
warned her not to, because of possible danger, much to the
indignation of the French authorities in Jerusalem. Caroline was
impressed by the kibbutz at Deganiah – 'It seems on the face of

it,' she wrote, after describing the cheerful well cared-for children, 'an admirable system for working women.' Helen took them, with a driver, on another tour, to Amman.

On the final day of her visit, Caroline called on a friend to discuss the Evelina School; visited a government teachers' training college and its associated school – 'too much embroidery of garments taught in upper school'; visited Miss Landau in hospital; lunched with friends in Ein Karem; shopped in town; and dined at Government House, a farewell party to the two girl cousins who had been staying there – 'very noisy after dinner but amusing. At 10 we left & went to the circus, all except Arthur. Rotten show but pleasant & friendly.'

It had been announced that Field-Marshall Plumer was to be the next High Commissioner, and Helen and her friends were apprehensive – needlessly, as it turned out, for Plumer's three years in office were notably peaceful, and Helen and Norman soon grew to like him and his wife. On paper, Plumer's credentials could well have worried Helen – aged 68, Eton and army, hero of the Boer War and Passchendaele – Helen referred to him, before she met him, as 'the Ancient Warrior'. But since the war he had also distinguished himself as Governor of Malta, which prepared him for his work in Palestine. He had one son, three daughters, and was enthusiastic about music and cricket.

30.5.25: It seems awfully flat now that you have gone, & I'm sure I won't be able to bear out my resolution not to come home this summer. Already I feel I must have something to look forward to – besides the depressing certainty of the stiff & elderly regime ahead. The more everyone thinks of it, the more hopeless they become. There is a rumour afloat that Milner had been appointed to the job, but died at the tragically wrong moment. I can't say if it's true – except that Ormsby-Gore[8] told Weizmann that the Jews would be intensely pleased & gratified at the appointment, a few weeks back – & that they certainly aren't now. And Milner was the one non-Jew they had longed for more than anybody. Anyway – it's all beastly.

There was a long series of farewell parties for the Samuels, and various rumours about the Plumers – wife not Catholic but very churchy and 'aggressively ungenial'; one daughter married to a Jew, another daughter 'stuck-up & conceited' with a husband to be ADC; all appointments to change at Government House when he arrived. And the prospect brought even more doubts about Helen and Norman's own future. The letters are full of '*if* we're still here', and 'we *do* mean to leave, almost for a certainty'; Norman tried to see if there were openings at Cambridge or Oxford, but he had missed his chance there.

An exciting archaeological find near Lake Galilee provided a distraction:

4.7.25: Yesterday we went to see *the* skull, about which you must have read a great deal in the papers. It's a Neanderthal skull, which proves that this type of man existed in Asia, as heretofore he's only been discovered in Europe. It was found in that cave you visited near Tabgha – & by Turville-Petre, the long-haired lanky youth there. So you'll be able to talk very intelligently about it – the cave I didn't visit, & which you then thought it a waste of time to go to.

10.7.25: After a sleepless night, I got shingled at 8 yesterday morning, & feel much better & able to cope with the intense heat-wave. *I* like the look of it, but Norman says it looks as if I've some awful disease – that it's a good thing I'm married, as nobody'd ever look at me now, & some other very rude things. It's where my neck changes from brown to dead white that it looks like a disease, & that'll soon get cured.

The kindergarten goes on well – there's a great difficulty about getting any water there, which has taken me a long time to arrange. The water problem is most acute in regard to distribution – there are 600 tins to be filled each time this particular stand-pipe in the Jewish Quarter is opened. 120–150 tins can be filled an hour. Think of these poor wretches waiting in the heat, all those hours! It costs up to 8 times as much if they buy it from the men who fetch it & resell.

That July Helen had, as she confessed in the following letter, a frightening, and what could have been a tragic, accident:

17.7.25: I came up here to Haifa alone in the car with John – he returned the next day by train to look after Norman. On the way, for the first time since I've been driving, I ran over someone. It was at Nablus – a most awkward place for it to have happened. We had just got past the Police barracks about 200 yards or so, when a woman in a black native dress, walking on the right side of the road, jumped across the road as I sounded my hooter. I was going very slowly, & drew up against the left-hand wall in trying to avoid her. But she got caught, I think, by her clothes, & drawn under, & I was perfectly certain I'd gone clean over her head. Anyway, I lost my own rather badly, as I can't bear to look at things bleeding & mangled; I jumped out, & left John to deal with it, & shamelessly went down the road by myself while he & some crowd lifted the car off her, put her in it, & went off to the hospital. It never entered my head that she wasn't dead – one does think queerly in an emergency – & I'd never felt so bad about anything before. Some effendis came up – John had already given my name – wiping blood off their hands & clothes, & some boys & policemen. 'What happened to her?' I asked. 'She will die all right,' the effendis said. 'I've killed her then,' I said. 'Never mind, Mrs Bentwich,' they assured me, 'She is only a poor servant-woman, & shouldn't have got in your way. Nobody will mind. But it is not nice that you should stand like this on the roadway. Fetch a chair, somebody, & shall I call another car for you?' It was a funny attitude of theirs, & I must say they were all very nice, although it was Nablus, & I was known, & quite alone. However, I walked back to the police-station – bare-headed as I'd left my hat in the car, & that didn't make me feel any better, as it was 2 pm & awfully hot. I was nearly fainting when I got there. No officer was there, but a Scotch NCO. I told him I'd killed a woman, & he said 'That's awkward, but I don't know what to do with you. Go on to Haifa, & report there. But don't worry, you'll get off.' I wasn't worrying about that, but I wanted someone to take an interest in the *woman*, & I told him so, & made him come & ring up the hospital, much to his annoyance, as he had been asleep. He kept saying on the phone 'Is that woman Mrs Bentwich ran over dead yet', about twenty times because they didn't understand him & I sat by his side on a little wooden bench, & thought any moment I'd be sick. However, after half-an-hour, John came back, & said the woman *wasn't* dead. I did feel relieved – & dashed in the car to the hospital, woke up the matron out of her siesta to tell her about it – I think she thought I was quite mad – & then discovered from John that they hadn't even kept the woman there, as she was too frightened to stay, but he'd taken her home, & she'd walked in & out of the car quite happily. I don't know why he didn't tell me at once – he was so frightened I'd get into trouble, he was nearly as upset as I was. She'd cut her face & knocked a tooth out – hence the blood. The matron promised to make all enquiries, & I came on here. I still get haunted by the thought of it. But the matron of the hospital says the woman wasn't at all bad, & having made all my depositions to Mr Mills, the assistant-governor here [Haifa], they say I needn't worry any more.

24.7.25: On Sunday morning we went to the monastery here [near Mount Carmel] for the Feast of Mar Elias – St Elijah. Crowds of all religions come – it's really a relic of the Baal worship that went on here, only they like to give it a more Christian & civilized meaning. A few people go into the Church, but it's a real Bank Holiday crowd, with the most attractive costumes & colours. They camp there two or three days, en famille. They are very fond of 'peep-shows', with a man to wind the handle & tell a tale in Arabic.

I wish I could find somebody to give a show in aid of our kindergarten! We only want £250 a year, so it shouldn't be so difficult to raise it. Can you give me any suggestions, as we have only enough for 3 more months.

In that hot and tiring summer, Helen became idle:

31.7.25: It's so glaring & sunny here – & every morning I seem to get full up with meetings, & dashing round the town after the wretched kindergarten, or the new playground we are trying to start, or the girls' school furnishings & things for the farm place at Nahalal. Then I have to fetch Norman, & it's nearly 2 before we have lunch. I rest till 4, & then, whenever I can, play tennis till dinner-time, having tea at the Club & gossiping by the hour about everybody & everything. I'm sure heat is the backbone of gossip, because it's too hot to talk sensibly or read.

8.8.25: The French are having quite a lively war in Syria, which they successfully prevent from getting into the papers … The Druses objected to the French governor, & asked for his removal. The French wouldn't concede, & asked the Druse leaders to come to Beyrouth & discuss it. They accepted the invitation & were promptly arrested – the same dirty trick that we did in 1920 in Baghdad. And so the trouble started. It's fairly near the Trans-Jordan border, but there are no Druses in T.J., so it's hoped they won't come over & cause trouble. The French are bombarding the towns from the air, women & children & all, which doesn't make things any better. I'm afraid most of us feel a little less sorry than we ought to when the French get the worst of it. And, Maugras being away, we don't have any Francophile influence here at the moment. They *are* so aggressive with their subject peoples, & so pig-headed about suppressing papers & speeches etc. The die-hard element here hold them up as an example, because last year they hanged people publicly in Beyrouth, & are so brutal.

On the day before Plumer's arrival, there was a tragedy in Norman's family once again when Michael Lange, widower of Norman's sister Nita, shot himself at Zichron. Shocked and upset, Norman dashed off to Zichron, but had to be back for Plumer. Helen had Lilian Friedlander's two youngest children over from Zichron to stay. She found everyone 'frightfully kind & sympathetic, as they always are when one is in trouble'.

On first impressions the Plumers were '*exactly* like what we expected. He is less prepossessing-looking even, but has a good & attractive voice which is always an asset. She is very thin & scraggy with a high voice, one of those people to whom being gracious doesn't come naturally.' There was a lot of prejudice to be overcome.

9.9.25: Sunday afternoon we went to tea with the Plumers – they are having the Administration up on Sundays, by twos & threes, to get to know them, which is awfully sensible. I'll confess that we had a *most* pleasant surprise – they were very nice indeed to us. We had a 'schoolroom tea', as Plumer called it, in the dining-room, & they were both very anxious to make us feel at home & to like them – which we did. Afterwards, they showed us all their interesting things – caskets with freedoms of cities, a gold sword from S. Africa, one from France, photographs of generals & war incidents, & crowds of miniatures, which, honestly, I can't much appreciate. She has nice things, but very un-modern in the way they are laid out. They have removed the more offensive parts of Ashbee's furniture (be careful how you repeat this to Aunt Bee), & have painted the walls blue-grey, & have a sort of royal blue covering for the chairs. The big mother-of-pearl table has gone, and they have the shelves from the library there, covered with their trophies & photos, & the miniatures are on a long table in the place where the awful blue & gold cabinet was. They have made it look 1880 instead of 1901, I feel – & somehow 1880 suits out here better. One day, perhaps, it'll look 1925 – but not with the Plumers. Lady Plumer is keen to see all the institutions & things …

This was vandalism. Ashbee, under the auspices of the Pro-Jerusalem Society, had furnished and decorated Government House with wonderful care, using local materials and craftsmen in the spirit of the Arts and Crafts movement. Lord Plumer, who kept Ashbee's Hebron glass chandeliers if not much else, is reported to have said, when they were smashed in 1927, that at any rate one good thing came out of the earthquake.

Fred Kisch thoroughly approved of the Plumers: 'Plumer's attitude to our [the Zionist Commission's] submissions will be: "Is the request justified under the policy of H.M. Government? – If so, I must grant it, and carry it through." The last High Commissioner's first reaction was: "What will the Arabs say to this?" '9 As for Norman, he was delighted, when warning Plumer that some action was not permitted by the law or the Mandate, to be told: 'What I want of the Attorney-General is not a legal adviser, but an illegal adviser. He should tell me how I get round a legal obstruction to achieve the right object.'10 Storrs, who admired Samuel's achievements and his 'orderly, creative and passionless intelligence', thought that the Plumers had made a good start, 'but I am always irritated by the chorus of adoration projected upon the rising sun. Everything that either of them does is construed to the disadvantage of their predecessors, and that by those who but a few months ago were roaring for a prolongation of the Samuel regime.'11

Helen's letter of 9 September continued:

... The playground has started, & promises to be a great success. Anything between 200 & 400 children each day – mostly Jews, but 40 or 50 Moslems & a sprinkling of Christians. It takes longer to get them, because they live a bit further off. The very orthodox Chassidic children, with their old-men's clothes & side-curls, are the most difficult, but we've got a few already. The sand-pit is a great success, we are to have some more swings soon, & there is a basket-ball ground, lots of bats & balls & ropes. It's open every day from 3–6. We are trying to arrange for a nurse to be there, as the eyes of the children are so terrible. Water is a problem, as the ground has to be watered, or the dust is unbearable – things are certainly more difficult to run here. Lots of big boys of 16 or 17 begged to come, so they come from 5–6, or they may come earlier if they'll help with the supervising – & a number do.

9.10.25: Ethel Harris & I have just offered to paint Mrs Magnes's house – inside – if she'll pay us the money she'd give a man, for the kindergarten.

We went to Tel Aviv for the opening of the Exhibition. They have one pavilion – the largest – all Palestinian-made goods, & it's wonderful what they make here – soap & oil & tooth-paste, excellent furniture, stockings & silk & knitted goods, embroideries, ice-chests, beds, toys – all kinds of things. And then other pavilions of things from outside, mostly machinery. But here it's amazing – no *English* firm has bothered to exhibit, although they've begged them to, over & over again. But plenty of German, & Russian & American stuff – no wonder England loses trade – everyone here *wants* English things, & machines, but there are no agents for anything. It's the same with cars – there isn't one agent here for English cars, not any sort, but nearly every kind of American & Continental car can be bought here. The Crown Agents tell us to buy English cars, but there isn't a spare part to be got here for any of them. It does seem hard that thousands of people in England should suffer from unemployment because the people who control the industries are incompetent to compete with America & Germany & Russia.

The Government House dinner was surprising good fun ... I didn't talk to Lady P., because after dinner I was going to, & then she said to Mary Clowes & me – 'You two young ones go & sit the other end of the room,' & I was very annoyed, because I'm quite senior, & shouldn't be treated like other people's daughters. [Helen was then 33.] I talked to him [Plumer] some time – he's rather an old dear, & I feel I shall like him very much.

31.10.25: Maugras is not yet back – he is having appendicitis, but I should think it's rather a diplomatic sort of operation. Things are so bad in Syria, he's probably got good reasons for not being messed up in them … It all started, they say, because the French heard of some brigands just outside Damascus & sent a contingent to round them up. The contingent caught instead some perfectly innocent Damascenes going out of town early in the morning to work in the fields. They killed 24, & hanged their bodies in the town square, in the nice French way. Then the relatives saw them, & were furious. And the brigands, who saw reports that they had been captured, determined to prove the contrary, & attacked the town, & were helped by the people who were indignant about the murdered men.

7.11.25: It's significant – the French bombard Damascus, but when we want a gun to fire on Armistice Day the only one in the country is the one belonging to the Mufti for firing at Ramadan. As Plumer says – a Field Marshal having to borrow a gun from an Ecclesiastical Dignitary for the Armistice Day is the best sign of our peacefulness here.

The Plumers are marvellously energetic – Aunt Bee would faint if she knew the old lady's itinerary. One day: starting at 8, & seeing all the notables of Nazareth & 3 schools; then lunch at our farm school at Nahalal, & visiting it & the colony most thoroughly; then on to the children's village for an hour or so; then back to Nazareth for a tea-party, an inspection of the hospital, & more notables; & out at 8 next morning for Safed. She has no maid on these tours.

21.11.25: We went to a musical reception at Government House – most amusing, as it was so much more Jewish than Uncle Herbert would ever have dared make it. The music was the orchestra of the Police Band (all Jews), Thelma, & two opera singers who sang in Hebrew! I can't think what the Mufti, the Latin priests & bishops etc thought of the Hebrew songs! It was very good for them, & will help the Jews to get rid of their inferiority complex, & to like the English, more than anything could. It's quite an asset to have such an unpolitical-minded High Commissioner.

I've been busy every morning, either gardening here, or painting the doors & windows of the Magnes house, for which they pay us for the kindergarten. They started dark ugly brown, falsely grained, & we are making them white. It's not easy, but it's going to be rather well done, I think. Then I'll fix their garden after, also for pay.

28.11.25: I have so much to thank you for this week – the coat, the two books, and the chocolates, which are so good, & so exactly what we like, that we (I regret to say) keep them in our bedroom, & don't let other people have any. But they're too nice for the unappreciative. By the way, it's all right to send things letter-post, as we have to pay customs here – assessed by John & the man at the counter in the most haphazard way, it is true. Chiefly done according to size, because John thought the 2 evening dresses you sent me in the summer weren't worth £5 each, & the man agreed, as there was so little material! And we paid accordingly.

On Monday we dined with Fred [Kisch] & went to the opera – 'Carmen' – which was really very well done & well performed, & is anyway a very good opera & nearly as cheery as a Gilbert & Sullivan. It's rather 'it' now, the opera, as Plumer & his suite went in full force to the 'Royal Box', which they have taken, & declare themselves very delighted with it.

I am most interested in the nigger problem, as my American friends here talk so much of it, & lend me many books about it. There is so much parallel, in some ways, with various racial problems here – only here the Jews have the exclusiveness, although they are the minority, whilst in America at present it's the majority who are exclusive.

5.12.25: The Plumers have upset their own community, & have a first-rate feud on with the Bishop, because the old man doesn't want any more of our combined services in the Cathedral, which were a great feature of Jerusalem life – & the Bishop insists. With the result that the Bishop is holding one on the day *before* Deliver-

ance day, & someone else having a purely English service on the
9th, which Plumer has more or less definitely said is *only* for
Church of England. Maugras says the Vatican is at the back of
this.

We plan to go to Sinai over Xmas, & ride on camels from
Akaba to Tor – I think it may be uncomfortable, difficult & expensive, but very interesting.

12.12.25: We are getting very thrilled over our Sinai trip – we propose to start on the 23rd, motor to Beersheba, & then onwards
south-west as far as we can get. Then pick up an escort & camels,
& ride or walk for 4 or 5 days to the monastery at Mt Catherine,
stay there 2 nights, & ride or walk 3 days on to Tor (on the Red
Sea) & up by ship to Suez, & so home. We can't find anyone who
has done it this way since the war, but all say it can be done. Tor
to Sinai, & back to Tor, is the usual way. But we always dislike
doing the same country twice. We are warned against a) snakes, b)
freezing nights, & even snow. We can't take tents, & opinions are
divided as to whether to risk a), & avoid b) by sleeping in the sand
– which Maugras, who did the trip from Tor in war-time recommends – or risk b), & take camp beds against a) which the
gendarmerie officer at Akaba recommends. We had hoped to do
it via Akaba, but that's too long a trip, & there are no good camels to be got there. Dr Magnes, Kisch & two other men are our
present party – a very congenial crowd. Storrs complains of my
'polyandrous picnics', but I can never find any other congenial
women who have the time or the inclination to accompany us.

Norman & Magnes gave a reception to the professors & students of the University – a very nice show, where bearded &
hatted orthodox men & short-haired, short-sleeved, short-skirted
girls, all met on equal terms, as students. It's the most instructive
thing at the University – how, at the Jewish Studies, the old & the
new get on so well.

19.12.25: I'm arranging all the food for our Sinai trip – 120 boiled
eggs, for instance, & 20 tins of bully beef, 20 tins of sardines, &
jam, cheese, biscuits etc – they take up no end of room. But I've
worked it all out most carefully, so it should be all right. Magnes is
the most difficult, as Americans are much more fussy travellers

than English. They love having things in schedules. I find the ex-soldiers, like all the other 4 men are, much easier than the Rabbi.

Norman got hurt at hockey last week, & had to have 3 stitches in his head, near his right eye. He stayed in bed, beautifully bandaged, on Sunday, but insisted on getting up Monday and going about as usual, with the stitches in. He was very foolish to go to work so soon, as tho' he has no pain, he seems rather knocked up. But the doctor says this desert trip, in the open air all the time, will do him a great deal of good. It can't be postponed. I have had a good deal of censure, in which doubtless you will join, because he said he only wanted one person to look after him, & Mrs Drayton, who is a trained nurse, said she was much better able to take him home & to the hospital than I was – so I went on playing hockey.

Mrs Brook, Plumer's daughter, was heard by Norman to ask Dizengoff, the Mayor of Tel Aviv – 'And do you have a big Xmas Tree for all the children of Tel Aviv?'

---

[1] By then Earl of Balfour, aged 76.

[2] Helen's sister and eldest brother.

[3] A former missionary living in Haifa, strongly anti-Jewish and critical of the Administration,

[4] Norman and Helen Bentwich, *Mandate Memories* (London: Hogarth Press, 1965), p 39.

[5] The English Chief Rabbi.

[6] 'Palestine and Lord Balfour', June 1925.

[7] Hyamson was Head of Immigration; Nurock was now Assistant Secretary; Edwin Samuel was a District Officer.

[8] Ormsby-Gore was Under-Secretary at the Colonial Office.

[9] F.H. Kisch, *Palestine Diary* (London: Gollancz, 1938), p 201.

[10] Norman Bentwich, *My 77 Years* (London: Routledge & Kegan Paul, 1961), pp 83–4.

[11] Ronald Storrs, *Orientations* (London: Nicholson and Watson, 1945), p 437.

1926

Too Many Tourists.

The packet of letters from Jerusalem is very thin this year. Helen was away from May to September, and there is also a five-week gap in February and March when Caroline and Arthur were visiting Jamaica. But once again Norman returned from his leave earlier than Helen (about six weeks this time) and there are letters to him from Helen. It was a time of calm in Palestine (in this General Strike year it was England that had greater political worries) and this seems to be reflected in Helen's mood – the restlessness and frustrations of the earlier years are much less evident and there was hardly a mention of moving. Her only problem was an excess of visitors, and they irritated her because they interfered too much with her normal life, which she was enjoying.

There must have been a long diary of the Sinai trip, but this has got lost and Helen's later account lacks the spontaneity of the letters. So the first letter of the year finds her feeling rather flat now she is back in Jerusalem, and sorry to learn that the French Consul, Maugras, was to be moved to Persia. 'We'll miss him horribly,' she wrote, 'He has quite the best intellect & wit of anyone here, & is very charming. You quite misjudged him – & so did Aunt Bee – but he has been one of the greatest friends we have had.'

She wrote of a visit to the Gymnasium (high school) in Tel Aviv, with Norman's brother José, who was an English master there:

23.1.26: There are 880 children, & it is very overcrowded, because of the immigration. Some of the things are very good – they do plenty of handicrafts & gardening now. But some are old-fashioned. There are 40 or 50 in a class; & they have 2 parallel classes for each form, but they don't interchange, like we did at St Paul's, but a child stays in the same class for every lesson, & if he's bad at English & good at arithmetic he has to do just the same as the child who is the reverse. José says it's disheartening to teach under these conditions, & that really only 30% of his pupils (the mediocre ones) can ever get anything out of his teaching.

Bomberg, the artist, & his wife dined with us on Tuesday. We are contemplating another picture of his – an attractive study of Jerusalem from the roof of his house opposite the Citadel, with the Mount of Olives in the background. But it's a bit expensive! It's hanging in our house at present, whilst we try to make up our mind. [They continued to dither – two weeks later they still thought they hadn't enough money and would send it back.]

I shall be very interested to hear from you how the black people [in Jamaica] impress you, & especially what are their conditions socially regarding the whites & the half-castes. I imagine it's much better there than in the southern part of the U.S.A.

29.1.26: We did a wonderful walk on Sunday. We motored to Ram Allah in Maugras' car, & had the car meet us again at the Trappist monastery on the Jaffa road ... I was rather appalled, on reaching the monastery, to find it very up-to-date, with electric light & a telephone! Why Trappists should want a telephone, I can't think.

6.2.26: We saw a very interesting scent factory at a colony the station before Zichron – Benjamina. It's one of Baron Edmond's [Edmond de Rothschild's] enterprises. There are 25 acres of flowers – jasmin, tuberose, lavender, roses etc, & they pick the narcissus & acacia wild. And they give jasmin & acacia plants to the colonists, & buy back the flowers. They send the essence to France – it's worth as much as £100 a kilo, & of course the transport is practically nothing. It seems an ideal industry for here, as the flowers grow beautifully there. It's only been going a year, but is very successful already.

12.3.26: Nothing frightfully thrilling has happened during these five weeks ... I've been to a dinner party at Government House, which was quite nice. I sat between Lord Plumer & an old warrior called Marling, who had won the V.C. when trying to rescue Gordon about 44 years ago. He seemed to expect me to lament the modern times with him, so I did. When I said something about the good old days to Plumer, he said, 'Good old days? Not a bit of it – slow old days, I call 'em. Give me these days any time,' so then I felt I could be more natural.

There are, & have been, an unpleasantly large number of three-day tourists – the Mauretania, Homeric, & all other biggest American liners have been disgorging at Haifa. There were 1200 tourists in Jerusalem at one moment. How we loathe them! It makes everything so uncomfortable & impossible ...

Helen had, she said, to 'join the ranks of the beggars' who hoped that the wealthy tourists would contribute to Jewish funds and charities, as she needed money for her kindergarten. There was also an endless stream of visitors from remote bits of the family and distant friends, all expecting to be shown round, and not all easy. One group, the letter continued:

... seemed so very sorry for us, having to live out here – rather like the attitude people take up towards East-Enders when they slum. They were so nice about it – but seemed to think it almost indecent when one friend of ours said he wouldn't live in England again for anything, & this was much better. It was an English officer, not a Jew, who was guilty of this treason. It made us think what a much wider life we have here, & what a great many more interests, than people like this at home. And also, how very out of touch with distant relations seven years abroad makes one. Near relations & real friends are different. But we seem to get more than our share of visitors, & one's sense of hospitality gets badly strained.

Norman is working tremendously hard – Saturdays & all at the moment, as Plumer never seems to realize that Saturday is Norman's day off, & fixes meetings, & Norman never tells him. They are doing things about Land Surveys.

20.3.26: We fed 40 extra people in one week – & are verging on bankruptcy in consequence. But I can endure that & I can endure (vicariously) the overworking of my household. But I can no longer endure the conversation of the tourists, & their questions, & watching them eat, & arranging & re-arranging my time to suit them, & the invasion of my privacy at every hour of the day. They come in the morning & leave letters of introduction, when I'm gardening, or washing the dog. They come when I'm just dressed to go out for hockey or a country walk, they come when I've arranged a tête-à-tête with a friend. Government House does little entertaining – Storrs & Symes [Clayton's successor as Chief Secretary], who are the only other people who do any now, get entertainment allowances. And anyway they don't get all the Jewish extras that we do. They are mostly quite nice, but there are *too many* ...

Not unnaturally, British tourists all pestered her with questions about Zionism and Arabs and Palestine, while she hoped they would talk about London plays and books and politics – 'After all, here am I in exile. I'll feed people – but in return, I require them to amuse me.'

... The Order of St John's visit here will be written up in the papers for you as a Grand Success, because they brought Colonel Pirrie-Gordon, their special correspondent, of *The Times*, with them. But don't you believe a word of it – it was the most laughable show that ever was, & *so* badly organized. The climax was the reception at Government House. We were all asked at 9.15 for the investiture. We got there & sat about, & talked, & waited for it to begin. But unfortunately, they had lost the cross & the banner, without which no investiture would be legal. So they had to send to the town to look for them, whilst we all waited till 10.30, & Lord Plumer fumed. His military soul was outraged at this happening when he was the host. Then they had prayers read by the Bishop – saying the object of the order was to fight the Infidel etc. (They didn't mention the Jew, but I'd read in a book they were out to fight the Jew too, so I supplied the information broadcast afterwards.) They had the Mufti & the Rabbi – & lots of priests, & the acting Latin Patriarch. He nearly burst at having to listen to these Protestant prayers – & rightly. They were never warned, & the Roman Catholics *never* are present at Protestant ceremonies. As Maugras said, Uncle Herbert would never have been so tactless.

27.3.26: Aunt Bee arrived on Wednesday, & is staying with us till Monday, when she goes to Hadassah's people for Passover. She is quite an easy guest – except that we live on boiled fish & chicken, which is slightly monotonous. I don't know what would happen to her if she ate anything more exciting, but she doesn't seem to be taking any risks. Norman's father arrived yesterday, to spend Passover at Zichron.

Tonight I'm going for a picnic to the Dead Sea with Fred & some American friends, whilst Norman goes to an Oxford & Cambridge dinner to celebrate the Boat Race.

2.4.26: De Jouvenel[1] arrived Monday & left Thursday. We lunched with Symes to meet him, went to a reception for him at Government House, & dined there to meet him. He is a typical politician – the silvery-tongued orator. He seems utterly cynical – not in the least interested in Syria except as it affects his career – & entirely insincere. He is supposed to be very charming & fascinating. France is strewn with his ex-wives,[2] & many candidates for the future, I understand, but although I sat next to him at lunch he quite failed to charm me. Maugras was very much to the fore, but leaves tomorrow – he goes in his own car, with all his luggage, from here to Teheran; it takes about 10 days from Baghdad. I'm most awfully sorry he is going, & so is Norman.

You will probably see a lot in the paper about the 'strike' when De Jouvenel was here.[3] But it was non-existent. Only the Arabs shut their shops – but, as it was Passover holydays, & all the Jewish shops were shut too, nobody noticed. And they didn't come to the Government House reception – but the very orthodox Jews didn't either [because it was Passover], so that wasn't noticed. Plumer took Jouvenel all over Jerusalem – & Lady Plumer went too because, as she told me after, the Arabs weren't so likely to 'do anything' if a woman were there. She is a sporting old soul – a regular military wife.

We had Seder [Passover] night at Fred's – a party of about 24, with Hall Caine there. He is still writing a life of Jesus, but he got such an enormous amount of information from Norman, both during the service & after, that I feel Norman should at least get half the profits. Seder with Hall Caine seems so funny, somehow ...

Hall Caine, now unread, was at one time an immensely popular novelist − over a million copies of *The Eternal City* (1901) were sold. He had visited Poland and the frontier towns of Russia, at the request of the Russo-Jewish Committee, to investigate the facts of the Jewish persecutions. His *Life of Christ* was unfinished, and was published posthumously.

... Sophie is hectically shortening all my summer dresses. They look so *very* left over from last year if they are below one's knees, nowadays. I see people get arrested in Athens for having short skirts − so I expect I'll get stuck there on my leave, & Norman stuck in Italy for talking against Mussolini, which he is rather inclined to do.

They intended to spend about a month on the journey back to England, via Greece, Yugoslavia and Italy (including a visit to Herbert Samuel at Lake Garda). Norman planned to join Wyndham Deedes for a two-week walking tour in July.

17.4.26: Our great excitement this week has been Heifetz. He plays marvellously − very restrained & dignified, but with an amazing amount of feeling all the same. He plays a lot of slight, modern, rather unworthy stuff, which is a pity. He is only 26 − & seems a fine sort of fellow, remarkably unspoilt considering that he receives £700 a night in New York, & is nearly a millionaire. He is very keen on Palestine, & certainly was most generous here. He played in Tel Aviv 3 times − once to workers, where he had an audience of 6000 − & at Haifa, & to the workers in the Plain of Esdraelon, 2500 of them. He made £1200 at the concerts, & has given it all to Palestine for musical education − & left it in the charge of a Committee with Norman & Magnes running it. He came to lunch here Sunday; Norman's father & sisters were here, & 2 other couples − at 2.30 we started lunch without Heifetz, & he came at a quarter to 3. It wasn't his fault − they'd taken him to the Dead Sea & Jericho & didn't allow time − but it put things out of gear, & it wasn't a great success.

The Archaeologists begin next week – we were asked to have a German & a Frenchman & his wife – but the spare-room ceiling fell down yesterday, much to our relief, so we can't. I'm sick of putting up strangers – it's such a strain. We are having 6 to dine instead. Meanwhile, we have the workmen in & a lot of mess.

24.4.26: I play a lot of tennis – will the court in London be usable? We have so much exercise here, that I feel we'll miss it at home. If not, I'll take to sculling again, at Regent's Park, in the mornings. It should be easy, if we have a car – anything round about £100 ought to get one.

Thursday night there was an enormous reception at Government House. I'll have to get lots & lots of new evening dresses if they will do so many evening shows there.

We are opening a new kindergarten, having no money. But we hope the money will come.

1.5.26: One day Plumer's daughter, who has been visiting her family here for a few weeks, came with me to see the kindergarten & other institutions in the Old City, & back to lunch here. She is awfully nice & very easy & clever too. She is Warden of the Passmore Edwards Settlement – Mrs Humphry Ward's – & she also very enterprisingly runs a Public House in Mile End, to prove that a pub can pay selling good wholesome food as well as drink, even among the poorest & most untamed population. She goes two or three times a week & serves them herself – & says that in that way an influence can be got over people who are never touched by any other body or organization. She is full of humour, & most refreshing, as she told us so much & asked no stupid questions. I'm going to visit the settlement – & the pub – when we are home.

We went to the Courtyard of the Holy Sepulchre, to watch the Washing of the Feet, by the Greek Patriarch. It was a sort of Passion Play – very interesting in a way, & they all wear lovely embroidered robes. The Patriarch washes the feet of 12 disciples – Peter protests – then he goes away, & coming back finds Peter, James & John asleep on the steps. They never liked us to go to these things a few years back – but now they mind nothing, & sent us the best seats, in the same balcony as Storrs.

8.5.26: From the tone of your last letter – & of the home papers – we gather that this strike must have been as much of a bombshell for all of you as it was for us. I wonder which side most people take at home. Here, even among the ordinary army-colonial type, there is a surprising amount of sympathy with the miners – very definite in the case of a few who live near mining districts. I suppose we'll have to accept the fact that more coal is produced in the world than is needed – & that the English methods are too muddly & old-fashioned to compete with foreign ones … But it must be a queer time you are going through. I suppose, before we come home, in 4 or 5 weeks, it will either be terribly serious (which Norman seems to think) or finished, but a very bad state of trade depression resulting. We are going off, all the same, to Greece – & if Uncle Herbert is not back at Garda by June 4th or so,[4] we may come home.

John is ill with blood-poisoning – & Sophie's daughter, who married Abdullah's chauffeur, is having a baby today. So my house is rather muddly, & there's a lunch-party coming.

Helen's letters when she stayed behind in England this time do not have the anxieties and soul-searchings of 1923. She travelled often, with family and friends: a walking tour with Evelyn Waley; the Lake District and Scotland with her brother Hugh and his wife; Belgium and Holland with Wyndham Deedes and his mother; Cornwall with her brother Ellis and his family – where her report on her niece Rosalind Franklin (the future scientist) then aged six, was that she 'is alarmingly clever, & spends all her time doing arithmetic for pleasure & invariably gets her sums right'. Helen seemed calmer, more tolerant, and for once she was not pushing Norman to move:

6.9.26 [to N.B.]: We get quite a lot of fun one way & another out of it all, don't we? I feel you'd be miserable if you didn't stay when they wanted you to. You give me such a good time over life in general; & money, & freedom to do just as I like, that I often feel I couldn't seriously ever try to make you live where you don't want to for *my* sake. Hitherto, I've thought very strongly that the move would be for your benefit – but now I rather feel that it's not, in reality, the right thing just now, so I'll promise not seriously to try & persuade you during the next year or so.

After talking with Wyndham Deedes about objective and subjective views of life and people, she came out with this self analysis:

> **[to N.B.]** I see now that my great fault in life is being *unwilling* to be objective. Unlike many women, I believe I *can* be. But I prefer the other, as it gives one's personality greater play in the limelight. I think objectivity is the secret of everything – from being a power in the world, to playing tennis or driving a car well. Wyndham has it, but largely artificially. You have it, from sheer love of truth & fineness of character. I'll try & have it from will-power.

And the last letter before she returned has this:

> **[to N.B.]** You ask if you stunt my life – what a thought! It still is a great & jolly adventure, & you have no prejudices, no selfishnesses & no limitations, which makes it so very perfect ... It's not really so bad in Palestine, if only one doesn't have to *be* a Jew or an Englishman, or anything labelled. To be human & *a* human is all I want to be, & it's less than nothing to me if people are Jews or Christians or Pagans. I can run clubs for Jews alone, because of practical difficulties. But ethics & ways of life, & ideals, are like hospitals – they must be for *everyone*. It's only in that way that Palestine is cramping – one can't preach or stand for this brotherly love stunt without being condemned at once as an assimilationist. I *am* an assimilationist – I want to assimilate to myself the best of every nation & every people & every religion. Anyway, that's my view at present.

Back in Jerusalem, she was glad to report to her mother that Norman had just got £100 a year more – £1600 in all.

> **30.10.26**: We dined at Government House, where there was a small informal party, & we played roulette after, & each lost 1/-. I sat next to the old man, who was very nice & easy to talk to. He is very fond of Norman – & says he is always trying to make him annoyed, & hasn't done so yet!
>
> I've got a new cook today, & if she's any good I must start in on dinner-parties in grim earnest, bother 'em. But the consular corps have all got quite musical wives – French, Italian & German particularly – so we shall have one of them at each, to start with,

& music. I know the kitchen is so unpleasant in the rains that the cook will leave, so I'll get the parties over as far as I can whilst she is here.

I went to visit Nevinson, the journalist, in hospital, & found him very charming. We talked of everything – of Labour things, & Jewish things, & life in general, & things he had done. He's a big personality – the sort of champion of lost causes that you'd never find except in England. He told me about how he'd helped free the slaves in Portuguese West Africa, & fought with the Greeks against the Turks, & all sorts of things.

Col. & Mrs Wedgwood are here. Mrs Wedgwood is very deaf & rather stupid, but very gentle & nice – rather the sort one associates with Liberty tea-gowns & indeterminate greens & browns. He is very nice too, I think, but a bit pugnacious. She is his second, & fairly new.

Both these last encounters, with Henry Nevinson and with the Wedgwoods, were the start of lasting friendships. Nevinson, who had in fact seen these struggles for freedom as a crusading reporter rather than as a participant, was to become their near neighbour in Hampstead. Mrs Wedgwood seems to have improved on further acquaintance, while Josiah's thundering on behalf of Zionists and Jewish refugees made him a natural ally; 'The Last of the Radicals', as his niece C.V. Wedgwood called him in her biography,[5] was a member of the first Labour Cabinet, and had a vision of Palestine as a Dominion of the British Commonwealth.

6.11.26: I took Mrs Wedgwood to the kindergarten & Infant Welfare Centres. And I've been going other mornings & having rows with the teachers, as they don't do enough, & are rather lazy. This idea of 'free play' is all very well, if it doesn't develop into the children standing idly doing nothing, as it's apt to do here.

Have you read Trevelyan's 'History of England'? If not, take it away with you. It's *very* good, & tells history from such a much more interesting point of view than all the ordinary history-books.

13.11.26: We get on very happily with the Plumers now. We dine there this week with some big Italian general, when Norman plays music – I told Plumer that it was a pity he had never heard Norman play, as he professes to like music so much. So he is going to, much to Norman's embarrassment. Thursday was Armistice day – at 9 we watched Plumer lay a wreath on the cenotaph; at 10.30 we went to synagogue – I went to the Sephardic one, & sat down with the men, because they have the 11 o'clock business, & you have to go somewhere for it. And after, Kisch & his Jewish ex-soldiers were inspected by Plumer in the Russian Compound. Norman, although he wore his khaki, refused to take part, as he doesn't approve of the Jewish ex-soldier business. I watched it from the flat of a police officer there, & when it was over, we danced till lunch-time.

Storrs comes here to a farewell dinner tonight,[6] and we say good-bye to him at Kisch's, at Miss Landau's, at Government House, & at a British officials' dinner. The German Consul & his wife come tonight too – she is very charming & musical, & he is said to be the most intelligent & high-class of the consuls here. I've not met them yet. But all feeling against Germans seems at last dead, & they & other intelligent ones are much sought after.

They had their own party for Storrs too, and he left them on the best of terms, 'full of invitations for us to go & stay'. Plumer took Storrs' place as president of the Music Society, while Norman took Lady Storrs' place as chairman.

---

[1] Henry de Jouvenel, the new High Commissioner for Syria.

[2] Including the novelist Collette.

[3] The Arabs protesting because the French had bombarded Damascus.

[4] Herbert Samuel had been summoned urgently to England to deal with the coal strike.

[5] C.V. Wedgwood, *The Last of the Radicals* (London: Jonathan Cape, 1951); Josiah Wedgwood had suggested the title himself.

[6] Storrs had just been appointed Governor of Cyprus.

1927

Only Half a Year

Once again Helen was away from Palestine for half the year. She went in March to join her parents in Mentone, on the French Riviera, where they had taken to going for the winter since Arthur had been ill with TB. She returned with them to England, Norman joining her later. In June she went to Geneva, as the Palestine delegate to the Conference of the International Council of Women. There are no surviving letters from her to Norman for the periods of separation. They returned together in September, having missed the hot weather, and, as it happened, having also missed the drama of a severe earthquake.

The year started with seasonal jollities, and with a large bazaar to organize – 'I've been very busy about the Bazaar. I've done the raffia mats, I'm now going to try a blotter. Either it's very easy or I'm very clever – I don't think it's very easy, though.'

1.1.27: We went to a cosmopolitan New Year's Party – all the Consuls & their circle, & one other English pair only. Norman is asked to these shows because of his music – & he is very popular with all the Consular wives. I go because I am Norman's wife, tho' I feel lost among the Consuls without Maugras. There was music, & a huge din with rattles, tom-toms, crackers etc at New Year – apparently to keep away devils – & afterwards a huge spread & a lot of gaiety. They are an amusing crowd for occasional times – though not for too long at a stretch.

The Sports Club New Year's dance tonight, fancy dress; ours is from 'Quality Street' – Norman is awfully pleased with his – & looks ever so nice, with an opera hat, pale blue coat, white trou-

sers, black Wellington boots, a gay cummerbund, a white cravat,
& a monocle on a broad black ribbon. Mine is biscuit-yellow
muslin with orange ribbons, white frills & mob-cap & black
shoes. It is so long, I feel positively indecent in it. It's so like a
nightgown …

It is hard to imagine Norman, always in my memory soberly
dressed in a dark suit and waistcoat whatever the occasion or the
weather, submitting to such indignities. Earlier he had refused to
dress up for these parties, and he must surely have done it, in spite
of what Helen says, more in a spirit of tolerance than of enthusiasm. Though fancy dress, like party games, was more usual then
than now.

… Norman & I went for a walk from Caesaria to visit the Jewish
colony of Hudeira. We walked along the seashore, on hard sand,
seeing lovely coloured shells & jelly-fish, & not a sign of other
life. We had a mounted policeman, who was going that way, as a
guide. We came to a river which was very full & deep. Some Arabs were near, fishing. I rode the horse over, & Norman, much to
his surprise, was suddenly hoisted onto the back of one of the
Arabs & carried over. I rode the horse a lot of the way, led by the
policeman, as it was very frisky. Hudeira is the nicest of the colonies I've seen – built all among woods chiefly eucalyptus. It is 35
years old, & tidier & better-kept than the others – & quite the
most prosperous of the lot. We had never been there before. We
met a man we knew, & had a lovely tea in his house, of all country food, including milk. Then we got into a motor-bus to go to
the station, but, as they had been having terrible rains there, we
couldn't go all the way, & had to get out in the pitch dark, &
walk. First, we walked into the swamp of a river, & had to come
back, & get onto the railway line, & walk along that to the station.
As the line went over the river, quite high up, & as there was
nothing except wooden sleepers on piles, & the rails, & we had to
step quite wide distances from sleeper to sleeper, with the river
below, & only one lantern, & very slippery boots, I didn't enjoy it.
But the only other female occupant of the bus – a real Yiddisher
old woman with a shawl over her head, talking Yiddish, skipped
along like a goat!

Two days later they went on an even more disastrous walk, from Zichron, getting lost and hot and cross '& full of flies, & we hated it & each other & everything'.

22.1.27: We bought you a birthday present, tho' it'll probably be a white elephant! It's a drawing of Bomberg's of Jerusalem – fairly large, & I think pleasing. Let me know if you'd rather not have it. We are doing 3 plays, including Sheridan's *Scheming Lieutenant* – I am one of the two women in it. We rehearse Wednesdays & Saturdays after hockey.

Last night, we dined at the Italian Consul's. There's a flutter in the consular dovecote. The Italian & his wife are not at all Fascisti, & his interesting brother – who does social work in south Italy – is distinctly not. So they have heard – not even directly – that they are to leave here almost at once, & their place will be taken by a Fascist deputy, who has never been a consul before. The English die-hard crowd here, too, are very indignant & sur prised, as they never thought Fascism was a 'tyranny like Bolshevism'. This'll learn them.

Three work parties this week – & lots of raffia in between times. I'm awfully busy – & haven't opened a book for weeks. I do want the Bazaar to be a success.

29.1.27: I'm fed up with tourists, & still more with Americans. To kow-tow to these people because they are rich is even vulgarer than to kow-tow to a duke. And these people love lords & aristocrats, & if you aren't rich or titled you may be 'interesting' as a freak, but you don't 'count'. Anyway, they are the biggest pest of this country – & I turn with relief to my suburban Bazaar sewing-parties, my school-teachers, my hockey-teams & my dramatic gangs, as being something very much more real. The more I like the country here, the more I resent tourists.

Ponsot, the French High Commissioner [for Syria] was here for two days. We dined at Gov. House to meet him, & Norman & the French Consul's wife made music after. The next night, a reception there, with quite good music provided by opera singers (in Hebrew) & the Police Band – all Jewish.

12.2.27: The new Chief Justice, McDonnell, was at school & college with Norman – Irish & Roman Catholic, which much upsets all the people here. He has 20 years' government service, as he went straight into it. Anyway, the Colonial Office would never give the job to Norman, as he is a Jew, & also much too Labour & progressive for them. They only like hide-bound, die-hard conservatives in their legal branches, full of traditions & precedents. They've never forgiven Norman for all the reforms he brought in whilst he was legal secretary, & not under them.

19.2.27: The big event of this week has been snow, quite a considerable amount of it. It was lovely – for those who had dry houses & warm clothes. It was hell for the others. They have to do a lot of relief & feeding for the poor. I've set them making soup in my Old City kindergarten, to give to anyone who is hungry, & to take round to their houses. The American element want details & statistics – but I think my old-fashioned way is best in an emergency; even though the wrong people may get some, it may get to the right ones at the right moment. The Nathan Straus[1] soup kitchen is feeding thousands of all sorts, but many haven't enough clothes to go out & fetch it. A few houses fell in, but there is so much united effort here now, & so many social workers – especially in the Old City – that I really think everything has been very well & promptly done.

Yesterday we had a Women's Council meeting. We are very exercised on the question of beggars. They continue to get worse each year.

Dame Millicent Fawcett & Miss Garrett came to lunch. They are wonderful old ladies. They came out again, resolved to see Trans-Jordan. Their niece Dr Louisa Garrett-Anderson turned up, & they went off, spending the night in Jericho. They tried to go to Jerash, but it was flooded & they went to Amman. They tried to leave Amman, but got in the snow near the Circassian village, Swaley, & had to return. They stayed at Amman till Monday – in the very primitive local hotel – & then went by train on the Damascus line, stayed two nights at Tiberias, & returned here by car – looking very well & full of life. Everyone was expecting them to be nearly dead.

The Bazaar things increase at a huge rate – great cases from Marks & Spencer until my house is full to the brim, as well as being flooded. And the cook's ill; & no washing can be done, & odd people keep strolling in to meals. However, John bears up, tho' Sophie is in tears because she can't wash, & rather thinks it's all my fault. She has to use the 'new sheets' as she calls them, which I bought nearly a year ago, instead of keeping them beautifully tied up in a cupboard, & that makes her very unhappy.

Writing on 12 March, the last letter before going to her parents in Mentone, Helen said her one wrench in leaving was the garden, which was in all its glory. She did not say that it was a wrench leaving Norman – perhaps that was assumed – but only that she hoped he would join them in England in May.

The next letter is dated 14 September. They had been back four days and she was immersed in tennis, preparing for the Jerusalem tournament. The Armstrong Siddeley tourer they had bought in England was due to arrive shortly. Everyone had their earthquake stories:

> **14.9.27**: I've not actually seen much of the damage, because in the Old City it's hard to distinguish ruins from the earthquake from ordinary ruins. Our house, apparently, had ceilings down & holes in the roof, but John so persistently badgered people that it has been perfectly repaired, & now looks nicer than ever, as it's all clean & done up. It's marvellous, considering the damage, that so few people were hurt. All our friends seem to have had hairbreadth escapes ... The Plumers [who were also on leave when the earthquake struck] are having a miserable time in their Convent – no place to receive people or entertain, no electric lights, miles from anywhere, & in supreme discomfort. But everyone says they were bound to have been hurt if they'd been in Government House at the time.
>
> My kindergarten rather worries me. The boys' school next door collapsed, & we have to give up our buildings to them. I think I shall give it up – the whole financial situation is so bad, I couldn't contemplate another bazaar, & there's no way of getting the money. And when all education is being so starved, it doesn't seem to matter what happens to the children under 6. I'll think further, but I feel it's not worth the effort – it's such a drop in this chaotic ocean.
>
> I think the new [Zionist] Executive of Kisch, Sacher & Miss Szold[2] may prove of value. Father should be glad – perhaps he'll support them now there's no Russian influence at all.

Everyone seems depressed about conditions, & worried & rather nervy after the earthquake & intense heat. Norman is up to his eyes in work, & rather finds himself, for once, with more than he can manage. Still, as he says, 6 months leave in 2 years is rather asking for overwork in the rest of the time.

21.9.27: Last night I got Ruth [Franklin]'s cable, saying she was marrying Fred Kisch. Of course, we're most frightfully glad – it will make all the difference to the Zionists here to have her as a sort of centre, socially & in every other way – & it's very nice for us as she's a most congenial companion for us both. I wonder what all the family at home think about it? I shall be most grateful if you will sink so low as to give me all gossip & comments you hear about it. It's very exciting, anyway.

Will you please send me the address of one Curtis Browne, an agent for plays & books. I'm finishing a play I wrote, & want to send it to him. Aylmer Harris – our dramatic expert – says the dialogue & theatrical part are very good, but there is too little action. I've got various articles – if Cecil[3] or anyone knows any agents for them I'll send them & see if they can be taken.

Nablus had been particularly badly hit by the earthquake. They went to see the damage:

19.10.27: It's a pitiful sight. In the main bazaar were houses three stories high, every room of which was built by & belonged to a different man. They all collapsed – & the chaos about new building permits, loans etc may be imagined. That was why Norman had to look at it. All the houses leaned against each other – & even now, when they take out a dividing wall, others still collapse. 3 people were killed the other day doing that. We mountaineered over piles of ruins, & into deserted buildings & onto roofs.

We are starting a horticultural society & flower shows – Lady Plumer is awfully keen.

That was the start of competitive gardening. With monthly flower shows and frequent tennis tournaments the letters give an impression of an increasingly competitive way of life. Helen's collection of silver cups grew.

12.11.27: Yesterday – Armistice Day – Norman had to turn out in immaculate khaki & command the parade of Jewish ex-service men. There were only about 100 of them this year – generally there are about 50 more. But Friday is a bad day for certain trades to take a day off & come up from the districts, & many of these ex-service men are butchers or bakers, & Friday is their busiest day. Norman had been most carefully dressed & coached – & really looked very smart in borrowed medals (he's never bothered to get his own) & puttees, & my gloves to hold, & all the rest his own. They say it's the first time an officer has ever commanded a parade bearing his wife's gloves. He had practised elaborate sword drill – but in the end everyone thought it easier not to have it. Plumer said he didn't mind – he was quite used to getting out of the way of swords. But it was a funny situation for such a pacifist as Norman now is.

24.12.27: I enclose a letter of Norman's – which tells you about the loss of the hoped-for job in England.[4] If he had accepted outright last spring, he might have got it. But once they had to wait a year, they had a chance of finding real professors from all over the world, & have appointed one from Canada. It can't be helped – I think the only career left for him now is politics. Personally, I would much prefer that. He'd be so good at it, & the Labour Party does so need people like him. So perhaps we'll come home & be very poor & try that. But it's only a vague possibility, & depends very much on things here.

We go off to Akaba in two days, & will probably be more cheerful about life then. It should be very good fun – & if it rains much we may have to winter there. The return via Trans-Jordan can't be done in the rain – & the return the way we go can't be done ever, in a car, as it's steps cut in the rock, which you can go *down* in a car (presumably) but not up.

---

[1] Nathan Straus was a philanthropic American Jew.

[2] Henrietta Szold was the American founder of the Hadassah organization for medical work in Palestine, and later organizer of 'Youth Aliyah', to bring Jewish refugee children to Palestine.

[3] Helen's brother, who was a publisher.

[4] There is no further clue about this 'hoped-for job'.

1928

A New House and a New High Commissioner

It did not rain in Akaba, and they were away only eight days. They went with two colleagues: Jerome Farrell, from the Education Department, 'full of classics and tells limericks in Greek, & a red-hot Tory, but all the same very good fun', and Eric Mills, from the Secretariat, 'a mathematician, full of learning & long words, but very amusing, & a liberal-labour'. They had two cars, with drivers. Helen was proud of her catering, which rose to tinned asparagus and marrons-glacés, but cost only 26/- each for the week. Down on the Red Sea, where there was now a wireless, they heard to their surprise a concert from Paris, and could get Moscow, though not London.

3.1.28: We walked a few miles southwards along the east side of the Gulf of Akaba, innocently looking for shells – enormous ones, just like landladies always have in lodging houses. After 4 miles or so, we were caught up by a gendarme on a camel, who shepherded us back. They wouldn't let us loiter an instant on the way. When we returned the officer told us we had been in Ibn Saud's territory, & they were very nervous. We asked a lot of questions, finding out how long it would take by car from there to Jeddah – we simply wanted to compare it with Lawrence & other people who had written of these parts. But later we heard someone had been complaining about us entering strange territory & trying to find out too much! I hope we shan't cause a war – or even a question in Parliament – because of my innocent desire for lodging-house shells.

They catch enormous fish at Akaba, & we bought two. One we ate there, & one they salted & we brought back here, meaning it for Lady Plumer. But, as John biblically put it, 'it bred maggots & stank'. It was used to manure the garden.

On to Petra, where they found that tourism had moved in:

> We were appalled at being met by 2 Arabs from a hotel here, who knew us, & who 'run' Petra for Cooks – they have stores of food, beds etc in caves, & asked us if we'd like 'caves' on the ground floor, first floor or higher up. It did seem an anti-climax. We scorned them, & slept in the open, at the foot of a large ruined temple. We refused to hire their primus, & cooked by a wood fire, & slept round it under the stars – it was amazingly warm. The second night, when the moon had sunk & we were asleep, with the 2 guards & their horses at the foot of the temple, a little way above us a shot rang out – very near – & echoed & re-echoed. I was frankly scared, & sat up & called the guard. The corporal rushed to me & said 'matahafsh'. That means in Arabic 'Have no fear' – but traditionally it is what an Arab or an Egyptian always says when the last hope is gone – they say it as the car falls over the precipice, or the horse bolts, or the saddle slips off the camel, so I wasn't reassured. And whilst we were talking, two more shots rang out. Then we really got alarmed, & Cooks men came running down, & all the dogs in the valley barked … Nobody knew what it was – it may have been raiders after our stores, or Bedouin having a feu de joie, or firing at a cheetah. Anyway, we'll never know. But it has provided me with an inspiration for re-writing the third act of my play – at Petra, with the curtain going up in a camp, & a shot ringing out & waking the sleepers. It'll be some act.

She did write such an act, for a comedy which caricatured British and American tourists. It has some witty lines, and a plot like a weak version of *Private Lives* – but Noel Coward did not write that until a year later. More seriously, Helen wrote a play called *Whither Jew*, which she submitted to the management of the Garrick Theatre in 1933. It was rejected as anti-semitic and anti-British –

'the pictures you give of Palestine and the new culture arising
there are hideous in the extreme' – though praised for its clever-
ness and promising dramatic sense. In fact it is not anti-British,
but critical of the British colonial administration, and not anti-
semitic, but critical of orthodox extremism. It portrays the Jewish
colonists with surprising sympathy, but it contains impassioned
speeches against nationalism which reflect Helen's own deep
beliefs: 'In the Bible we are told that Israel shall never be a nation
as other nations. And today you are all occupied in trying to make
her one. But that is not Judaism; that is something you have
caught like a bad disease, from the post-war world ... Don't let
this passion for nationalism be your final assimilation.'

Helen now had, she wrote later, 'the pleasant occupation of
designing a new house in which to live. Ours was at last to be
returned to the German owners, & for some time we had been
looking for another. We found an Arab, whose house had been
destroyed in the earthquake, who was willing to build a new house
on the site, to our design, if we provided the money.'[1] They would
live in it rent-free for ten years, and it would then revert to him –
they were putting down roots at last, albeit not very permanent
ones. 'It may be bad finance,' she explained to her mother, 'but it's
less trouble. And as one's chief effort in *having* money is to use it
to save one trouble (i.e. servants, cars etc) well, then, why spend it
to *give* one trouble?' The site, with wonderful views of the Moab
Mountains, was reputed to be on the piece of ground that Judas
had bought with the thirty pieces of silver – there was an old Judas
tree in the next garden. It was also known as 'The Hill of Evil
Counsel', which was pleasing for the house of the Attorney-
General.

> **21.1.28**: I think making plans for houses that one proposes to live
> in oneself is frightfully thrilling. I'm afraid you've brought me up
> very badly, because my tastes are so expensive – I mean, I always
> want windows & doors in the *right* places, & lots of cupboards &
> things, & they always cost more than the badly man-planned
> houses one usually sees. I wonder what building costs at home –
> here it is £7 a square metre, if one has the very best. Personally,
> so long as the house is comfortable, & keeps the rain out, I don't
> mind second-rate materials, because I never have a sense of per-

manence, & what's best today may be second-best next year. I'd
rather have it airy & comfortable of cheap stuff than cramped of
expensive. We both agree on not wanting to buy it outright.

28.1.28: We went by train to Jir Mejarni to see Rutenberg's big
electrical scheme. It's most interesting – I'm no engineer, but all
who saw it were extremely impressed. There are 250 workers
there now – the chief engineers are Swiss non-Jews, & there's a
Scotsman in charge of some very fascinating excavating machines.
They have model houses & are beautifully welfared – it's necessary in the summer there. But although they began in August they
have had no malaria. It'll be done by 1930.

Then I had to go & address the Haifa Social Service Association – about 100 women of all breeds – & I talked of the Geneva
Conference.

I have read 'Desperate Remedies' – I'd started reading Hardy
before he died, because of having been to Dorset. It's the third
I've read lately. I get sick of modern books at times, & Hardy is
so really good. It's really tragic to think he is dead.

In mid-February they learned they had to leave their house by the
end of March and they had not yet made a contract for building
the new one. Helen drew up a plan, modelled on their current
house 'with all the wrong things put right' and handed it over to a
local architect ('trained in Surbiton!') and the owner of the new
plot of land said he would probably have it ready in four or five
months. Helen felt sufficiently rooted to ask for her grandfather
clock and desk to be sent out from England.

Much time and thought was being put into a major arts and
crafts exhibition. Helen brought out a catalogue, 4000 copies,
making a profit on the printing by getting advertisements. But
nine days before the exhibition opened she was in hospital, having
a course of injections for painful septic sores which had started
with an infected burn; she wrote cheerfully of being well looked
after and having over 50 visitors. The exhibition, open 12 hours a
day for a week, was not the best sort of convalescence, and when
it was over, Helen went to stay with friends on Mount Carmel to
recover. She wrote from there: .

16.3.28: I'll forestall you, & say I was an unspeakable fool to be so careless about my burn, & then to dash around & not rest properly, even when I came out of hospital. Anyway, you'll have to admit it's a trait I've inherited from you, & remember all the times we've tried to tell you you're overdoing it, & the little heed you always pay to us. I'm to go on getting these inoculations for weeks, apparently, & they certainly take it out of one a great deal & make me feel very depressed, & make the sores all bad again each time. But they are declared to be an infallible cure, & if they are they're worth it. Because I'm sick of all the blood poisoning I've always had ever since I came here.

Now as to the Exhibition – all the world says that it was a howling success. And really, it was. From 9.30 till 11.30 each day school children were allowed in free. And they came! Jews & Christians of every sort & country & Moslems & Government Schools & Germans & French & Americans & English ... It was the most popular thing the town had ever had, & I can think of nobody of any class or community whom I didn't see there, from patriarchs to bazaar porters. We sold a good deal of stuff, & took in many orders ... The teas were done by the ladies of Jerusalem, each vying with the other in the lavishness & variety of cakes & sandwiches ... I expect we'll end up £100 or more to the good [a later letter says it was over £200], which isn't bad for an exhibition – considering that the Ashbee one in 1922 ended up £270 to the bad! We didn't use Father's loan because the Plumers put up £100.

The Plumers were wonderful – they were there every day & brought all their friends & had people staying with them from all over the country to visit it. And they are now both frightfully keen on an Arts & Crafts shop in the Citadel every winter. In fact when I told Plumer that we should shortly be paying back his loan, he said he didn't want it, but that it was to go for the shop.

Boy scouts helped us a great deal, & one day I had a message 'go easy with the scouts today; two of them are royalty' – they were the sons of Emir Abdullah & King Ali, at school in Jerusalem. We never found out which they were – & Plumer hoped they were those who helped wash up the tea, as it would have been so good for them.

Clearing up the Exhibition has been quite a job. We had 2 tickets on every article, one taken off & stamped by the cashier

when it was paid for. It seemed fool-proof, but there are all sorts
of fools, & curiously enough we have ended up with more money
than we can account for.

31.3.28: Life is too hectic here for enjoyment at the moment – it's
enough to make one a Communist for life, the way young royalty
has to be served. Tomorrow the Crown Prince of Italy arrives, &
there are receptions, dinners & concerts all week – Norman is
once again the 'Jew Süss',[2] & has to play for his amusement both
at Government House tomorrow & at the Italian Consulate next
Saturday. And when he's done, Princess Mary & her impossible
husband [Viscount Lascelles] arrive, & it all has to be gone
through again. I like meeting people who *do* things, but people
who just *are* I find irksome, as there seems no way of reaching
beyond conventionalities & platitudes.

I had Dame Millicent [Fawcett] & her sister here – terribly
energetic, at 83 & 85, & having their cold baths every morning,
much to John's horror & amazement. Miss Garratt is a little vague
& wandering, but Dame Millicent is as clear as ever, & full of
good stories of bygone days & political life. She was greatly excited yesterday at a telegram which came for her saying that the
Suffrage Bill had a large majority for the second reading.

The country was also, Helen reported, 'stiff with missionaries'
who had come for an international conference. She enjoyed their
problems:

7.4.28: The 'native' element of India, China, Korea, S. Africa etc
are talking the purest nationalism, & much upsetting the Imperial-
minded missionaries from America & England. In fact, I gather
it's altogether quite advanced, & the old-fashioned crowd are
quite dumbfounded. The general plea is that missionaries need no
longer go from the West to the East, but that each country can
now run & keep together its own Church. The Arabs here are
furious at the insult to Islam at having it here, & all cried 'Down
with the Missionaries' at the Nebi Musa procession yesterday.
What with Easter, Passover, Princes, Pilgrims & Tourists, Jerusalem is really overwhelming.

We've just averted another war, & are quite relieved at our
escape. Vandervelde, the great Belgian socialist, is here, with his

wife. He was put under our care all today. Norman is again performing before royalty, at the Italian consulate, & in the
innocence of our undiplomatic minds we thought we'd take the
Belgian & his wife to the reception. Norman asked his accompa-
nist, the wife of the French Consul, to find out if that would be
all right. Her husband asked the Italian Consul-General, & the
answer came back, *any* other friend of ours, or *all* our other
friends, but not Mr Vandervelde! Apparently he didn't hit it off at
all with Italy when he was Prime Minister, & the Italian ambassador left Belgium & wouldn't return until he'd resigned! So he's *not*
going, & we've put him onto some Jewish labour people instead.
He is charming – deaf & talks only French, which is difficult.

Then there's our flower show coming off in 10 days, & I'm
getting hectic over that. [She came first for tulips and for table-
plants and fourth for her garden, winning small money prizes,
which went to John.] I feel almost that nothing can happen here
unless I do it, which is very demoralizing & shows that it's time I
left. I also go to Cyprus on 18th, as I'm sure that the country
couldn't win the tennis unless I played!

I'm restarting my kindergarten as an open-air nursery school
quite soon.

Our contract has been signed, & our new house is to be
started almost at once. We leave this on June 5th, & will stay
temporarily in a friend's empty house next to our site, hoping to
get in the new one in the autumn.

16.4.28: Princess Mary arrived Wednesday, & had an amazingly
good reception from all the population. She was not scheduled to
visit any institutions except the Order of St John & the Princess
Mary Ward in the hospital, & Norman thought she ought to see
something Jewish. Plumer eventually allowed it, & Miss Landau
heard about 9 pm Thursday night that her school was to be visited the next morning – Friday is normally a holiday. But they
went round & knocked up the children, & 400 were there next
morning, & Miss Landau quite at her best, with guides, eurhyth-
mics etc all going strong. Then Saturday she visited the
University, & Norman did the showman; & yesterday she visited
Dilb, the Jewish colony 10 miles out on the Jaffa road, & again
Plumer asked Norman to be showman ... Norman sat next to her
at a Government House dinner & played afterwards – he's a

regular Court Musician now … The royal family's all right – it works very hard – but it's the aristocracy & the hangers-on who ought to be abolished.

I don't think I'll be home this year. Norman certainly can't, & what with moving, & the expense of a new house, I expect we'll be rather short of funds. I want the new house to be extremely nice, & I want some new things for it, & a good garden, & it all costs a lot.

The next letter comes from Government House, Cyprus. Helen had gone out as part of a Palestine tennis team, and was staying with the Storrs. There should have been a cricket team too, but most of the members were in the police, and police leave had been stopped because of a disturbance at Gaza, a protest against the missionary conference.

24.4.28: Well, I'm having a most entertaining time, & I tell you, they *do* do things correctly here – not like our informal post-war Palestine. Why, a week-end at Buckingham Palace would be pure child's play to this. Precedence really *means* something here – & at functions I feel super-regal in the car behind the Union Jack & with the Anthem playing, in a way I've never felt with Herbert or Plumer. Anyway, they are most frightfully kind to me. I'm the only one of our 17 that came over who is staying here [in Government House].

It's most amusing among colonial service people. 1) They always think the last place was perfection. 2) They always say their present place is appalling unless 3) they're talking to anyone from another colony, when their present place, too, is perfect. Cyprus is *infinitely* superior to Palestine in the eyes of the officials here (who've never been there). And we all try terribly hard not to show how awfully sorry we are for the miseries who are stuck in this off-the-map island, when they might be living in the perfections of Palestine. But really, though the people are very nice to us indeed, they are a limited crowd. Beyond Storrs & his ADC & one other man in the Secretariat, I don't think any of them ever read a book, or think seriously of anything beyond qualifying for a pension. And though our Palestine officials may be as bad, in a way, yet we have our Jewish & Continental intelligentsia as a refuge.

The Greeks hate the idea of this Jubilee year – it *is* so silly, as why should they be asked to be glad at having been 50 years under England, when all the time they are begging not to be – & so they turn up at nothing. Storrs calls everything this year 'Jubilee' – so they boycott the horse-races, police-sports, tennis-tournaments etc, & are worse than either Jews or Arabs in Palestine.

We won our matches, but the glory was taken out of it by the fact that they weren't taking it seriously! It's a bad sign when English people don't take games seriously! But we've been given to understand that had it been *golf* – which is *the* game here – they would have been all out to beat us.

2.5.28: I attended a session of the Legislative Council [in Cyprus] in order to instruct our people here on the idiocy of having such a farcical institution. It certainly seemed absurd. Storrs – the Governor – is Premier & Speaker. There are 12 Greek members, who are naturally the opposition, & speak on everything, as long as they like, in order to get it in the local press & acquire votes. Storrs, being Premier, can't squash the opposition, so each speaks in turn. There are 3 Turkish members, & 9 British officials besides Storrs. If all Turkish members back the government, it wins. But they don't always, & threw out last year's budget, & generally it's most chaotic. Every remark has to be translated into two other of the official languages, Greek, Turkish & English. Government people talk of wanting one here, but it would be hopeless. You can't govern a subject people as if they were a democracy, when all the time it's a pretence & you mean to anyway. This was all right in the good old 19th century days, when people were quite happy being governed. Now, when they're instinctively the opposition on *every* point, you must either be thoroughly despotic – which is bad – or clear out – which few have the courage to do. The more I see of colonial government, the more I wish we were in some other branch of the Civil Service.

Helen thoroughly enjoyed the trip, playing more matches in Beirut on the way back, and having a happy day motoring in Lebanon with Maugras, who was then Acting High Commissioner in Syria.

On her return, she learnt that the Plumers were to leave in August:

9.5.28: 'We are both so fond of the Plumers, that the thought of their near departure saddens us very much. He's so very much the right type of man for the country … I wonder what we *shall* get. Smuts is mentioned – he would be good, & we'd soon like him. But the Colonial Office haven't any sense, & I *know* it'll be a dud.

19.5.28: My new house is 5 feet high today. The water will be on tomorrow, & the garden started at once. It's reinforced concrete all through, with stone facing – much steadier for earthquakes than all stone.

26.5.28: I'm very anxious to make my house very modern & attractive internally – very little furniture, & lots of colour. I wrote to Heals asking for designs for curtains etc, & they sent me the most awful cretonnes – very old-fashioned flowery designs. So I wrote & said they were delightfully quaint, but hardly suitable for my kind of house. I'm thinking of having each room done all over one colour – for instance my bedroom primrose yellow; walls one shade, ceiling a little lighter, paint & curtains & bed-spreads a little darker. Dining-room perhaps green, & drawing-room rust, & my sitting-room jade, & Norman's study darker green.

We forget the horrors of the future [without the Plumers] in our tennis & parties, gardening & meetings.

16.6.28: We are in our temporary house – quite comfortably – after a fairly hectic three days' move. There's a continual breeze blowing up on this hill; & there's no dust. I think we shall like living here very much. The first storey of the new house is built, & it's growing rapidly.

A month later the downstairs was plastered and the roof was soon to go on – 'It has been built so quickly that it will probably collapse.' And Helen planted a hundred petrol tins of seeds for the spring.

There seems to be rather less emphasis on Good Works in the letters now, though she considered herself busy: breakfast 6.30, garden 7–10, meetings etc until she fetched Norman for lunch, then tennis and club until it was time to change to go out to dinner. Such a life brought more requests for smart clothes to be sent from England – outfits for the expected farewell parties for the Plumers, and even tennis socks with dark yellow tops to go with her jacket with yellow Yemenite embroidery.

7.7.28: A friend in the Education Dept has gone on leave, & left me his gramophone & a lot of very high-brow records for 3 months. The idea is – a plot between him & me – to make Norman enjoy it, & buy one of our own in the new house. I think it's working – Norman is quite keen on it.

Well, our new High Commissioner is appointed. We know nothing of him, but are depressed at his Colonial Office record.

Sir John Chancellor, the new High Commissioner, was an army staff-officer, who had been Secretary of the Committee of Imperial Defence, and had served as Governor in turn of Mauritius, Trinidad, and Southern Rhodesia. 'Personally,' Norman wrote, 'I found him rather detached; and not anxious to consult me about the Jewish community of Palestine or the policy of the Jewish National Home. He had not the sense of history which his two predecessors signally felt for the country.'[3] Like Plumer, he was in office three years, but they were to be troubled years which contrasted sadly with the previous calm.

28.7.28: I hope the Chancellors like a) gardening b) good works c) arts & crafts d) books e) music f) Jews g) simple pleasures & games. And I hope they dislike a) bridge b) missionaries who try to convert Jews c) American tourists d) large functions. Especially bridge. It's getting a perfect nightmare here now. But it'll be no easy task for an ordinary colonial governor to succeed two such outstanding personalities as Uncle Herbert & Plumer.

4.8.28: The Plumers went off Tuesday – very old & tearful at the farewells on the platform, where they went round & shook hands with everyone. The P & O people treated them *abominably* – they always do, people from here. But they gave them rotten low-deck cabins, & never even put them at the captain's table, & told them to get there 12 hours before the boat came in, which meant a night in a rotten hotel in Port Said.

29.9.28: My house looks a little vulgar now – I won the Ladies' Singles Palestine Championship at tennis, & carried off a huge &

blatantly shiny silver cup, which I keep for a year, & a smaller cup
which I keep for ever.

I expect you've seen a lot about this silly business of the
Wailing Wall. The Jews were silly & unnecessarily troublesome in
not taking down a screen when they were told to, & the government – i.e. Keith-Roach – were incredibly tactless in sending quite
the wrongest sort of police officer to deal with it, who pulled it
away in the middle of the service, & caused a 'scandal'. Norman,
Luke [the new Chief Secretary], Fred etc have spent hours in
talking of it – but there's nothing to be done. The Government
regrets its mistake, & that's all there is to it.

This 'scandal', mentioned by Helen dismissively in her letter
between accounts of tennis and dances, was a disaster of the
interregnum before Chancellor arrived. In Norman's opinion,
'none who worked with Plumer can doubt that, had he been in
Palestine when the troubles about the Jews praying at the Western
Wall began to brew, these troubles would not have passed the
dimensions of a cloud no bigger than a man's hand. And the
history of Palestine might have been written otherwise.'[4] The
screen Helen wrote about had been placed the day before the Day
of Atonement, to separate men and women at the service; but it
was resented by the Moslems, who saw it as an intrusion on the
Temple area. Keith-Roach, the District Commissioner, anxious
not to upset the Arabs, refused to listen either to Norman or to a
deputation of rabbis who begged him to leave it until after the
fast. In his memoirs,[5] Keith-Roach wrote unrepentantly:

> I gave instructions to Noah Gladstone, the Jewish beadle, to have
> the screen removed before continuation of devotions the follow-
> ing morning. He promised to remove it & I accepted his
> assurance; but I also took the precaution of informing the British
> police inspector that in the event of Noah failing to carry out his
> undertaking it would be his business to see that the screen was
> nonetheless removed. Noah did not keep his promise. So the po-
> lice removed the screen. Opposition was shown and one rabbi,
> who clung onto the screen, was carried bodily, with the screen,
> outside. Justice had been done. The status quo had been pre-
> served with as little force as possible.

It was the start of a period of high tension which led to serious Arab riots.

Everything was calm enough at first for Helen and Norman to be able to take a ten-day holiday, an adventurous tour in Lebanon and Syria. And when they got back they were planning big parties in the new house, a musical evening for 90, and a dance for about 150.

> **17.10.28**: I think we'll tent in all the balcony, & dance there & in the drawing room on the dance night, & eat there on the music night.
>
> Then, on 14th, a chrysanthemum show at the Citadel – I'm secretary of the society now, & that means a lot of work too.
>
> Poor Norman is up to his eyes over this 'Wailing Wall' business. It is all so trivial & petty, & yet potentially so very dangerous, especially when the Jews talk of acquiring or expropriating the wall, which inflames the Arabs at once. They are a difficult crowd here – but Keith-Roach's tactlessness is having very far-reaching results.

Still not too worried, Helen went off in the middle of November to join her parents in Mentone once again, not returning until after the New Year. The musical evening, she reported, was rather a dud, but the dance was the success of the season.

---

[1] Manuscript memoir.

[2] The 'court Jew' in the novel by Feuchtwanger, first published in English in 1926.

[3] Norman and Helen Bentwich, *Mandate Memories* (London: Hogarth Press, 1965), p 129.

[4] Norman Bentwich, *Wanderer Between Two Worlds* (London: Kegan Paul, 1941), p 142.

[5] Edward Keith-Roach, *Pasha of Jerusalem* (London: The Radcliffe Press, 1994), p 119.

1929

The Storm Breaks

For the first half of the year life seemed to go on as normal. In January, Helen was happy to have her friend Evelyn Waley visiting her again. Evelyn helped run the arts and crafts shop, which was to be open for twelve weeks, and the letters give the impression that this was the most important problem in Palestine. The garden came a close second. There is not even a mention of Palestinian politics before the riots broke out in August. It is only with hindsight that one gets a feeling of fiddling while Jerusalem headed for an explosion.

There is the usual chronicle of dinners and parties, and Helen seems increasingly concerned with clothes, detailing what she wore on each occasion. Here are her impressions of the Chancellors, after a dinner party:

16.1.29: They were very friendly & nice to us but I don't think we shall have much in common with them. I can't think why everyone described them as 'charming'. He's polite & courteous, a little laboured, wears an eyeglass, & doesn't look as if he took enough exercise. And she seems very ill & delicate & frankly hating the house & country, & telling everyone so.

Chancellor started off rather brilliantly by saying he hated his house because he had to go through a ghetto every time he went out, & asked if I knew what a ghetto was! I was sorely tempted to say I had been born in one – but refrained. ['It's like sitting next to a leg of mutton to spend an evening with H.E.,' she complained the next month. 'I don't know what interests or attracts him.']

The gramophone continues a great success. I'm getting quite an authority on records. I've enough dance ones for the present, but will get classical ones now. I play it while I brush the dog, do the flowers etc, to liven up the house. And in the evenings. It's quite the best one here. Norman says a gramophone should play only Mozart.

A little later she wrote that she had bought, and liked, Rimsky-Korsakoff's *Scheherazade* and Stravinsky's *Petrushka*; Norman's family were making progress with Helen's musical education.

The letters rarely mention Norman's law work, but when she was reminiscing about the casino at Mentone, Helen added, 'By the way, someone has just applied to be allowed to set up the equivalent of "franc machines" here, & Norman refused – isn't he a prude?' This admirable puritanism persisted in Palestine and Israel – there is now a state lottery, but the Israeli cabinet is bitterly divided about licensing a casino.[1]

Aeroplanes, as well as gramophones, were becoming a more usual part of life – by 1929 it had become possible to send letters air mail from England in four days. One letter shows the hazards:

2.3.29: Norman's new assistant was sent to Baghdad on a job, & flying back they had such a strong gale, that though they registered 100 miles an hour, they only went 40, & came down in a field 15 miles before Gaza, after 13 hours up, for lack of petrol, & had to stay in the machine there all night, with no food for 24 hours. There were 2 ladies, one aged 84; but they said she was the calmest, & slept most peaceably all night.

Thursday was Norman's birthday, & we had all his family, Sachers, Hadassah, Millses, Magneses & a few others in for roulette. José [2] has an alarming talent for it, winning 12/- on farthing stakes! And he'd never seen it before.

23.3.29: We had a successful & enjoyable trip on the Dead Sea, in spite of being a party of 14, rather larger than I really like. The whole party was organized by one young man so that he could ask one of the girls to marry him, in the moonlight on the return journey. Alas – the young girl didn't want to marry him, being rather a young lady of character, & he being rather weak, though very nice. So on the return journey he, poor dear, sat alone on the motor boat, whilst the girl sat by my side in the large tub we were being towed in, & talked 5 hours without stopping of her future career, & all she wanted to do as an independent young woman. All rather like a modern novel, & I felt very grandmotherly towards her, & gave her lots of advice … We tried to climb to the top of Masada – a very easy climb before the earthquake, but almost impossible now.

Norman & I & the Magneses took Rudyard Kipling round the Hebrew University. He is here about War Graves, & sick of seeing people & being entertained. He was charming – much more alive & alert than I had imagined.

31.3.29: Evelyn & I & three very nice archaeologist girls walked about 12 miles – one of them is Miss Garrod, & she & Evelyn have become great friends. The three go off tomorrow to dig in prehistoric caves on the slopes of Carmel; rather sporting of them, all alone with a man cook & a guard.

This turned out to be the famous dig that discovered a treasury of Neanderthal and early *Homo sapiens* fossils. Nine years later Dorothy Garrod became Cambridge's first woman professor.

19.4.29: One night we went to see the film 'Ben Hur', & found it very thrilling. Being a Jewish cinema, they had eliminated everything about Christianity. It was amusing to guess where the cut-out bits should have come in.

I suppose you've heard all about the shlimozel when Edwin & Hadassah [Samuel] & the others were lost on the Dead Sea for a few hours? They *were* mugs. They broke all the unwritten laws of these camping trips, & gave all of us here a ghastly 24 hours trying to get a motor boat to rescue them, & to locate them with aeroplanes & police. [The 'mugs' included Harry Sacher and Marcus Sieff, future directors of Marks and Spencer.] …

One amusing feature – Norman went to open a show at Tel Aviv, and they were so certain those people were lost for ever that there were no speeches. The first thing that had ever stopped Tel Aviv making speeches. So we all plan to disappear in future when there are functions.

Later in the month she wrote that she did not see very much of
Edwin & Hadassah these days because 'they never play tennis, &
do so dislike our other friends, the English Sports-Club crowd'.

In May 1929 the first government with a Labour majority in
Britain was elected, and Helen was full of hope, for both Britain
and Palestine. Herbert Samuel's Liberals had only 58 seats (in spite
of polling 5 million votes out of a total of 22 million).

> **1.6.29**: A Labour victory is worth while if for no other reason
> than that it has made your son-in-law wildly & deliriously happy.
> I've never seen him quite so pleased about anything. It's like a
> religion with him, a genuine faith. Fortunately, it's a feeling I quite
> share. Chancellor is grieved – Baldwin is a personal friend of his.
> Poor Uncle Herbert – although he bears the balance of power in
> his hand, his small total is a depressing result of his terrific labours
> & expenses. It has quite surprised everyone here – I think we
> probably had too much faith in him – but all our forecasts gave
> Liberal many more votes & Labour less.

> **8.6.29**: When the wind here goes east, my bedroom gets full of
> the strangest creatures, blown straight up from the Jordan valley.
> The other night, the floor was lit up by glow-worms. And huge &
> rare moths & spiders & beetles, praying mantises, locusts; &,
> worst of all, sand-flies.
>
> So we've got Sidney Webb [as Colonial Secretary] – there's
> been great excitement as to whom we *would* get. I think he'll be
> good – not revolutionary, but tremendously efficient.

It was a sadly misplaced faith. In her manuscript memoir, Helen
wrote that 'It soon became apparent that Sidney Webb had little
understanding of, or sympathy with, the Jewish aspirations in
Palestine. He regarded the Jews in the same way as he regarded the
white settlers in Africa, and thought it his duty to protect the
Arabs as "exploited natives". And he was more under the influence of his permanent officials, and less independent in his
outlook, than any former Colonial Secretary of whom we had had
experience.'

Helen and Norman left Palestine cheerfully at the end of June,
planning to spend a month motoring to the Hague, where Norman was to lecture for a week, and then go to England until the

beginning of October. John went too, to help with the driving and
the car. 'Every Consul here has given us a sort of laissez-passer
about customs, so that it should all be very easy. And every British
legation has been warned by the Foreign Office to give us help &
do anything if we need it.'

Sir John Chancellor was in England on leave; no-one had
expected a crisis. But on the journey across Europe Norman read
of a disturbance on 15 August at the Wall. As soon as he arrived
in London he saw Chancellor to discuss the situation and draw up
temporary regulations, but it was too late. Eight days later serious
riots broke out. The lack of soldiers, which had been a source of
pride in calmer times four years earlier, proved disastrous, and the
police failed to keep control. In 1926, when Plumer was abolishing
both British and Palestinian gendarmerie, Kisch had worried
about what might happen if there were a wave of Islamic fanati-
cism or an Arab rising, and had warned the Chief Secretary [Harry
Luke] 'that Government are taking an unjustifiable risk in regard
to the Jewish lives for which they are responsible'.[3] Norman later
described the start of the troubles:[4]

> Suddenly the situation was out of hand. An Arab mob was stirred
> to frenzy one Friday in a hot August by the Mufti after prayers in
> the sacred Mosque of Aksa in Jerusalem, a day or two after Jewish
> Revisionists had staged a demonstration at the Wall. They burst
> out to attack the Jewish quarters and murder any stray Jew in the
> streets. The fever spread rapidly. Before Chancellor could return,
> brutal group murders were perpetrated, particularly of the old
> religious Jews, in Jerusalem, Hebron, Safed and several villages.
> For a few days, till troops could be brought from Egypt, the very
> scanty security forces, augmented by British volunteers, official
> and non-official, were hard-pressed. Luke incurred the resent-
> ment of the Jews by forbidding British Jewish subjects, including
> Government officials, to be armed.

Norman's brother José was one of those refused permission to
carry arms.

The Colonial Office did not ask Norman to return, but he of
course did so, with Helen, as soon as they heard the news over the
wireless. Norman's father arrived to see them off bringing a

bullet-proof waistcoat, which Norman refused. (The following month, when Herbert Bentwich was setting out, in spite of the troubles, to live in Jerusalem for his last years, Norman wrote to him: 'You must be careful of yourself here, and I may make you wear that mail waistcoat.') Writing from Port Said, on the journey, Helen seemed confident that everything had calmed down. But when she reached Jerusalem the full horror slowly hit her:

> **5.9.29**: My head is in a whirl – I've heard so many versions & stories of the affrays. We are in our house, & one feels absolutely safe & normal, though we have a British guard, who will sleep in my little sitting-room each night, & guard the exposed side of the house. My Arab boy has proved devotedly faithful; he sleeps the other side, in the garage. The curfew is still on, between 6.30 pm & 6 am, but it's considered perfectly safe to go anywhere in the daytime. There seems no special work for me to do yet, tho' Norman told Chancellor I was available for anything. I shall avoid the Sports Club as some of them are, I hear, bitterly anti-Jewish, & I don't want to make feeling any worse by coming up against them. I think I shall re-make part of the garden.
>
> Norman has seen all the official crowd. The blighters are, so many of them, again talking of 'bloody Bolshevik Jews', because the Jewish people used the arms they had, & thus protected their new quarters & colonies, when the government couldn't. If it hadn't been for that, all the new quarters & colonies would have suffered as badly as the ghettos. Safed is the bad spot at the moment – once again, they failed to get the troops up in time. Nobody is very happy about the retired Chief Justice[5] who is to direct our commission of enquiry – we know what Colonial Chief Justices are![6]

Why was there hostility rather than sympathy for Jews, when Jews had undeniably been the victims of a brutal outrage? Unfortunately it was always easy to blame the Balfour Declaration for all troubles; and this time the Zionists, by fighting back, and by accusing the Administration of negligence and incompetence over the riots,[7] managed to antagonize still further the British officials and their wives. Storrs wrote that when he revisited Jerusalem in 1931 he 'found the British Administration fully convinced that in

any future crisis, while the Arabs might be their enemies, the Jews
certainly would be'.[8]

7.9.29: Things seem quite quiet here now, on the surface, but of
course everyone is a raw mass of nerves. This curfew is rather an
advantage, as one doesn't have to give dinner parties or go out at
night. I've not got a car yet [hers was being sent back from England],
but I believe I'm having an old one belonging to Mills. It's very
necessary – Arab drivers are afraid to go into Jewish quarters, &
Jews into Arab ones, & one has to get out & walk in the sun,
which I did yesterday. And then one takes a car with Hebrew
numbers, thinking one has a Jewish driver, & finds oneself with
an Arab who has put up Hebrew numbers to get custom. All the
drivers take two hats, to wear a tarbush or an ordinary hat according to the district.

I've started in on some relief work – I went to the head of the
Hadassah [Hadassah Medical Organization], who was running it,
& was welcomed by him. My contention – & of course theirs – is
that as much of the immediate relief as possible should be done
by the Government, & the fund saved for reconstruction pur-
poses. At present the Government only feed about 400 people
from Hebron here in Jerusalem, & the Safed people. But there are
2000 here, in various schools & lodgings, from unsafe places. So I
want the Government to say first which places are definitely unsafe, & we will make everyone else return, & the Government
must feed the rest, & help us in emptying the schools & putting
them in a permanent building. And also in giving them free transport ... Here & Safed are the main places, with a little in Haifa.
At present, everyone is being housed & fed who needs it – but
there's fear of an epidemic if it goes on in this crude way.

The baby-home had Arabs round attacking, but soldiers de-
fended them, & they were brought in under escort & housed in
the city. It's amazing how many of the Jews – even in Hebron –
were saved by Arabs. And – more extraordinary – how already
the Hebron Jews are talking of returning to their houses right in
the ghetto there. Human nature is queer. The Arabs have asked
them to return, as they were the only money-lenders there. Terrible stories – true, for the most part – are rife, of the butchery.
Though there is a degrading debate between the Public Health &

the Zionists as to whether or no there were any technical 'atrocities'.

14.9.29: Well, I've done a lot of really hard work this week, & it's been quite hot too. On Sunday, I went with the two others of my committee to see Mills[9] &, having primed him beforehand of what we wanted, he had talked it over with H.E., & we got our answers, instead of having to wait for further consultations, which was most useful. It was really embarrassing, to hold a pistol, as we did, at the head of the government, & for them to reply by heaping coals of fire on the head of the Relief Committee. We said they must ensure safety for the people to return to their homes, except in special cases like Hebron & Safed & the colonies; or else they must be prepared to feed everyone who had left their homes in fear. And the answer was – we can't give you the guarantee at the moment, but how many would you like us to feed? We replied, 2500 in Jerusalem, 1500 in Tel Aviv, 2000 in Haifa, & (I think) 2000 in Safed. They said right – & from Wednesday they did it! We do it through the Public Health Department in each district, & they give Hospital rations, which are much more generous than even the American Hadassah dietician had asked for. And all the other points were granted too.

The distribution of rations in a place like Jerusalem is terribly difficult ... But to make people feel secure – to feel the government is their friend, as we have by getting them these rations, & keeping them healthy in very trying circumstances, & at the worst time of year, is all we can really attempt ... Giving rations to the people who lived in other places than our hostels – with friends, or in any empty holes – was a great difficulty. And from tomorrow we are having the soup kitchen at the Straus Health Centre giving double its usual number of rations, so as to get over that. That is, about 2500 lots a day ...

It needed a huge amount of organization, with families housed in schools and synagogues. And there were critics – the Americans said it was wrong and demoralizing and was pauperizing, but had nothing else to suggest: 'They only wanted committee meetings to discuss the problems, whilst we were all working from 7 am to try to get things done.' Occasionally Helen took an afternoon off to play tennis, avoiding arguments by refusing to talk at the Club

about anything other than tennis or her leave – 'almost all of that
crowd are openly hostile to Jews.'

...I went round the hospitals & saw some of the wounded. All
the children have fractured skulls from clubs, if nothing worse.
One woman had her child killed on her lap & her husband killed
in front of her, her skull fractured & her fingers cut off; she was
quite out of her mind. Another, who had lain under a heap of
dead bodies for hours, is also mad. One woman, whose husband
was killed, put her arms round her children, & they cut each
child's head, & slashed her arms so badly, she has died too. The
massacre happened on the Saturday morning, & they didn't get
them in here till the Sunday evening. Nobody here knew it was
going on. Safed was a ghastly blunder, as the troops arrived late.

They won't consider the Old City safe until 100 of the new
police arrive on Tuesday, because troops are no good in a
crowded area like that.

21.9.29: To such people as you may meet who pooh-pooh the
seriousness of the riots here, will you show such parts of Norman's & my letters as may seem relevant? The press – both inside
& outside Palestine – is being as false, as partisan & as harmful as
only the press can be.

We still have our 3200 refugees in Jerusalem being fed by the
government; 1500 in Safed; 800 in Haifa & I believe 1000 in Tel
Aviv. As the government will only feed either those who have
had their homes utterly destroyed or those whom, in the opinion
of the police, it is not wise to force to return, that shows how the
country stands. I can get nothing about their future in writing
from the government, only telephone messages & verbal remarks.
As I refuse to act on these, there is an impasse.

We have got things organized so well here, I decided to have a
look at Safed & Tiberias. Norman couldn't get away so soon, but
Eric Mills came with me, as I couldn't have gone alone. He hired
a car from here & had no escort, & the country is safe ... Safed is
really in a sad plight. And the worst aspect of it is that the Jews
there have an entire lack of confidence in the government, & the
Arabs an open contempt for it. There are troops, but the same
Arab police force as witnessed & in no wise checked the outrages;
& no responsible District Officer, only a very nice but very inex-

perienced young Persian of about 25. It was a very good thing that Mills came, as he is recommending immediate action on these things – sending a very senior British commissioner to live there; changing the entire Arab police force; retaining the troops in Safed through the winter, & other things. From the other point of view, it was a good thing I went with him, as the Jews are naturally not loving just any British official who turns up, but seeing he was with me they gave him a good welcome. And he dealt with them so kindly & sympathetically that they were really touched.

We went through the Jewish quarter, & Mills declared that the only thing he had ever seen at all comparable was Ypres. They had fired the Shell petrol store which was right in the middle of the ghetto, where we had walked when we visited it with you, & taken the oil & poured it over other places. Only the stone shell of the houses was left, blackened & marred. Sixteen persons were killed outright; one was the only lawyer – deliberately murdered before his family. I saw his widow & two children, & her father, who is the best Arabic scholar in Safed & often consulted by the Arabs ... An orphanage was attacked & a number of small boys wounded, tho' not killed. The very old rabbi was killed.

124 living rooms – they mostly had one room each – were utterly burnt & destroyed, & 50 shops or stores. 202 houses were damaged & looted. There are 1500 refugees – & there is not a big building anywhere available for housing them. The Hadassah doctor there has done wonders – run his hospital, looked after wounded, & taken charge of the refugees. There are only two non-Safed people there – one a schoolmaster, sent to help, & one an old Safed native, now a doctor in Beyrouth, who had been there on holiday, & is giving his services as long as required.

We talked of the problems of relief. There is a claims commission, & 50% of the claims can be paid quite soon. The claims come from the collective fines which are to be paid by the towns & villages which caused the damage. This makes people think twice about taking part next time. Tulkeram had to pay £20,000 in 1921 – & was one of the places which kept quiet this!

They were desperately in need of clothes – they'd had their shirts on for 3 weeks, & no change of anything. 12 cases of clothes were waiting at Haifa to come up; Luke had promised to arrange for them to come Customs free, but he hadn't bothered

to see it through. Mills arranged it all on the telephone, & they'll
have them tomorrow.

They had many stories – no doubt true in many cases – of
intimidation of witnesses, & lack of help by the police … Hebron,
I believe, is far worse & bloodier in every way.

We went to Yesod Hamallah, the Jewish colony on Huleh.
Nobody was killed there, but the place was sacked, houses pil-
laged, & cattle looted … The Bedouin had stolen a horse, & when
the police found it & ordered it to be returned, the Arabs cold-
bloodedly cut its eyes out. I saw it there, a sickening sight.

At Tiberias there were 250 refugees from Baisan. They had
been attacked, & their shops looted, & they had been wounded,
& were afraid to return, but we went to Baisan, & Mills saw the
District Officer, & they go back on Monday, we hope in safety.

Symbolic of the attitude of some British wives to all Jews was their
exclusion of Helen and Norman from a subscription list for the
British police, because 'as a matter of principle'[10] Jews could no
longer count as British in Palestine. Norman was upset, but sent
£5 saying he was sure he had been left out by mistake – and got
strong support from Mills and from Chancellor. 'We're both good
fighters,' Helen added, 'I'm making every possible effort to win
the tennis tournament – a Jehad, as Mills now calls it.'

5.10.29: There has been much agitation about Norman this week
amongst the Arabs – the usual thing; it's almost a matter of routine now, after '19, '20, '21 & '22. But Chancellor takes it very
seriously, & has put a special guard on Norman. I'm very thankful, really, as he's so careless, & it saves me worrying. He insisted
on going to the Wailing Wall this morning – but as he has gone
with 6ft 6 of ex-guardsman as escort, I don't mind. We have a
guard now day & night on the house, always a British constable,
& we take him when we go out to dinner.

The refugee work goes on – but I was very fed up about that
last week. Fred [Kisch] 'took charge' in a rather overbearing way,
without a word of thanks to us, or even telling us he *was* taking
charge. He appointed a relief & reconstruction committee – without a woman on it! – & when I'd got everything ready for the
people to return to the Old City, he, together with Keith-Roach,
decided to 'postpone' it. That was 9 days ago. They've vainly tried

to get the people home since, & the people got scared at having it postponed once, & won't go, so it's all chaos. The government rightly decided that as it was safe for them to go back, they wouldn't pay for their food. So the relief fund is paying for feeding over 2500 people, & heaven knows when it will be able to stop. It has all got so 'political' since Fred took it on, with rabbis & labour people & agudath [ultra-orthodox Jews] & everyone represented on the committee, & not a soul who understands relief work. Meanwhile, the people from Hebron are being neglected, & are still left in acute discomfort in the schools. But nobody will make up their minds as to their future at all. I wrote a letter in the press, & as a result the English people have sent me large quantities of old clothes, which I've given them; & I've had money, too, from them – about £50 – & with that I've been buying stuff for them to sew themselves, & make into shoes. And I've been supplying them with blankets & mattresses, which I insisted the relief fund should pay for. Their great idea is to save money for reconstruction – which is only a political way, to some extent, of making capital out of the situation. The Hebron people were even becoming verminous, as they had no change of shirts or underclothes. There are so many people looking after things, that nothing gets done now. So I go ahead & do it, & they all get very angry, & hold long meetings about it, & meanwhile I go ahead further ...

In her letter of 7 September Helen had advocated keeping relief fund money for reconstruction, but that was so that the Administration would finance the emergency feeding; there was no government money on offer for clothing, so relief fund money had to be used.

> ... The country really feels no quieter. There are weekly murders in Jerusalem, & occasional shoot-ups outside. It's sad that the commission delays so much. We are all – especially Norman – peculiarly confident of its entire futility, as those sorts of commission have never been known to achieve anything. But meanwhile, nobody settles down to anything, & everyone is preparing the right sort of evidence to suit themselves. Read Kipling's poem 'Cleared' in the Barrack Room Ballads.[11] It seems an excellent prophecy.

A week later, more trivial thoughts started to creep back:

12.10.29: About my evening dress. I've had lots of consultations
with various friends on the subject – because anybody's new best
evening dress is rather an event here – & I'd definitely like a jade-
green or a dark dahlia-red; & something soft, like georgette or
crepe-de-chine, & not too stiff; &, if possible, not lace material. I
expect it'll be very dear, with a coat too, & fur. But seeing I got
practically nothing when I was home, that's all right. It'll cheer me
up enormously, too, which is a good thing.

The Jerusalem refugees are still occupying the schools, &
practically none have returned to their homes. One woman gave
birth to a child on the floor, with about 30 others in the room.
Most of our people owe rent to Arab landlords, & can't return till
that's paid. I expect we'll have to pay out a lot in the end.

There's more trouble about the blowing of the shofar[12] at the
Wailing Wall. How unutterably childish it all is! If it's going to
lead to more massacres & bloodshed, for heaven's sake don't
blow it, is my view. And personally, I'd give up the whole place
rather than one Jew more should die. The government is so afraid
still, it does nothing … Luke suggested the other day that Norman should be asked to 'continue his leave'. In the government's
present state, anybody so downright as Norman is a nuisance –
especially when he is Jewish, & blatantly honest.

Everyone who walks around alone tells of stone-throwing in
the villages. I'm very careful, & never go anywhere unless well
guarded.

It was not only Luke who felt that it would be easier to govern
Palestine if Norman went home. Chancellor wrote to Passfield
that Michael McDonnell (the Chief Justice) 'felt strongly that the
Government was being seriously hampered at the present time by
the presence of Mr Bentwich, a Jew and an ardent partisan of
Zionism, in the high legal office of Attorney-General'. Chancellor
explained that he himself did not want Norman to resign, pointing
out that the McDonnells 'are devout Roman Catholics and like all
the Latins in Palestine are strongly anti-Semitic'.[13]

Norman's position as a Jewish, and therefore presumed
prejudiced, Attorney-General, was becoming, under McDonnell's
influence, more and more difficult. When the Zionist Organiza-

tion had attacked, not only the Arab leaders for responsibility for the riots, but also the government for negligence, Norman had not been allowed to advise the government about their defence. He was not consulted by the High Commissioner, and did not appear before the Commission.[14] The Arab leaders resented his position as law officer, holding him responsible for the sentences against the rioters, and even organized a strike – 'in my dishonour', as Norman put it. Helen made light of it:

> **26.10.29**: Norman's strike went off quite happily – nobody would drive him in a car, so I went & fetched him home, with the policeman, & took him, as I was afraid the crowd might throw stones at him if he walked ...

The rest of the letter was more relaxed, mostly about gardens and clothes and dinner parties and tennis – having failed to win the singles championship in Jerusalem, Helen did win in Jaffa. She seems to have begun mixing a bit more with the British community again. Towards the end of the letter she returned to the problems of the refugees; she had now been put on the executive committee for the whole country, and in entire charge of the Hebron people:

> ... The refugees are all now housed in rooms they have found themselves, & been given some money for furniture, & 4 months rent paid. They still draw government rations; & we are now seriously tackling the clothing problem. We have set up one man as a tailor, & pay him to make suits for others. And we give the mothers material for the children. Next week we shall set up a cobbler or two, & some sempstresses. I expect to have about 10 families employed in clothing the others.

In early November Helen wrote that the curfew was off, though cafés still had to close at 9, and cinemas and performances at 10. Things were not yet quiet; a Jewish eye doctor was stabbed in front of his hospital; Arabs were trying to enforce a boycott of Jewish shops.

22.11.29: A year ago today I was just arriving in Mentone. What a difference there is. We've got so used to an atmosphere of suspicion & hatred & uncertainty, that we can't really realize how very different it is to what we lived in before. And there seems no end to it ... The Commission will probably sit till after Christmas, & give no report till March. Meanwhile, this foolish boycott goes on unchecked, & trade is dying. At present, the tourists are crying off in numbers, & that will mean more distress. I'm afraid it all sounds very gloomy.

The Hebron refugees still need daily attention, in finding work now, & giving out the clothing which has just arrived from the Union of Jewish Women. But I'm glad to have that to do, & it's a good excuse for not seeing the British women except at the Club & on the tennis-court or hockey-field. Some are all right – but they are such sheep!

I do so envy you the peaceful, safe, contented sort of life of the Riviera. I'm so tired of agitations & hatreds & armed guards & shots at night & the everlasting talking of it all!

24.11.29: What I've been dreading for the last three months happened today – & I suppose one's first & deepest feeling must be one of intense relief that the result is no worse. Norman was leaving his office at lunch time – alone – & as he came down the last flight of stairs & walked along the corridor, he heard a loud explosion behind him – but says he felt nothing. He thought it was someone playing a trick, & turned, & saw a lad dressed as a government messenger. He was just going to speak to him, when the lad rushed past him, & stood in front of him, with his pistol in his hand, & fired twice more. Norman turned tail & fled up the stairs – two stories up, 4 flights – to his clerks' room, & told them to phone the police, as there was a boy shooting at him. Then he felt queer in his leg, & went to his own room, & took off his trousers, & saw an enormous lump about half-way between his thigh & knee. His silly old clerk said this was 'caused by shock' – but then Norman found he was bleeding from a hole a good deal higher & further back – & the lump was the bullet. The clerk rang me up to say 'Mr Bentwich has been shot,' & I was very alarmed, till Norman himself spoke, & said it was only a boy with a very small pistol. I rushed down there in the car, with the gendarme, & found Norman sitting in a chair with his leg up, rather shaky, but otherwise as cheerful as usual ... He was put on the table, given tea & brandy, & the wound dressed, & taken in an ambulance to the government hospital. His father went in the ambulance with him, & I followed. They took the bullet out with a local anaesthetic.

Meanwhile, the guard at government offices caught the lad who attacked him – a messenger boy from the police office, an Arab, who was an ex-inmate of the Government Reformatory. Aged 20, & probably a half-wit. Almost certainly someone's tool. The lad couldn't control his automatic pistol, & has shot himself too in the leg.

Of course all Jerusalem got excited. First, every Jewish individual & organization – they seemed to get wind of it within half an hour. And now all the English people. Everybody is frightfully nice & kind, & keep asking me to stay & all that. I'm spending the night with the Saunders next door. Not that there's any real reason to, but it was rather a shock, & I know I'll dream & think about it.

Norman had a long & sympathetic telegram from the Arab Executive. I wonder how sincere!

Helen added in a letter to her brother Ellis:

I'm convinced this has genuinely shocked even the most rabid anti-Zionists here; & Norman, in his philosophic way, says it's a tremendous asset politically. In fact, one friend says it's such a good thing for the Jews, that he believes we arranged it all. Anyway, I hope they're right. We need a bit of luck! And this assassination business is pure hell.

In the House of Commons, Josiah Wedgwood asked: 'In the first place, why was not police protection afforded to Mr Bentwich and his wife, in view of the many threats that have been made; in the second place, are any steps being taken to purge the police force of those who think it their duty either to murder Jews or to allow them to be murdered?'

30.11.29: Norman came home from the hospital yesterday, & is writing away in his study now, quite happy. His leg is stiff, naturally – he has to be helped in & out of his clothes a little, & hasn't walked on it much yet. And he still has the irritating rash from the anti-tetanus ... People flocked in so rapidly to see him in hospital, that after H.E. had been, a special British policeman was put on the door with orders only to allow in family. He got rather puzzled at the amount of Norman's family; when I turned up he had already let in a father, dozens of sisters & brothers & cousins, & he tried to keep me out.

Police orders are that Norman is to have a British constable by his side wherever he goes, & sitting outside his room all the time.

The man who did it is from a village near Jenin, & was put in the Reformatory for 4 years for being an accessory in killing his sister. He is now 20, & a little weak in the head & fanatical. He was an orderly with the police. Some people think he was put up to it – others that he was merely worked on by all this foolish talk & journalism &, being weak-minded, wanted to be a hero. Norman wants to have the man let off lightly, but fortunately it doesn't rest with him. Not that I don't really feel the same, only if you don't punish the first one, it will go on, & there'll be no end to it.

All the week I've been feeding with other people, who have been very kind, & sleeping at the Saunders' house, next door.

7.12.29: Norman is really all right again. He still goes to the hospital every other day for dressings – but he walks up to his office in the mornings, as fast as ever, with the poor constable trying to keep pace by his side.

We dined with the Chancellors & went to a concert with them, Norman got on the platform in the interval & made a speech – he was much clapped. And he couldn't get down, & instead of asking for help, he jumped. A lady sitting behind said to Chancellor 'What swank.' 'Mr Bentwich never swanks,' Chancellor replied.

---

[1] *Jewish Chronicle*, 15 October 1999.

[2] Norman's brother.

[3] F.H. Kisch, *Palestine Diary* (London: Gollancz, 1938), p 236.

[4] Norman and Helen Bentwich, *Mandate Memories* (London: Hogarth Press, 1965), p 132.

[5] Sir Walter Shaw, former Chief Justice of the Straits Settlements.

[6] Helen is almost certainly thinking of McDonnell, the new Chief Justice of Palestine.

[7] Norman Bentwich, *England in Palestine* (London: Kegan Paul, 1932), pp 189–91.

[8] Ronald Storrs, *Orientations* (Nicholson and Watson, 1945), p 364.

[9] Eric Mills had become Assistant Chief Secretary.

[10] Helen put the phrase in quotation marks in her letter.

[11] 'Cleared' refers to the Royal Commission which investigated Parnell and his party in Ireland in 1890:

> 'Cleared', honourable gentlemen! Be thankful it's no more:–
> The widow's curse is on your house, the dead are at your door.
> On you the shame of open shame; on you from North to South
> The hand of every honest man flat-heeled across your mouth.
> 'Less black than we were painted'? – Faith, no word of black was said;
> The lightest touch was human blood, and that, you know, runs red.
> It's sticking to your fist to-day for all your sneer and scoff'
> And by the Judge's well-weighed word you cannot wipe it off.

[12] The ram's horn traditionally blown at the Jewish New Year.

[13] See Bernard Wasserstein, *The British in Palestine* (London: Royal Historical Society, 1978), pp 212–13.

[14] Norman Bentwich, *Wanderer Between Two Worlds* (London: Kegan Paul, 1941), pp 153–4.

Conclusion

From the Hill of Evil Counsel to the Vale of Health

Riots and shooting did not destroy Norman's idealism. Shortly after he was wounded he was sympathetically discussing the 'Brith Shalom' ('Covenant of Peace') movement, which sought peace with the Arabs and a non-aggressive Zionism, a movement in which Magnes was prominent. But although he had not himself changed, Palestine had been changed in a way which was to make Norman's future there impossible.

Early in 1930 Helen and Norman and Eric Mills had a few days' holiday in the north of the country, complete with a guard. Things seemed quieter, though there was a perpetual undercurrent of worry. Helen's letters are filled once more with gardens – she was writing monthly gardening articles for the *Palestine Bulletin*. The Women's Council re-appeared in her life, she went back to the Sports Club, took up golf, and got excited about a big fancy dress party at the French Consulate (notable because Edwin Samuel went as a Bedouin, complete with a sheep which misbehaved in the drawing-room although he had been house-training it all afternoon). Helen continued this determinedly busy social life, though she knew it was all very artificial. Looking back later, she wrote that she was behaving that way out of defiance; she was determined to show she did not care about such things as not being elected to the Sports Club committee – but of course she did care. Later in the summer, to escape problems, she played a lot of tennis and went partying with Air Force officers who were not remotely concerned with problems of Zionism – 'a foolish life of which I am now ashamed'.[1]

But the problems did not go away. Helen visited Hebron, six months after the riots:

8.2.30: We went all over the ghetto & the other destroyed houses. They haven't been cleared up yet, as most of the trials haven't taken place, & they may be needed as evidence. Blood-stains are still on the walls & floors, & great heaps of rags from the mattresses, broken glass etc. Apparently it was all over in a few minutes. Some houses they got in through the top, & threw down huge rocks. And they broke into the ghetto through a door at the back. But most of the people were killed in the isolated houses outside – 19 in one house. 61 altogether were killed there.

22.2.30: Politically, things are quiet, but increasingly depressing. The Jewish papers are now having a concerted attack on Norman, for the results of some cases where Jews have been convicted, or Arabs let off. They are perfectly revolting in their remarks – saying he is afraid of being shot again, & that's why he panders to the Arabs! … The English people are most of them fairly nice to us now, & try to forget we are Jews. But now I see nothing of the Jewish people, who can't forget we are English. But I've acquired such a contempt for my fellows here, for the most part, that it no longer worries me.

In a later letter (19 April), Helen complained that many of the English were avoiding them:

People we've been out-of-the-way kind & hospitable to never ask even Norman to their house, & pass quickly on if they see him in the road sometimes … And open anti-semitism & even persecution is practised by the Public School type of Englishman. As for the army here – the officers & their wives are the dullest, least interesting, most bourgeois people I've ever met.

The 'American Colony' were having their own minor crisis at this time, which gave Helen some malicious pleasure:

22.3.30: There is a complicated business about the American Colony, which will probably be the end of it – law suits by the younger people, to prevent the Vesters making themselves into an American company, under the directorship of their immediate family. The young ones ask for their share of the money back – & it's all very complicated, & Norman gets dragged a lot into it, & it'll almost certainly be the end of Mrs Vester. Nobody sees her or speaks to her now, & she is cut by everyone everywhere. It's a curious position – but I am sure deserved. The way she spends money on herself & her family, & stints the others, has been scandalous for years.

The American Colony did become a company and did survive this unhappy time, with 40 members staying with Mrs Vester and 11 leaving.

29.3.30: You ask if we think we shall ever settle down to pleasant conditions again. Quite frankly, & speaking for us two, & not for the whole country, the answer is no. I don't know what will happen or how long we shall be able to stick it, or they us. It's an experience, & the danger & the hostility we've been through gives one rather the feeling one had during the war. The danger seems over now – I think there are too many soldiers & police for further outbreaks – but the hostility on all sides still exists. Sometimes I get quite detached, as if it were all happening to someone else, or just wonder what will happen next. Sometimes I get absolutely raving at the injustice & persecution of it all. But mostly we go on from day to day, not talking of it except to each other, or to Mills. One can't talk to the Jews about things, as they are always hostile to the government. And most of the government are hostile to the Jews. It'll be funny to be in a normal atmosphere again.

In April the report of the commission of inquiry into the riots came out, 'as supremely unimportant & mediocre as Norman expected':

5.4.30: There have, as yet, been no changes in the government here because of the riots. Norman has been offered a Chief Justiceship in some utterly insignificant Colony,[2] & by refusing it has lost his last chance of a knighthood, he is told ... He's a white elephant to the Colonial Office, & we wonder what will happen to us next.

The one encouraging feature in this depressing time was the development of the University:

19.4.30: Tuesday was a University day – H.E. opened the library in the morning, & there was a concert in the amphitheatre in the afternoon. H.E. made a pleasant speech – he is fond of Magnes, & likes the university atmosphere, I think. Magnes made a too-long speech, & the librarian made a particularly futile one. There were huge crowds.

All the Easter things, so far, have gone off well – today's a nasty day, the Hebron people going home, & the Holy Fire, & the Latin Easter, & the last day of Passover. There are a lot of precautions – Norman is getting slightly irritable at the watch kept over him!

4.6.30: We had Hore-Belisha to dinner. He is a Liberal M.P. of 32, very brilliant, ex-President of the Oxford Union, with a doting Christian mother [and a Jewish father]. He says the only way for a Jew to get on in the House is to take up Palestine, so he came here to study it, & has, I think, reverted very strongly. Most of the officials treated him as a Christian – & he was appalled at their frank anti-semitism. That may do a lot of good. He is very noisy & overwhelming.

Tuesday we went to a new colony, & then all over the famous Kebarah marshes they have drained & made cultivatable, between Zichron & the sea, & to see the Arab village by the sea they had made for the dispossessed Bedouin who used to squat in the swamps. There they live in stone houses, in a wonderfully healthy place, & are all employed – but one hears nothing of *that* sort of thing in all these prejudiced reports. I won't write any politics to-day – I feel too depressed about it all. It's no good making you all annoyed by comparing England's lack of faith to the Jews to her lack of faith for so many years in Ireland – or saying how wrong it was of the Jews to trust her so utterly. The Labour Government is to blame – but they are too worried, & have their hands too full, to see the full significance of their acts. As an English person,

it's the most painful thing one can suffer; to live among a betrayed people, as the representative of the betrayers. Norman is
terribly upset ...

Now, furious at the pro-Arab prejudice of the Administration, it
was Helen who was determined not to leave:

> ... It's no use throwing his hand in, I keep telling him, because
> it'd only be worse in the day-to-day persecutions. The Hope-
> Simpson report[3] is, I fear, a foregone conclusion – when he met
> me, not knowing who I was, he told me more or less not to
> worry, as the country would *not* be allowed to be run by the Zi-
> onists! And that was when he first arrived. *Everyone* is hostile. He
> goes round Jewish places with Arabs, & hears the most awful lies,
> & you've no idea how hard it is to disprove things, when *nobody*
> except those who are considered partial are interested in correct-
> ing the lies. The *facts* are obvious, if they would take the trouble,
> & have the good faith, to give them. I think I – & probably Nor-
> man too – have been more deeply shocked in the way things
> happen here today than ever before. The depression of the Jews
> is only balanced by the jubilation of the British. 'At last' – that is
> their present attitude. As you may imagine, it doesn't make for a
> pleasant life!
> However, by dint of seeing few people, working in the garden,
> & reading a lot, one gets on happily enough.

Helen admitted that her depression, though justified, was aggra-
vated by feeling unwell: for some weeks she had been living on
invalid food, and unable to indulge her addiction to sport. They
planned a leave in September – 'Our future is as rotten & uncer-
tain as ever it was, but we will be better able to face it after leave.'

> **26.6.30**: Norman, of course, has even more work than usual. Life
> is very hard for him in every way. I can't tell you in a letter just
> how beastly it all is. But I'm quite sure all you respectable people
> at home have no conception of what British government officials
> *can* be like in their less happy moments. Of course, he's a born
> martyr, & the persecution which is meant to make him go, only
> makes him sorry that the other people should behave so badly!

'The policy of the Administration,' Norman wrote later, 'became steadily more hostile to Jewish enterprise, & I was impotent to check its course. The trials of those involved in the outbreak were protracted for months by every device of the lawyers ... The deliberate purpose was to keep passions hot; and when in the end the High Commissioner confirmed the death sentences against three of the twenty who had been condemned for murder, and the sentences were executed in the summer, there was again passionate outcry. The three, who had committed particularly brutal murders, were turned into national heroes; and the blood of the 'martyrs' became the seed of the Arab rebellions.'[4]

Chancellor went on leave at the end of June, although Eric Mills, the Assistant Chief Secretary, was in hospital and the next man in his department was also away; so there was very much a second team in charge. Davis, the acting High Commissioner, Helen described as 'a dear old thing, fatter than ever'. 'It'll look very bad for the colonial service,' she added, 'should anything happen again.'

> **3.7.30**: I've seen quite a lot of the Wailing Wall commission.[5] They are a very different calibre of men to the last rotten lot – all, I think, the right type for the job ...

Helen's assessment was right. The Wailing Wall Commission, composed of a Swedish ex-premier, a Swiss judge, and a Dutch ex-governor, managed to produce that rare document in Palestinian history, a report that solved the problem. The recommendations were accepted by the British government, and there were no further questions about the rights at the Wall during the period of the Mandate. But the Commission under Sir John Hope-Simpson, investigating problems of immigration and land settlement, was another matter:

> ... Hope-Simpson is a little too clever; he is all things to all men, & I'm afraid the Jews, tho' they are pleased with him now, will get a jar about his report.

> **10.7.30**: I had a wonderful trip in a Moth. They are marvellous machines, so easy & so comfortable. In a few years, it will be as

accepted to have your own Moth as it is to have your own motor-
cycle. They are more like that than cars, & essentially things for
owner-drivers. They cost about the same, to buy & run, as a
Studebaker big car. I think flying is *really* fascinating, & very much
more comfortable & less noisy in a Moth than in the big airliner
that I had been in before.

I've been roped in as chairman of a collecting committee for a
lot of children's charities. It's quite a good scheme, to have one
collecting committee, to control the budget of each of about 6
organizations, & prevent separate appeals. We are trying to get
most of it here, at first, in small donations. The condition I've
gone in on is that this includes my kindergarten, which otherwise
won't be able to open next term as I've no money. Some of the
committee are difficult, but I'm, as usual, very autocratic.

17.7.30: Miss Garrod, the prehistoric-man expert, has been staying here with us. She is very entertaining, game for anything, & an
expert on X-word puzzles.

We went with Mills & Norman to the talkies; Norman sat
through ¾ of it with a pained, grieved look on his face, so then
we left for a really good supper. The only thing that interested
him was in the news part, to hear the Guards Massed Bands at
the Cenotaph last November!

My gardener tried to murder his wife yesterday, & when I sent
for him, to give him to the police, he bolted to town & came back
with a divorce, & says she is no longer his wife, & he is working
happily again, & she has gone to her home. It's a queer country.

24.8.30: There is an Arab strike on today, & Norman is having to
be careful again. Much of his & Davis' time is spent in trying to
bring about an agreement over the Wall, but I think it's all wasted
effort. I can't think the Arabs will be pinned down to anything
unless they are forced to. And they've not had much evidence of
the desire to force things on them, so far. But the Commission
asked them to do this, so they feel they must at least try.

Helen and Norman went on leave at the beginning of September,
fully expecting to be back. Soon after they reached London the
Labour government, acting on the reports from Sir Walter Shaw
and from Sir John Hope-Simpson, published the Passfield White

Paper on immigration and settlement. Lord Passfield (Sidney Webb) was totally unsympathetic to Zionism. Christopher Sykes, son of Sir Mark Sykes, called him 'the most anti-Zionist Secretary of State with whom Zionists had to deal at any time',[6] and his wife Beatrice Webb is reported to have once said to Weizmann: 'I can't understand why the Jews make such a fuss over a few dozen of their people killed in Palestine. As many are killed every week in London in traffic accidents, and no one pays any attention.'[7] Norman wrote that the White Paper 'shocked the Jewish people throughout the world. The tone was hostile and, as Lord Plumer observed to me, unnecessarily rude.'[8] The proposals, that there should be no further Jewish purchase of agricultural land in Palestine, and that Jewish labour immigration into Palestine should be severely curtailed, predictably caused a Zionist storm, but they also caused strong protests in Parliament. There was a debate which ended with the Prime Minister (MacDonald) reading out a letter to Weizmann 'explaining' – in fact repudiating – much of the White Paper. The Arabs, calling this explanation the Black Letter, claimed that the Zionists had too much influence in England. The British Government had succeeded in upsetting both sides.

Norman was told that feeling in Palestine ran so high that there would be disturbances if he returned as Attorney-General. It distressed him deeply that, after all his efforts to bring peace and to deal fairly with Arabs and Jews alike, the one place in which he, as a Jew, could not have a government post was Palestine. 'It is not often,' Storrs wrote, 'that too great love of a country proves a bar from dedicating to it the maturity of one's experience and qualifications, but such was the pathetic fate of Bentwich.'[9] He was again offered a post as Chief Justice, this time for Cyprus; but he refused to be hounded out of office. An unhappy and unsettled year followed, only relieved by a six weeks' visit to Russia. Norman was 'in purgatory' as he put it, frustrated and under-employed at the Colonial Office.

Helen broke her right shoulder in a taxi accident in London and was never able to play golf or serious tennis again. The accident seems symbolic, the breaking of her old life. There were signs of her new life starting when she joined the Labour Party, supported her brother Hugh in his unsuccessful stand in the 1931 election, put her name forward as a prospective candidate herself, and bought the house in the Vale of Health, Hampstead which was to be her and Norman's home for the rest of their lives. She was finding an outlet for her energy and ambition.

That is where I, her niece, remember them, in a Victorian house littered with oriental rugs and pictures and enviable clutter. There was a Bomberg over the mantelpiece, big Epstein flower paintings, Lear watercolours of Palestine bought at a time when he was famous only for nonsense rhymes, and silver tennis cups on the sideboard. Helen could never make contact with small children, but when we grew older she taught us the pleasures of old bookshops and took us to explore the odder parts of London. For London became her home and the centre of her work, although there was always a pull towards Jerusalem – she managed to spend some time there nearly every year throughout her busy life.

Shortly after the Colonial Service decided to retire Norman, he was offered the newly founded Weizmann Chair of the International Law of Peace at the Hebrew University. He accepted, on the understanding that he would be in Palestine for only half of every year. Anxious that she too should have a definite new role, Helen arranged to be the *Manchester Guardian*'s correspondent in Palestine while she was there with him. She started with articles on the orange trade, on Haifa harbour, and on the Dead Sea potash works.

Over the years, Norman was to contribute greatly, and with enormous pleasure, to the life of the Hebrew University. But his inaugural lecture, optimistically titled 'Jerusalem, City of Peace', was a terrifying shambles:

11.2.32: I cannot think why such a calm, peaceable, easy-going person as Norman should always be such a pivot for disharmony wherever he goes. It was, really, what I expected when I begged & begged him not to come. And it was tragic, this lecture on which he had set such great hopes, & given such hours of time to preparing, to be greeted like this. I wish to God he hadn't come, & cast these really good words of wisdom before such utter swine. The first outburst alarmed me – I heard the word 'Mufti', & thought it was another Arab going to shoot. But then I found it was only stink-bombs & not pistols. The disturbances lasted over an hour – a very miserable hour, as far as I & Margery & some others were concerned. But Norman remained quite calm, though it was absurd, really, to try & get out words of peace in these surroundings ... The students protest, firstly because they consider such a chair an unnecessary luxury at present; & secondly, because Norman has always opposed the University being an undergraduate place too quickly, & a refuge for students from anti-semitic places in Europe, which is what they want it to be ... He's not the first Jew to be persecuted for preaching peace on the Mount of Olives ... I long for a peaceful life.

The University was certainly not being quick about becoming an 'undergraduate place' – the first 13 undergraduate students had been given their degrees in a ceremony only two weeks earlier. And Norman was supporting Magnes and other Brith Shalom sympathizers in thinking that 'the principal political aim should not be the maximum immigration but an understanding with the Arabs',[10] and in applying these views to the University in spite of the rise of Nazism. One leading protester was Abraham Stern, later to be the leader of the notorious Stern Gang. 'We don't want to hear peace talks when the students at Vienna University are being beaten,' the students shouted, and 'Go and preach peace to the Mufti, not to us.'[11] Fifteen young Revisionists were arrested, and order was restored for the rest of the lecture; but Norman's hopes of co-operation and gradual growth were unrealistic, and were overwhelmed by the tragedies of the thirties.

Helen and Norman were back in England after only four months, and there are no more bundles of letters. They were both too pugnacious in their idealism – to use the adjective Norman had used to describe Magnes – ever to have a really peaceful life. The rest of Norman's life was to be devoted to the causes of international peace, Jewish refugees, and the Hebrew University. Helen fully shared and supported his ideals, but she became increasingly absorbed by her own career. After failing to get into Parliament, she joined the London County Council, where she felt she could at last use her ideas and abilities. She was particularly active and influential on the Education Committee, and ultimately became, to her enormous pleasure, Chairman of the Council.

Norman died in 1971 and was buried in 'the land of his ancestors', on Mount Scopus; Helen died the following year, and was buried in London.

---

[1] In her manuscript memoir.

[2] Mauritius.

[3] Sir John Hope-Simpson was reporting on the problems of immigration and land settlement.

[4] Norman Bentwich, *Wanderer Between Two Worlds* (London: Kegan Paul, 1941), p 156.

[5] This was a new international commission, concerned with rights at the Wailing Wall.

[6] Christopher Sykes, *Cross Roads to Israel* (London: Collins, 1965), p 140.

[7] Chaim Weizmann, *Trial and Error* (London: Hamish Hamilton, 1949), p 411.

[8] Bentwich: *Wanderer Between Two Worlds*, p 159.

[9] Ronald Storrs, *Orientations* (London: Nicholson and Watson, 1945), p 368.

[10] Bentwich: *Wanderer Between Two Worlds*, p 206.

[11] Report in *Jewish Chronicle*, 12 February 1932.

Index